DAILY LIFE OF

THE INUIT

Recent Titles in
The Greenwood Press Daily Life Through History Series

Civilians in Wartime Twentieth-Century Europe
Nicholas Atkin, editor

Ancient Egyptians, Second Edition
Bob Brier and Hoyt Hobbs

Civilians in Wartime Latin America: From the Wars
of Independence to the Central American Civil Wars
Pedro Santoni, editor

Science and Technology in Modern European Life
Guillaume de Syon

Cooking in Europe, 1650–1850
Ivan P. Day

Victorian England, Second Edition
Sally Mitchell

The Ancient Greeks, Second Edition
Robert Garland

Chaucer's England, Second Edition
Jeffrey L. Forgeng and Will McLean

The Holocaust, Second Edition
Eve Nussbaum Soumerai and Carol D. Schulz

Civil War in America, Second Edition
Dorothy Denneen Volo and James M. Volo

Elizabethan England, Second Edition
Jeffrey L. Forgeng

The New Americans: Immigration since 1965
Christoph Strobel

DAILY LIFE OF

THE INUIT

PAMELA R. STERN

The Greenwood Press Daily Life Through History Series

7/10

 GREENWOOD

AN IMPRINT OF ABC-CLIO, LLC
Santa Barbara, California • Denver, Colorado • Oxford, England

Library of Congress Cataloging-in-Publication Data
Stern, Pamela R.
    Daily life of the Inuit / Pamela R. Stern.
        p. cm. — (The Greenwood press daily life through history series)
    Includes bibliographical references and index.
    ISBN 978-0-313-36311-5 (hardcopy : alk. paper) —
ISBN 978-0-313-36312-2 (ebook)   1. Manners and customs.
I. Title.
    E99.E7.S8248   2010
    971.9004'9712—dc22   2010009533

ISBN: 978-0-313-36311-5
EISBN: 978-0-313-36312-2

14   13   12   11   10   1   2   3   4   5

This book is also available on the World Wide Web as an eBook.
Visit www.abc-clio.com for details.

Greenwood
An Imprint of ABC-CLIO, LLC

ABC-CLIO, LLC
130 Cremona Drive, P.O. Box 1911
Santa Barbara, California 93116-1911

This book is printed on acid-free paper ∞

Manufactured in the United States of America

—for Peter

CONTENTS

Acronyms and Abbreviations   ix

Introduction   xi

Chronology   xxv

 1. Family Life   1

 2. Language and Intellectual Life   21

 3. Economic Life   37

 4. Community Life   55

 5. Material Life   69

 6. Political Life   81

 7. Religious Life   103

 8. Sports and Recreation   115

 9. Expressive and Popular Culture   125

10. Visual Arts   143

11. Health and Medicine   157

12. Inuit in International Political Arenas   173

Glossary   187

Appendix: Places Mentioned in the Text   191

Further Reading   195

Index   201

ACRONYMS AND ABBREVIATIONS

AEWC	Alaska Eskimo Whaling Commission
ANCSA	Alaska Native Claims Settlement Act
ANILCA	Alaska National Interest Lands Conservation Act
EU	European Union
GN	Government of Nunavut
HSP	Hunter Support Program
ICC	Inuit Circumpolar Council
IQ	*Inuit Qaujimajatuqangit*
ITK	Inuit Tapiriit Kanatami
IWC	International Whaling Commission
JBNQA	James Bay and Northern Quebec Agreement
MLA	Member of the Legislative Assembly
NQIA	Northern Quebec Inuit Association
NSB	North Slope Borough
NWT	Northwest Territories
OAS	Organization of American States
UN	United Nations

INTRODUCTION

The Inuit are an Arctic people indigenous to the tundra regions of Alaska, northern Canada, and Greenland. A small number of Inuit also live on the Bering and Chukchi sea coasts of Chukotka, Russia. The ethnonym *Inuit* means "the people" in Inuktitut, the Inuit language. Inuit, like other North American Native peoples, are descended from the waves of ancient peoples who crossed the Bering Sea from Siberia to Alaska during and following the last glaciation. Contemporary Inuit are descended from the last wave of Siberian migrants, people archeologists call *Thule* (pronounced *too-lay*), who settled first along the coastal areas of the Bering and Chukchi seas. Toward the end of the first millennium of the Common Era some of those Thule ancestors spread northward and then eastward to North Alaska, Canada, and Greenland. Like modern Inuit, they were coastal dwellers, dependent upon marine resources for most of their food, clothing, and shelter. Archeologists recognize Thule sites from the remains of houses built from whale bone, and it seems likely that Thule people moved east into what is now Arctic Canada and Greenland as they hunted migrating bowhead whales (*Balaena mysticetus*). Thule Inuit, however, were not the first peoples to inhabit the North American Arctic.

PEOPLING OF ARCTIC NORTH AMERICA

The retreat of glaciers during a period of global warming 7,000 years ago allowed plants, animals, and people to colonize the high latitudes. Archeologists recognize a culture identified as Belkachi as an early migration of people into north central and northeastern Siberia. Between 4000 and 2500 B.C.E. people sharing Belkachi culture settled the area of Siberia from the Taimyr Peninsula to Chukotka, eventually spreading across the Bering Strait into the Norton Sound region of Alaska and beyond. American archeologist J. Louis Giddings excavated a site at Cape Denbigh, Alaska, in 1948, and discovered the same kinds of microblade stone artifacts previously identified in Siberia, indicating that they had been made by people from the same culture. Giddings called the archeological assemblage the Denbigh Flint Complex. Similar stone tools along with harpoon heads, lance heads, and fish spears made of bone as well as the bone remains of seals and walruses were subsequently found in Arctic Canada and on the north coast of Greenland, all dating from around 2500 B.C.E. Archeologists originally labeled this eastern cultural complex the Arctic Small Tool tradition, but have since renamed it Independence Culture and recognize it as part of the same cultural tradition as Denbigh in Alaska.

Climatic cooling around 4,000 years ago had important consequences for human activities in the Arctic. At sites in the northern Hudson Bay and Foxe Basin regions, Independence developed into a paleoeskimo cultural tradition archeologists call Pre-Dorset. People continued to make stone tools similar to Denbigh, but the sites also contain evidence of additional technologies such as toggling harpoons, composite bows and arrows, and fishing equipment. Dogs, which were present in earlier periods, seem to have disappeared from Pre-Dorset sites, but an innovation, small stone lamps in which sea mammal oil could be used as heating, represents a major technological advance.

DORSET CULTURE

In Canada and Greenland Pre-Dorset evolved into what archeologists call Dorset culture around 1000 B.C.E. Early Dorset culture was distinguished by large, semisubterranean winter houses that were heated with oil lamps. The Dorset people also had bone snow knives suggesting that they, like historic modern Inuit, built snowhouses on the ocean ice, where they probably also hunted seals. Snowhouses on the ocean ice, however, do not leave archeological remains, so it is impossible to be certain that Dorset people built them. The Dorset people are also noted for their artistic expression, which included small effigies of humans and animals carved from stone and bone as well as masks and decorated utilitarian objects. Dorset sites over a wide geographic area share many common artifacts, suggesting that the Dorset people traded both among themselves and with distant peoples.

Renewed climatic warming allowed Dorset people to expand their territory northward, and by the turn of the last millennium Dorset people once again occupied sites in the High Arctic and northwest Greenland. But by around 1200 C.E. following the arrival of both Norse and a new Arctic people—the Thule ancestors of modern Inuit—Dorset culture survived in only a few places including what is now northern Quebec and northern Labrador. By 1500 C.E. Dorset culture was gone.

ONGOING CONNECTIONS WITH SIBERIA

On the Bering and Chukchi sea coasts Denbigh evolved into a culture archeologists label Choris around 1500 B.C.E. Choris people had pottery and built large oval houses. More changes in the material culture have led archeologists to assign another name, Norton, to the people who continued to occupy the western coastal region of Alaska around 1500 B.C.E. The presence of toggle-head harpoons and fishing net sinkers indicates that Norton people depended heavily on marine resources including salmon and seals. They also hunted caribou. They lived, at least part of the year, in permanent villages and used pottery similar to that found in Siberia, indicating ongoing connections among people on both sides of the Bering Strait. Trade and other relations between Alaska Natives and Siberians continued without interruption until after World War II when the Cold War conflict between the United States and the Soviet Union prevented indigenous peoples from crossing the Bering Strait even while hunting sea mammals.

Cultural changes continued so that by 200 B.C.E, Norton developed into what archeologists recognize as the earliest manifestations of the neoeskimo Thule Culture. Called Old Bering Sea, Ipiutak, Punuk, and Birnik by archeologists, these maritime peoples on both sides of the Bering Strait developed the ability to hunt large whales in addition to other sea mammals. People spread to new regions of coastal Alaska and Siberia, and the archeological record suggests that local populations developed distinct social and political identities. Owen Mason calls these local populations "polities" and argues that rivalries between and within polities developed over control of the best whale hunting sites as well as over access to exotic, long-distance trade goods such as iron and to mundane essentials such as seal oil. Hostilities could be kept in check through marriage alliances, regional feasting, and the creation of fictive kin relationships, all cultural practices described by European and Euro-American visitors to the region in the 19th century. Nonetheless, archeologists have also recovered pieces of slat armor and other evidence of violence, suggesting that intervillage warfare was a reality for these proto-Thule peoples. Regional hostilities, occasionally erupting in warfare, are also known from historic Inuit communities in northwest Alaska. Some archeologists believe that the political divisions among proto-Thule communities during the first millennium c.e. represent the kind of social division that ultimately led to the cultural differentiation of modern Inuit and Yupik peoples.[1]

AN EARLIER GLOBAL WARMING

No one knows why for sure, but around 1000 c.e. some of the Thule ancestors of modern Inuit expanded their territory eastward from North Alaska. By 1200 c.e. they reached northern Greenland. Some archeologists believe that Thule people made the migration from North Alaska to Greenland over a very short period and only later occupied the region in between. The Thule period coincided with an era known as the Medieval Warm Period (c. 950–1250 c.e.) when the climate in the Northern Hemisphere, including the Arctic, was relatively warm in comparison to today. Changes in ice conditions allowed bowhead whales to penetrate the Arctic Archipelago, and it is possible that the Thule Inuit were simply following an important resource. It has also been suggested that political changes in Asia under Genghis Khan closed off the trade for iron tools. The need for metal may have caused some of the people living around the Bering Strait to set off in search of new sources.

Thule culture represents a technological florescence in Arctic Canada and Greenland. In addition to whaling equipment such as multiperson boats and large toggling harpoons attached to sealskin floats, the Thule developed technologies for hunting seals at breathing holes. They also had large sleds pulled by dogs and compound reinforced bows. The Thule built spacious semisubterranean winter houses with raised sleeping platforms.

MEETINGS WITH NORSE

Thule Inuit were not the only northern people on the move during the Medieval Warm Period, and as the Thule were moving east, Norse from Norway were moving west, establishing colonies first what is now Iceland before spreading into Greenland and Newfoundland. There is no doubt that there were contacts between the Thule peoples and the Norse, but neither archeologists nor medieval historians have been able to discover much about the nature or duration of these contacts. A small number of Inuit stories collected in Greenland in the 19th century describe encounters with the Norse, and Norse sagas make reference to people identified as *skraellings,* who probably included Inuit, Dorset, and Indians. Objects excavated from numerous Thule sites point to the likelihood that the ancestral Inuit had substantial interactions with the Norse especially in the period 1200–1350 c.e. Thule had access to walrus ivory that the Norse needed to pay taxes to the Norwegian crown, while the Norse had smelted iron sought by Thule Inuit.

LITTLE ICE AGE

The climate in the Northern Hemisphere changed again, and the period 1300–1850 c.e. was a cold period that is known as the Little Ice Age. The Greenland Norse became cut off from Europe and most likely died out. With the colder temperatures and more extensive sea ice, bowhead whales ceased migrating into the central and eastern Arctic. The Thule responded to this potential ecological crisis by abandoning their northernmost sites and concentrating their subsistence efforts on other species of marine mammals, notably ringed seals (*Phoca hispida*). Dorset culture also disappeared, but it is not clear from the archeological record if the Dorset people died out, if they were killed by the Thule, or if they were absorbed by the Thule. The evidence for interactions between the Thule and the Dorset is indirect. For example, the Thule adopted a number of Dorset technologies, including snow knives necessary for constructing snowhouses and soapstone oil lamps necessary for heating them. The Thule probably also learned the locations of valuable materials, including meteoric iron and soapstone, from the Dorset. Inuit traditional stories contain references to a people called *Tuniit,* who are widely believed to have been Dorset Eskimos. In some of these tales, the Tuniit are said to be very strong, but peaceful. Other stories describe conflict between Inuit and Tuniit.

With the end of Norse colonization in Greenland and the disappearance of the Dorset around 1400 C.E., Inuit remained the only people in the North American Arctic. Within a few centuries, however, Inuit again had to adapt to the presence of others in their homeland. Unlike their dealings with the Norse, these later interactions had profound consequences for Inuit culture, economies, and social organization.

NEW ARRIVALS

European exploration of the North American Arctic is usually traced to the three voyages (1576–78) of British privateer Martin Frobisher to southeastern Baffin Island. Frobisher, like many who came after him, was searching for a northerly sea route to Asia known as the Northwest Passage. Though Frobisher failed in that quest, he collected some rocks that he initially thought contained gold. His second and third voyages were mounted in order to mine what turned out to be, not gold, but worthless iron ore. On the first voyage, Frobisher also encountered a group of Inuit. At first their interactions were benign, but this did not last. Frobisher sent a landing party of five men ashore to trade. When the five did not return to the ship Frobisher regarded them as having been taken prisoner, and perhaps they had been. After unsuccessful attempts to find the men, Frobisher retaliated by kidnapping a Inuit kayaker who paddled too close to the ship, snatching the man, kayak and all, out of the sea, and sailing with him back to England.

Although not all encounters between European explorers and Inuit ended with kidnappings or other violence, during the first half of the 17th century, ships' captains working for the Danish-Norwegian crown captured more than 30 Greenlandic Inuit, becoming ever more convinced that they were descendants of the lost Norse.[2] In 1721, a Norwegian Lutheran priest, Hans Egede, persuaded the Danish king to fund his mission to Greenland to convert the Catholic Norse descendents to Protestantism. Finding no Norse, Egede set about to convert Inuit, thus beginning the Danish colonization of Greenland.

At the other end of the Inuit world, Alaskan Inuit were integrated into trade networks and other relationships that extended into Siberia and beyond. One of the first detailed descriptions of Inuit at Point Barrow made by a ship surgeon, John Simpson, noted that the people there had manufactured goods that arrived regularly via indigenous trade networks. Russia's colonization of Alaska did not extend into northwest Alaska, and so, few Inuit there encountered Europeans before the 1820s when British naval vessels began exploring and mapping the western edges of the North American Arctic.

Commercial Whalers

The first sustained contacts between people of European descent and Alaskan Inuit resulted from the 1848 discovery of whaling grounds north of the Bering Strait by the crew of an American whaling ship. Immediately American whalers flooded into the region and began moving east and west in search of their prey. By 1854 they had sailed beyond Point Barrow, and by 1889, they were wintering on Herschel Island (in what is now the Inuvialuit Settlement Region of the Northwest Territories) near the mouth of the Mackenzie River.

Encounters with European Explorers

Inuit in what is now Canada were the last to come into sustained contact with Europeans. Prior to the 1880s when commercial whalers began wintering in the Arctic, Canadian Inuit had mostly short-term and sporadic encounters with whalers and with the crews of British naval ships searching for a northwest passage to Asia. An exception was the meeting with the crews of the H.M.S. *Fury* and H.M.S. *Hecla,* captained by William E. Parry and George F. Lyon. The ships and their crews spent two winters (1821–22 and 1822–23) near Igloolik where they had extended interactions with local Inuit.

Interactions between explorers and Inuit accelerated after 1847 when numerous British, American, and other expeditions in search of the missing Sir John Franklin were launched. In 1845, Franklin, an experienced Arctic explorer, began his third Arctic voyage, commanding two ships and 129 men in search of a northwest passage to Asia. The ships became icebound, and after three winters in the Arctic and Franklin's death, the remaining crew abandoned ship and tried to walk to safety. None survived, but between 1847 and 1855, nearly 40 expeditions were launched to search for Franklin and his crew.

The activities of commercial whalers led to significant changes in Inuit communities, particularly in the areas most frequented by whalers: north and northwest Alaska, the Beaufort Sea coast of Canada, Cumberland Sound, and the west coast of Hudson Bay. It is common today to focus on the social disruptions whalers created among Inuit due to the depletion of game animals and to the introduction of diseases and alcohol, but Inuit were drawn into relationships with commercial whalers because of economic and social benefits the relationships offered to Inuit. Historian W. Gillies Ross equates it to the modern phenomenon of rural-urban migration, noting that, particularly in the sparsely populated Canadian north, Inuit relocated to whaling stations out of "curiosity and a desire for a more varied social experience. . . . [At whaling stations] they joined with scores of sailors of several ethnic origins in sports, dances, concerts, plays, and other activities, to partly learn a second language, to expand ideas, and generally to open a window upon another culture with its radically different concepts of time, work, and behavior."[3]

Colonization

The most significant changes in the daily lives of Inuit have come about as a result of the incorporation of Inuit lands into the nations of Canada, the United States, and Denmark. All three countries initially regarded Inuit as primitive and in need of acculturation to norms of the colonizers. For the most part Inuit disagreed while adapting to new challenges as well as to new opportunities. The end of World War II and the beginning of the Cold War mark the start of a new phase in the Inuit experience. Increased development, much of it driven by external forces, brought Inuit into increased conflict with colonial administrators over education, housing, wildlife management, and land use. Inuit in all three countries began to assert their civil rights as citizens as well as their indigenous rights as the aboriginal occupants of their lands. It took many decades to achieve success and Inuit continue to press their indigenous and civil rights, but today Inuit in Alaska, Canada, and Greenland enjoy both a measure of indigenous self-government along with national citizenship. The three nations vary in the ways that they provide education and health care, regulate trade and resource extraction, and permit Inuit to participate in decision making. Since the 1977, Inuit, along with Yupik peoples, have joined together to form the Inuit Circumpolar Conference, an international indigenous rights organization that promotes Inuit's shared concerns on the world stage.

Contemporary Inuit are filmmakers, politicians, artists, scientists, teachers, nurses, lawyers, poets, philosophers, journalists, homemakers, and hunters. They are citizens of the United States, Canada, and Denmark. They live in large towns and cities and small villages, and some make their lives in tiny hunting camps. The chapters that follow discuss Inuit daily life in the light of the changes Inuit have experienced in the last 300 years. It is essential to keep in mind that Inuit are neither isolated primitives nor simple victims of colonial exploitation. Many of the changes and challenges Inuit have faced have not been of their making, but they have not been passive recipients of external demands. Inuit culture, like all cultures, continues to change, *not* to diminish. Inuit are modern people, living modern lives as well (and as poorly) as others in the globalized world.

CONTEMPORARY INUIT REGIONS

Inuit across the North American Arctic continue to share many cultural attributes, but there are also regional and national differences in the way Inuit culture is expressed. These differences result from the great physical distances that separate Inuit communities as well as from variations in the ways that Denmark, Canada, and the United States administered Inuit lands and communities. Furthermore, contemporary Inuit may call themselves Inuit, but they also go by other names such as Inupiat, Kalaalliit, and Inuvialuit that reflect regional and linguistic differences.

Greenland

The approximately 48,000 Inuit in Greenland call themselves Kalaalliit, a label which may derive from *skraelling,* the term the Norse used for the indigenous peoples of North America. Today, Greenland has a Self Rule government with most of the elected officials being Inuit. Nonetheless, Greenland remains part of Denmark. As noted above, Greenland became a Danish colony in 1721. The Danish crown administered Greenland through a state trading monopoly, and kept very tight control on both the economy and abilities of Greenlanders to interact with the outside world until World War II. Other commercial entities were restricted from operating in the Danish colony, and very few outsiders were permitted to even visit the island. In some respects this insulated the Inuit there from some of the most exploitative forms of colonization, but many Greenlanders also chafed under Danish paternalism. Through the tutelage of Lutheran and Moravian ministers a cadre of Greenlanders was trained as catechists, teachers, and local administrators. Hunting and fishing remained important economic activities. These were simultaneously idealized as truly Greenlandic and disparaged as primitive and backward by more educated Greenlanders.

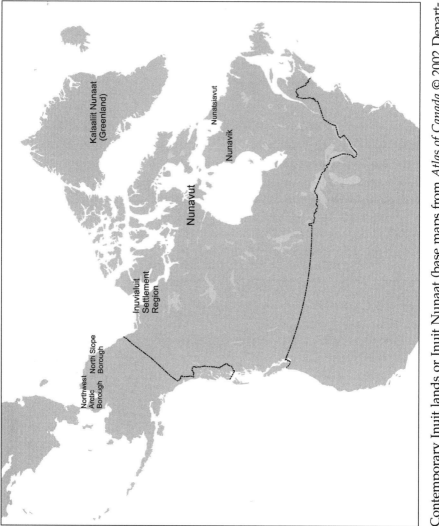

Contemporary Inuit lands or Inuit Nunaat (base maps from *Atlas of Canada* © 2002 Department of Natural Resources Canada. All rights reserved)

Denmark was occupied by Nazi Germany during World War II. The United States established military bases in Greenland, and introduced many new ideas and material items to Kalaalliit, making it impossible for Denmark to seal off the island and its residents after the war. Instead, in 1953, Denmark made Greenland a province of Denmark. Many Greenlanders did not regard this as a political gain and began pushing for Home Rule. This was achieved in 1979 when responsibility for many government functions, such as housing, health, and education, slowly transferred to Greenland over many years. The Inuit language, called *Kalaallisut* in Greenland, is the primary language of everyday conversation. It is also used in broadcasting, elementary education, and government publications. Though still formally a colony of Denmark, Greenland is a modern Inuit state. With Denmark's acquiescence Greenland has negotiated bilateral agreements with foreign governments, and in late 2008, Greenlanders voted overwhelmingly to assume control over most of the remaining government functions still managed by Denmark, including resource development and the administration of justice.

Alaska

Inuit in Alaska usually call themselves *Inupiat* rather than Inuit, and they are culturally distinct from Inuit living in Canada and Greenland. Inupiat means "the real people" in their dialect of Inuktitut. Inupiat make their homes in north and northwest Alaska in the region stretching from the Seward Peninsula (the area of Alaska that sticks into the Bering Strait) north and east along the coast to the Canadian border. The region has been continuously occupied by Inupiat or their ancestors for the past 4,000 years. They were, historically, a whale-hunting society, and whaling remains an important economic and cultural institution in many Inupiaq communities.

The United States purchased Alaska from Russia in 1867 without any consultation with the Inupiat or any other Alaskan peoples. Commercial whaling and mining during the late 19th and early 20th centuries had a significant impact on the lives of Inupiat through the introduction of new technologies, new diseases, and new ideas. American government officials regarded Alaska Native cultures as inferior and primitive, and Alaska Natives were subjected to social and economic discrimination. Today, however, all Alaska Natives are citizens of both the United States and the state of Alaska. A comprehensive land claims agreement signed in 1971 created a corporate structure that was meant to fully incorporate Alaska Natives within the American economic system (see Chapter 6). In a related process, Inupiat also established borough governments in northwest Alaska (Northwest Arctic Borough) and North Alaska (North Slope Borough). Both boroughs are super municipalities chartered under the state of Alaska and incorporate several towns and villages.

Canada

Inuit live in 54 Arctic communities in four regions of Canada. Three-fifths of the approximately 50,000 Canadian Inuit live in the Nunavut Territory, which covers 20 percent of the landmass of Canada. Formerly part of the Northwest Territories, the Nunavut Territory became a separate political jurisdiction in 1999. It was created through a side agreement to the 1993 Nunavut land claim.

The second largest group of Canadian Inuit (approx. 9,200) live in 15 towns and villages in northern Quebec, in a region they call Nunavik. Inuit in Nunavik signed a land claims agreement in 1975, which provided for local control over schools and health care. Another 3,500 or so Inuit live in one of six communities in the Beaufort Sea region of the western Canadian Arctic. They generally refer to themselves as Inuvialuit and call their area the Inuvialuit Settlement Region (ISR). The ISR remains part of the Northwest Territories. The final Inuit region, Nunatsiavut, is northern Labrador. It is part of the province of Newfoundland and Labrador. Inuit there signed a land claims agreement with governments of Canada and Newfoundland and Labrador in 2005.

Canada assumed ownership of the majority of Canadian Inuit lands from Great Britain in 1870 and 1880, but took little interest in either the lands or the Inuit residents until after World War II, leaving most administration to Christian missionaries and traders. Labrador remained a British colony until 1949, when it, too, became part of Canada. Up until that time the Inuit there were administered by the Moravian Church. In Canada as in Alaska, Christian missionaries and traders followed whalers, exerting pressure for change on Inuit communities. These might have been resisted, but for the serious demographic collapse Inuit suffered from introduced diseases for which they had no previous immunity.

ESKIMO OR INUIT?

The indigenous people of the North American Arctic are properly known as Inuit, but that ethnonym only came into widespread usage among non-Inuit in the 1970s. Before then Inuit were usually known as "Eskimos." The term *Eskimo* was once believed to mean "eaters of raw meat," but is now thought to come from an Algonquin Indian word that describes a style of snowshoes.[4] Nonetheless, most people like to be called by their own names, and Eskimo is no longer preferred as a general label for most contemporary and historically known North American Arctic peoples. An exception is in Alaska, where the term *Eskimo* continues to be used to distinguish between the historically related Inupiaq, Yupik, and Alutiiq peoples and unrelated Indian groups. Because we cannot know what past peoples called themselves, Eskimo also remains correct for archeologically known prehistoric North American Arctic peoples. For other uses, *Inuit* (sing. *Inuk*) is usually the preferred generic ethnonym. It signals both the common culture and the common language of the peoples of the North American Arctic. Stretching from the Russian Far East to the east coast of Greenland, Inuit lands cover half the Earth north of the Arctic Circle, making Inuit the most widely dispersed indigenous people in the world.

NOTES

1. Mason, Owen K. (1998) "The Contest between Ipiutak, Old Bering Sea, and Birnik Polities and the Origin of Whaling during the First Millennium A.D. along Bering Strait," *Journal of Anthropological Archaeology* 17(3): 282.

2. Oswalt, Wendell, H. (1999) *Eskimos and Explorers,* 2nd ed. Lincoln: University of Nebraska Press, 75.

3. Ross, W. Gillies (1979) "Commercial Whaling and Eskimos in the Eastern Canadian Arctic 1819–1920," in *Thule Eskimo Culture: An Anthropological Retrospective,* Allen P. McCartney, ed., Ottawa: National Museums of Man, Mercury Series, 247.

4. Damas, David (1984) "Introduction," in *Handbook of North American Indians: Arctic,* David Damas, ed., Washington, D.C.: Smithsonian Institution Press, 6.

CHRONOLOGY

c. 8000 B.C.E.	Small groups of Siberians move across Bering Sea and settle in Alaska becoming the first Arctic North Americans.
c. 2200	Paleoeskimos move from Alaska into Arctic Canada and Greenland. Beginning of Arctic Small Tool tradition.
c. 950 – 1250 C.E.	Medieval Warm Period.
986	Norse colonization of Greenland begins.
c. 1000	Thule ancestors of modern Inuit spread north and then east from the Bering Sea to occupy North Alaska, Arctic Canada, and Greenland.
c. 1400	Paleoeskimo Dorset Culture disappears.
1576	English privateer Martin Frobisher makes the first of three voyages to Baffin Island where he encounters Inuit. He kidnaps three and takes them to England.
c. 1300–1850	Little Ice Age. Thule people adapt to climatic cooling.
1721	Danish-Norwegian priest Hans Egede arrives in Greenland intending to minister to the previously abandoned Norse colonists, but finding no Norse establishes a Danish colony and mission to the Inuit living there.

1750	First dictionary for the West Greenlandic dialect of Inuktitut published by Poul Egede.
1763	Royal Proclamation of 1763 declares that Native Americans must not be "molested or disturbed" in their territories and that land not ceded by them belongs to them.
1800s	Majority of West Greenland population is baptized as Christian.
1850s	Activities of commercial whalers begin to affect Inupiat. A group of Inuit from North Baffin Island cross Smith Sound and reintroduce kayak and other Inuit technologies to the Inuit in northwest Greenland. Settlement of Greenland Inuit in permanent villages is completed.
1861	First Greenlandic newspaper, *Atuagagdliutit* (Readings), begins publication.
1867	United States purchases the Alaska territory from Russia for $7.2 million.
1876	Syllabic translation of the New Testament.
1884	First *tupilak* carvings are created for Gustav Holm. First Organic Act (Alaska).
1893	59 Labrador Inuit and 35 dogs are exhibited at the World Columbian Exposition in Chicago.
1901	Thomas Edison shoots first motion picture footage of Inuit during Pan-American Exposition in Buffalo.
1914	Last traditional Messenger Feast on the North Slope of Alaska is held in Wainwright.
1922	*Nanook of the North* is released.
1936	Indian Reorganization Act is extended to cover the Native peoples in the Alaska Territory. Alaska Natives are recognized as U.S. citizens.
1937	*Wedding of Palo,* a feature-length film directed by Knud Rasmussen in East Greenland, is released.
1939	Canadian Supreme Court rules that, under the Indian Act, the federal government of Canada has an obligation to safeguard the economic security of Inuit.
1941	Canadian government begins issuing disk numbers to Inuit.
1946	International Convention for the Regulation of Whaling becomes basis for regulating commercial and aboriginal subsistence whaling.

1948	Cold War tensions between the United States and the Soviet Union prevent indigenous peoples living on the Bering Sea coast from visiting friends and relatives on the other side of the international border. Right to vote is extended to women in Greenland.
1949	Canadian Handicrafts Guild exhibition and sale of Inuit art in Montreal proves marketability of Inuit art.
1950s and 1960s	Canadian Inuit are resettled in permanent government-administered towns.
1951	National Gallery of Canada holds its first exhibition of contemporary Inuit sculpture.
1953	Greenland is made a county of Denmark.
1959	Alaska statehood. First graphic print collection from Cape Dorset, Nunavut.
1962	*Tundra Times,* first statewide Native newspaper in Alaska, begins publication. U.S. Atomic Energy Commission buries radioactive material from a nuclear weapon test near Point Hope, Alaska, as part of a secret research project to understand the movement of radiation in soil and groundwater.
January 1968	Prudhoe Bay oil strike is announced.
1969–70	Project Surname in Canada.
1970s	Greenlanders leave small villages for larger towns and urban centers.
1970	Committee for Original Peoples Entitlement (COPE) is founded in Inuvik to negotiate Inuvialuit land claims.
1971	Northern Quebec Inuit Association (NQIA) and Inuit Tapirsat of Canada (now Inuit Tapiriit Kanatami) are founded.
December	President Richard M. Nixon signs the Alaska Native Claims Settlement Act (ANCSA) into law.
1972	State of Alaska enacts legislation requiring bilingual and bicultural education for students (Native and non-Native) whose primary language is not English. U.S. Marine Mammal Protection Act becomes law. North Slope Borough is formed.
1973	Labrador Inuit Association is formed. Spelling reform for Greenlandic.
November	Arctic Peoples Conference is held in Copenhagen, Denmark.

1975	James Bay and Northern Quebec Agreement (JBNQA) is signed. State of Alaska begins One Percent for Art Program.
1976	*Aqviqtiuq,* the last independent Inuit settlement on Baffin Island, is abandoned. The residents resettle in Clyde River, Nunavut.
1977	International Whaling Commission moves to ban Inupiaq whaling.
June	Inuit Circumpolar Conference (now called the Inuit Circumpolar Council) is founded at a meeting in Barrow, Alaska.
1978	Contemporary Alaska Native art is exhibited at the National Collection of Fine Art of the Smithsonian Institution.
May 1979	Greenland Home Rule is proclaimed.
1980s	Major galleries in Canada begin collecting, researching, and exhibiting Inuit art.
1980	First formal meeting of the Inuit Circumpolar Conference (ICC) is held in Nuuk, Greenland. ICC gains observer status at International Whaling Commission.
1981	Inuit Tapirisat of Canada (now called Inuit Tapiriit Kanatami) uses funding from the government of Canada to create the Inuit Broadcasting Corporation (IBC).
1982	United Nations establishes Working Group on Indigenous Peoples. European Economic Community enacts voluntary ban on importation of sealskin products.
March	Inuit Circumpolar Conference coordinates Greenlanders' testimony before Canada's National Energy Board opposing the shipping of liquefied natural gas in Arctic waters.
May	Referendum on division of Canada's Northwest Territories.
February 7, 1983	United Nations grants Category II Non-Governmental Organization (NGO) status to the Inuit Circumpolar Conference (ICC).
March 3	ICC charter is ratified by Greenland's Home Rule government.
1984	Inuvialuit Final Agreement is signed.
1985	International Whaling Commission cuts Greenland's quota for minke whales in half and forbids the hunting of humpback whales. Greenpeace officially apologizes for harm

	to Inuit done by its campaign against the Newfoundland seal hunt.
1986	Inuit Regional Conservation Strategy.
1988	Messenger Feasts resume on the North Slope of Alaska. Inuit Regional Conservation Strategy wins Global 500 award from UN Environment Programme.
1991	ICC organizes first summit of Arctic indigenous leaders. Nellie Cournoyea becomes first Inuit premier of a Canadian territory.
1993	Nunavut land claim is settled.
1994–95	Greenlandic commercial fishermen sell their quota for salmon to a salmon conservation fund in order to help rehabilitate salmon stocks.
1995	First annual Agpik Jam Music Festival in Nunavik.
1996	Arctic Council is established.
May 1997	Gender parity proposal for new Nunavut Legislative Assembly is defeated in referendum.
April 1, 1999	Canada's Northwest Territories is divided and Nunavut proclaimed a new territory of Canada.
March 2000	Association of Montreal Inuit is founded.
July	United Nations establishes Permanent Forum on Indigenous Issues.
September 2001	First Throat Singing Gathering in Puvirnituq, Nunavik.
August	ICC concludes a Memorandum of Cooperation with the governor of Chukotka, Russia, for ICC to aid indigenous communities in Chukotka.
January 21, 2005	Labrador Inuit Land Claims Agreement is signed.
December	62 American and Canadian Inuit hunters and elders, led by Inuit Circumpolar Council (ICC) chair Sheila Watt-Cloutier, file a petition with the Inter-American Commission on Human Rights, a department of the Organization of American States (OAS), alleging that the United States violates Inuit cultural and environmental human rights through its unwillingness to reduce greenhouse gas emissions.
March 2007	The OAS rejects Inuit human rights petition, but invites Sheila Watt-Cloutier to testify at a hearing on climate change and human rights.

September   United Nations adopts Declaration on the Rights of Indigenous Peoples.

October   Canadian Inuit leader Sheila Watt-Cloutier is nominated, along with former U.S. Vice President Al Gore and the Intergovernmental Panel on Climate Change, for the Nobel Peace Prize "for their efforts to build up and disseminate greater knowledge about man-made climate change, and to lay the foundations for the measures that are needed to counteract such change." Watt-Cloutier is excluded when the Nobel laureates are named.

June 11, 2008 Canadian Prime Minister formally apologizes to Canadian aboriginal peoples for subjecting them to residential schools.

September   *Before Tomorrow,* from the Arnait Video Productions Collective based in Igloolik, wins award for the best first feature film at the prestigious Toronto Film Festival.

November   In a referendum, Greenlanders overwhelmingly vote in favor of more complete self-government.

April 28, 2009 ICC announces its "Declaration on Arctic Sovereignty."

June 21   Self Rule replaces Home Rule in Greenland.

December   Copenhagen round of global treaty negotiations on climate change conclude without any binding agreement to reduce greenhouse gas emissions.

1

FAMILY LIFE

Folk tales and stories can often reveal a great deal about social values and relationships in a society. Inuit traditional stories often give clues about the most important relationships in Inuit lives: those between parents and children and between husbands and wives. These are relationships that do not end with death, but continue through the birth of new babies.

One widely told story concerns a young woman, known by several different names including Sedna, Taleelayuk, and Nuliajuk, who lived alone with her widowed father. She was a somewhat dreamy and spoiled girl who often became distracted from her work and failed to finish her tasks. Although Nuliajuk had long been old enough to marry, she refused all of the young men chosen by her father. Her father was troubled that his daughter refused to marry. So many young hunters, who seemed as though they would become good, hardworking husbands, were sent away. People begin to talk about Nuliajuk. Some thought that she did not want a husband because she did not want to leave her father alone. Others said it is because she was afraid to have sex. Still others thought that Nuliajuk refused to marry because her father spoiled her by treating her as his favorite child, giving her the best morsels of food and allowing her to spend her days doing little more than combing her long, beautiful hair. What people did agree was that it was time for Nuliajuk to be

married, and that a son-in-law could be a help to the father. But po-
lite and thoughtful Inuit do not question the motives of others, and
so no one asked and no one knew for sure why Nuliajuk remained
single.

One summer day when Nuliajuk was sitting by the seashore and
gazing off into the distance, she saw a handsome hunter paddling
a kayak. He was wearing snow goggles to protect his eyes from the
bright sun reflecting off the water. But even with his eyes hidden
behind the goggles, Nuliajuk knew that this was the man she had
been waiting for. He paddled to shore. Without hesitation, Nuliajuk agreed to marry the kayaker. She allowed him to take her to his
island home.

When Nuliajuk and her husband arrived at the island where they
would live together, the hunter removed his goggles revealing his
red eyes. He was not a handsome hunter. In fact, he was not even a
man. He was a fulmar—a sea bird. Nuliajuk was horrified. What had
she done! How would she ever get back to her home!

Nuliajuk's father was also distressed. He returned from hunting
and discovered his daughter missing. He set out to search for her
and after traveling many days discovered Nuliajuk imprisoned on
the fulmar's island. He waited patiently until the fulmar went out
hunting, and then he hurried his daughter to their *umiak* (skin boat)
and began the journey home.

When the fulmar returned and discovered his bride missing, he
was furious. Had someone stolen his wife? He seethed with jealousy at the thought that his wife had run away to another husband.
He took to the skies and began scanning the sea for Nuliajuk. Soon,
he spotted her with her father and flew low to demand that she
return to the island. The father continued paddling and the fulmar
continued squawking and flapping his wings ever more angrily.
The fulmar beat his wings so furiously that he raised a storm on the
ocean that threatened to swamp the tiny boat. The father continued
to paddle, but the storm caused by the fulmar's fury grew worse.
Finally, the father felt he had no choice; in order to save himself, he
threw his daughter into the sea.

But Nuliajuk was quick. She grabbed onto the side of the umiak
and tried to pull herself back into the boat. The fulmar was still
squawking and flapping overhead and the little umiak was in even
greater danger of overturning. Nuliajuk's father again felt he had no
choice. He used his knife and cut off Nuliajuk's fingers at the first
joint. Her fingertips fell into the sea and transformed into seals. Still
Nuliajuk grasped the boat. Again, her father used his knife, cutting

Nuliajuk fingers at the second joint. These, too, fell into the sea where they were transformed into walruses. But Nuliajuk used all of her strength to cling to the boat with the stubs of her fingers. The noise from the fulmar's squawks and Nuliajuk's screams was unbelievable. The father believed the world was coming to an end. He used his knife one last time, severing Nuliajuk's last finger joints at the knuckles. These also fell into the sea and transformed into whales. Without her fingers Nuliajuk could no longer hold onto the side of the umiak and she, too, slipped under the water.

With his bride gone, the fulmar gave up his demands and flew away. Immediately, the storm dissipated. Without the angry flapping from the fulmar's wings, the ocean settled back to calm. The father continued his sad journey home, alone, but he could not find peace. He was so distraught at what had transpired at sea and his role in the death of Nuliajuk that he committed suicide. But this is not the end of the story.

Nuliajuk sank to the bottom of the ocean where she became the mistress of all the sea mammals. She had the power to decide when to allow Inuit to catch seals, whales, and walruses and when to withhold them. Despite her powers over human affairs, Nuliajuk's was a lonely life. Without fingers she could not comb her hair, or sew, or do any womanly tasks. She was utterly miserable. As her misery grew seals and other sea creatures would become tangled in her hair. When Nuliajuk was especially unhappy, either from her loneliness or because she was displeased with the behavior of humans, she caused storms that prevented Inuit from hunting. Unless Nuliajuk released the sea animals and calmed the seas, starvation was a real possibility.

In order to appease Nuliajuk, a shaman would have to undertake a journey to visit her. The shaman traveled under the sea, where he would sing to her, comb her hair, and beg her to release the sea mammals. If the shaman succeeded in placating Nuliajuk, there would be food. If not, hunger would persist and death could follow.

There are many variations on the story of Nuliajuk, and as discussed in the next chapter the way a story is told depends upon many factors including the specific concerns of the storyteller. This version concerns many aspects of Inuit family life including what can happen when children refuse to listen to their parents and parents put their own needs above those of their children. Disaster is the result when people neglect their responsibilities to family. The story also touches on questions of proper marriage, sexuality, gender roles, and the connection between procreation and death and naming.

NAMING

Nuliajuk's undersea home was also the land of dead, where the name souls of the recently deceased resided until ready to return to the land of the living in the form of a newborn baby. When a person died, his or her name soul or *atiq* stayed near the body for about four days, but then went to reside temporarily with Nuliajuk. It was Nuliajuk who would then choose to send the name to inhabit the body of a newborn child. Naming, thus, is one way that relationships are perpetuated. Inuit naming practices varied somewhat in the specifics from region to region, but Inuit across the North share the same basic culture of naming—that is, a belief that the name carries some aspects of the personality and character of the holder. In most places an Inuk received several names either at birth or over the course of a lifetime. We often tend to think of names as a method of identification, a simple way to distinguish one person from another, but Inuit names are inseparable from the person and it is the name that brings the essential nature and many of the abilities of the holder into being. The name or atiq is the third of three types of souls that are part of a person's make-up. The first two, *tarneq* (personal soul) and *anersaaq* (breath soul), in the Greenlandic dialect of Inuktitut, are now regarded as similar to the Christian notion of the soul as the moral and spiritual essence of a person. Unlike the personal soul and the breath soul that go to an afterlife apart from living people, the atiq or name soul returns to the world of the living after a period in the land of the dead.

Discovering the Name

For Inuit, the process of naming was a process of discovering *who*, in fact, the child was and welcoming that person back to the community. Sometimes this divinatory process was aided by a dream that the mother or other family member had during pregnancy. Other times, a movement or gesture made by the newborn appeared reminiscent of a recently deceased person and helped people recognize the true identity of the newborn. Often the midwife's or another elder's judgment was deferred to in determining a child's name. Still other times different names were tried out until the infant seemed to recognize its own atiq. On occasion a child's name was misidentified, which could cause the child to fall ill or even to die. In those cases it would need to be changed. Anthropologist Bernard Saladin d'Anglure was told of a mother who had dreamed the correct identity of her infant, but had acquiesced to different names chosen by her mother-in-law. While the mother, Iqallijuq, was pregnant, her father-in-law, Iktuksardjuat, died.

He had been a shaman and a prestigious chief in the [Igloolik] region, and he had lost an eye in a hunting accident. . . . [The baby, a girl,] was given the name of Nataaq, a young cousin of Iqallijuq's who had died of cold and hunger the year before; it was desired, by means of the little namesake to warm and feed the deceased. The newborn also received the names of Taqaugaq and of Qattalik, two deceased brothers of her father. Several days after the birth, Iqallijuq dreamed of her deceased father-in-law, but she did not dare to evoke this dream in front of her mother-in-law who had just served as her midwife. . . . But the baby fell ill; an infection began in one of her eyes, the same eye which her one-eyed grandfather had lost. . . . [The frightened mother] decided to admit her dream, and under pressure from her family, she gave the name Iktuksarjuat [*sic*] to the baby, who recovered rapidly.[1]

Making Connections

For the most part, Inuit children did and still do receive the name of a recently deceased member of the community. A newborn baby is, thus, not a stranger, but rather a returned member of the community and bereaved family members are often comforted by the renewed presence of the deceased in the form of the newborn. For example, in Upernavik in West Greenland, "there is a sense that people are not naming/baptizing a new person, but are welcoming back a member of family and community."[2] And Nunavut political leader Peter Irniq described the reincorporation of a new old member this way,

My brother, who died about forty years ago, was named after my grandfather. When my parents adopted a child . . . they named him again so . . . he continues to have this new life each time. Same person, but living. He drowned in 1968. In 1969 they were given a baby [by traditional or "custom" adoption] . . . they named my grandfather again . . . I named my grandfather in our own family so that he's alive in our own family.[3]

It is common for members of the deceased's family to address the child by the kinship term they used for the namesake and for the child to respond also using the kin term that would have been employed by his or her namesake. This practice was depicted in the film *Atanarjuat* when the elderly Panipak addressed her much younger relative, Atuat, as "mother," and caressed her saying, "You're just as beautiful as I remember when I was a child in your arms."[4]

Inuit children today are still understood to receive their essential natures and many of their abilities as endowments with their names. From shortly after birth when the child's name is recognized, "a child possesses its entire life potential in capsule form; and the business of socialization becomes one of assisting the new member (who is really an old member) to realize the potential of his or her pre-established identity."[5] People look for and socially reinforce signs of the namesake in the personality and preferences of the child.

Inuit names are not gender-specific and a female may be named after a male and vice versa. There is a sense that all individuals with the same name are, in essence, one person, and living individuals sharing the same namesake often develop a special connection to each other. According to the Danish ethnographer, Knud Rasmussen, "Everyone on receiving a name receives with it the strength and skill of the deceased namesake, but since all persons bearing the same name have the same source of life, spiritual and physical qualities are also inherited from those who in the far distant past once bore the same name."[6] It should be noted that most individuals receive several names, and thus they receive characteristics with each of the names so that no two individuals are regarded as precisely identical. Sometimes a person's names are thought to fight with one another, and this can cause personality problems for the individual.

Changes with Christianity

Inuit naming practices began to change with the arrival of Christian missionaries. Christian missionaries throughout the North usually baptized Inuit with European names of biblical origin. In West Greenland, nearly all Inuit had Danish names by the end of the 19th century. Greenlanders also adopted the Danish pattern of patronymic surnames. It is not known whether Greenlanders were troubled by this change to their naming system or if they worried that name souls were being abandoned. Early Greenlandic converts to Christianity continued to use Inuit names through the mid-19th century, but they believed their new Christian names conveyed a kind of protection and they were sometimes baptized multiple times in order to take additional names.[7] At present Danish-style names are recycled in the same manner that Inuit names were with one primary difference. Danish names are gender-specific, so that namesakes are now also gender-specific. A child receives the name of his or her namesake at baptism. Nuttall described the way naming occurs in the Upernavik District of Greenland.

As an example, shortly after Josepi [the head of the family] died in October 1988, the news came through from Upernavik town that the wife of his sister's son had given birth to a baby boy. The family was overjoyed for, although it had not been formally announced what name the child was to receive, it was known that he would be called Josepi. Josepi's sons and daughters travelled through to Upernavik for the baptism in November and there was much celebrating afterwards. During this time, Josepi's youngest daughter was pregnant, expecting her child in March. In February 1989, when I was back in England, I received a letter from Juuna tell me Naja had given birth to a son. He went on to say that the child was to receive his father's name and that "we are all happy."[8]

In Alaska and in the Canadian Arctic, Inuit were also baptized with Christian names but continued to use Inuit names alongside the Christian ones. In most cases it seems that Christian names were adopted without much fanfare, but perhaps this was not always the case. Pond Inlet elder Apphia Agalakti Awa told anthropologist Nancy Wachowich that most of the time Inuit used their Inuit names except in the presence of white people, but that her mother-in-law had chosen only a Christian name for one of her sons out of fear of the missionaries.

My mother-in-law named him just a Christian name, just Peter. She wouldn't name him an Inuktitut name because she was scared of the missionaries. There were a lot of Inuktitut names to choose from. Some of her relatives and her older sisters had just died. Even though she was grieving for those members of the family, she wouldn't name her new son any other name other than Peter.[9]

In the Canadian Arctic at present, it is common for a child to receive a Euro-Canadian first name and one or more Inuit middle names. In most cases all of the names, both Euro-Canadian and Inuit, are atiit (*pl.*) and individuals may be addressed by one or the other of their names depending upon the circumstances. While many Inuit still regard the atiq as embodying personality and behavioral traits, it is also becoming common among some Inuit to regard an atiq relationship as symbolic and honorary rather than physical.

Disk Lists

In Canada government officials found Inuit names difficult to deal with. They were difficult for Anglophones and Francophones to pronounce, and consequently, had no consistent spellings. Missionaries used one spelling, police another, still a third might be used by medical personnel. Moreover, because Inuit did not have surnames, wives did not share their husbands' names; children did not share their fathers' names. Inuit names did not conform to the patriarchal nuclear family ideal of Euro-Canadian names. While Inuit had no problems keeping identities straight, the Inuit naming practices created official confusion for northern administrators who were unwilling or unable to adapt their recordkeeping practices. To address this problem, in the 1940s the Canadian government implemented a program of identifying Inuit by number.

The Canadian North was divided into East and West zones and the zones further divided into regions—12 in all. All Inuit were issued small fiber disks, similar to military-style dog tags, bearing a number that indicated zone and region followed by a unique number. A person from Ulukhaktok, in the Inuvialuit Settlement Region, would have a disk number that began W2-, while a person from Arviat, on the west coast of Hudson Bay, would receive a number that began E1-. Individuals were expected to keep their disk number tags with them at all times and the numbers were used in place of names on all official records. Many Inuit artists signed their artwork with their disk numbers.

Opposition to disk numbers came mostly from missionaries and other non-Natives who found the assignment of numbers in place of names to be dehumanizing. The disk numbers were part of a broader program to bring Inuit under the bureaucratic administration of the Canadian state. As recent critics of the disk number system noted, "the military 'dog tag,' like the hospital identification bracelet, is worn on the body precisely to identify someone who cannot, or will not, identify himself. . . . The Inuit disk . . . was invented as a device for outsiders to keep track" of or monitor the activities and movements of Canadian Inuit.[10] In 1970, partly in response to criticism of the disk numbers, the Canadian government initiated a program to assign surnames and issue birth certificates to all Canadian Inuit.

Project Surname

In many parts of the Canadian North it became customary for Inuit, in their official relationships with the government, to use their Christian names as a first name and their Inuit names as a surname. As Apphia Awa put it, "We changed to surnames so that the Qallunaat [white people] wouldn't get confused."[11] But this was far from universal and it did little to alleviate the bureaucratic problem of inconsistent spellings or the fact that close kin did not share the same surname. To deal with this, the government of Canada created Project Surname and appointed Abe Okpik (1929–97), an Inuvialuk from the Aklavik area, to direct the assignment and registration of Inuit surnames. Okpik was well known to northern administrators. He was fluent in English and had worked as the first government administrator at Taloyoak and as a translator for the Department of Indian and Northern Affairs. In 1965 Okpik became the first Native person appointed to the Northwest Territories Council, then the governing body for the territory.

Okpik carried out the assignment virtually single-handedly. He traveled to every Inuit community in the Northwest Territories (which at the time also included Nunavut) and Nunavik in the span of 13 months in order to record Inuit names. Although some in the government had expected that the assignment of an Inuk to carry out the task would accommodate Inuit naming practices, Okpik employed a standard Euro-Canadian naming pattern that assumed a nuclear family with a male head-of-household. For the most part, Okpik interviewed only men. While some individuals chose new names to serve as their surname—a Baffin Island man named Aksujuliak chose Pisukti, meaning "things that walk" for his family's surname because he was known for his ability to walk long distances[12]—in most cases a man's Inuit name was registered as the surname for the entire family. Women were given their husband's name as a surname and children received their father's name. This Euro-Canadian manner of naming was a source of distress for many Inuit women who felt that their identities had been arbitrarily reassigned. "Women were renamed in their absence, by men. One Elder remembered her confusion when her husband came home and announced their new name. It made no sense. Women didn't take their husbands' names, yet suddenly, both she and her husband had his father's last name."[13]

GENDER

It is often noted that men and women had distinct but complementary and interdependent roles in Inuit society. Men hunted to provide food and hides, while women prepared the food, and especially, the clothing that made hunting possible. But this is an overly simplistic understanding of gender roles and of the relationship between Inuit men and women. Inuit cosmology invests women with *the* essential role in attracting the animals needed for food, clothing, and fuel. Among Inupiat, for example, the tasks that are regarded as female such as sewing, butchering, and sharing are regarded as hunting rather than domestic skills. "Male/female interdependence is absolutely explicit in the cosmology of marriage; the generosity of the wife in sharing meat and the skill of her needle which 'makes the hunter' are central in attracting the animals to the husband."[14]

Women's contribution to the success of hunting is particularly explicit in the case of bowhead whale hunting, where the wives of the whaling captains are responsible for "calling the whales." Among other things, this involves maintaining the correct demeanor, particularly during the whaling season, by moving slowly, thinking peaceful thoughts, and acting generously. Given the tremendous amount of work and coordination of labor that are the responsibilities of a whaling captain's wife (see Chapter 6), this is no casual expectation.

An Inupiaq story symbolically equates the life force of the whale with woman and the whale's body with the house. In the story, a raven flying over the water falls exhausted into a whale's mouth, and finds himself in "a beautiful and lovely house where there was light and warmth."[15] The light and warmth were from a lamp (the whale's heart) tended by a young woman (the whale's soul). During the whale-hunting season, today as in the past, "the whale-woman in her house sees the whaling captain-woman in hers, senses her welcoming spirit [and] decides that this is a good place 'to camp' and offers itself to the whaling crew."[16] This story, which continues to have salience in contemporary Inupiat communities, likely has quite ancient roots. Archeologists have noted that Thule period winter houses closely resemble the shape of a whale, with the ribs used as upright supports, mimicking the skeleton of the whale. Oil lamps, though no longer used for light and heat in Inuit homes, continue to be symbolically associated with femininity in many parts of the Inuit North. For example, Pauktuutit, the Canadian Inuit women's organization, employs the *qulliq* (stone lamp) as the symbol of women's essential role in Inuit social and political life.

Non-Native northern administrators disregarded Inuit understandings of gender relationships and imposed their own notions of appropriate gender roles on Inuit communities. The result was that women were often excluded from formal decision making. Although at present, there are a number of Inuit women political leaders, this was especially true in Canada in the first years after Inuit moved from seasonal hunting camps into permanent towns and villages, when non-Native Northern Service Officers, the local administrators, would invite only men to participate in community councils and, for the most part, only men were offered wage employment. Canadian

Ulukhaktok elders and youth at International Women's Day gathering, March 9, 2001. (Photo by author)

government–sponsored economic development surveys from the 1960s employ the Euro-Canadian concepts of "head of household" and "breadwinner" when discussing men. This kind of sexism was apparent in other reports as well. For example, reports on social development speak of "promiscuity" among young women.

A Third Sex

Until relatively recently Inuit in parts of the Canadian Arctic recognized a category of persons that is sometimes described in the academic literature as "a third sex." It is more appropriate, however, to speak of a third gender (a social distinction) rather than a third sex (a biological distinction). Inuit regarded all fetuses as male, but believed that some changed their sex at birth. The fetus was said to hold its penis in the womb, letting go only at birth if he wants to remain a boy, but letting go earlier if he wants to become a girl. Some infants were said to have transformed their sex from male to female at the moment of birth, particularly if the labor was long.

Anthropologist Bernard Saladin d'Anglure, who investigated the occurrence among Inuit from the Igloolik region of Nunavut, connects the phenomenon to the infant's name or names.[17] If the namesakes of a girl were all or primarily male she might be regarded as a *sipiniq* (one who had changed its sex); raised as a boy, taught to hunt and to engage in other male-gendered tasks, and dressed as a boy. This continued at least until puberty, but Saladin d'Anglure offers examples of sipiniit (*pl.*) who, though married to persons of the opposite sex, continued their cross-gendered identity well into adulthood. It is important to note that identity as sipiniq related to an individual's gender role rather than to her sexuality.

Although there were also biological males who were raised as females, it appears that most of the individuals identified as sipiniit were infants whose penis and scrotum were "observed" to split at birth to form a vulva. There is some question as to whether, in the past, Inuit also recognized the possibility of transformation from female to male. Anthropologist Jean Briggs reports that Inuit she has consulted with "believe that an infant can change its sex from male to female at the moment of birth. Midwives see this happen occasionally; but it never happens in reverse—that is, the sex never changes from female to male."[18] Saladin d'Anglure, in contrast, offers two cases of sipiniit who were said to have "split the other way," but in both cases he attributes the phenomenon to a child born with an unusually small penis and scrotum. He does not try to reconcile the logical inconsistency of physical transformation from female to male at birth with the assertion that Inuit regarded all fetuses as male.[19]

MARRIAGE

Prior to the arrival of Christian missionaries and non-Native colonial administrators, Inuit accomplished marriage without ceremony or much fanfare. To be considered married, a couple simply started living together. Children were sometimes betrothed at birth, but betrothal did not always result in marriage, and it was more often the case that a marriage would be arranged once an individual was skilled enough to carry out adult tasks. For girls this usually occurred around the time of the first menstrual period, while boys were generally a bit older. As in the case of Apphia Agalakti Awa, born in 1931, it was not unusual for a girl to be married to a man 10 years her senior.

My father, Arvaarluk, he was getting old when I got married. He knew that he wouldn't be living on the earth for many more years. He knew that he was going to die early, and he wanted me taken care of. . . . He knew that when he died I wouldn't be able to live alone, so he arranged a marriage for me. He arranged it out of love. Even though I was his only daughter and the only one around to look after him, my father gave me to this man and his family. . . . I was so young I had never thought about falling in love or marriage. . . . I was maybe thirteen or fourteen years old.[20]

Apphia was so frightened of marriage that she ran away from her husband and back to her father, but soon her husband and in-laws moved to another camp taking her with them. Eventually, she came to love and respect her husband, but this was only after several years of marriage.

We used to go to bed, but we never had sex for a long time. I would be in bed with him and stay with him in bed, and thought this was the way married life was. Apparently I was wrong. I guess he was waiting for me to grow up. He wanted to be with me and be my husband, but he thought I was too young. . . . He never bothered me or tried to have sex with me.

When I started menstruating, that is when I found out about sex. . . . If it was today, with the RCMP [police] and Social Services here, I would report that I was raped by my husband. . . . I remember being so upset after it happened to me. I remember telling my mother-in-law about this bad thing that had happened to me. She scolded me. She screamed at me, saying, "Don't say things like that!"

. . . Sometimes couples who had never talked or slept together would get married. Women were just taken from their camps one day. We were taken away—we had no say. Once we got married, we would start sleeping with our husbands. It was really terrible that way. I had never slept with a man before I got married. When we got married, I had to open up and fall in love with my husband. That is how it was done in the old days.[21]

Despite the ideal of women's essential role in providing subsistence, in practice, women, especially young women, had very little power or control over their lives. Adults were expected to be married, and in fact, marriage was, and to an extent remains, a marker of adulthood; something that is necessary "to a full life" according to Ulukhaktok elder Sam Oliktoak.[22] As noted above, subsistence work involves both male and female labor. The Inuit understanding of "work" is something one does for one's spouse. In the Belcher Islands, Nunavut, in the 1960s, for example, young adults hoping to catch the attention of a potential spouse made concerted efforts to be seen to be working hard.[23]

No Traditional Marriage Rituals

Just as traditional Inuit marriage was accomplished without ceremony, divorce also occurred without resort to formal procedure. However, it was unusual for divorce to occur after a couple had been married for several years and had children together. Relatively high death rates combined with the economic necessity of being married meant that most adults married several times. Additionally, in the past, some Inuit marriages were polygynous. Polyandry was also permitted, but was not common.

With conversion to Christianity, Inuit marriage practices changed. For one, Christian missionaries outlawed polygyny and polyandry. They also insisted that Inuit couples be formally married in a religious ceremony, and there are descriptions of Anglican missionaries in Canada in the early part of the 20th century traveling from camp to camp formally wedding already married (according to Inuit custom) couples in mass ceremonies. In at least some places, this practice resulted in officially registered "legal marriages" of new couples who might not have remained together.

Contemporary Marriages

At present, Inuit marriage practices are similar to those of the majority populations in each of the nations in which they reside, although it should be acknowledged that the majority has become more similar to the Inuit rather than the other way around. It is common for teenagers and young adults to engage in multiple sexual relationships without the intent of establishing a marital bond, though Inuit teens in Ulukhaktok told anthropologist Richard Condon that they tried to keep their sexual activities hidden from their parents for fear of being pressured into marriage.[24] There is no stigma attached to pregnancy or childbirth outside of marriage—children are welcomed, and there is no shortage of people anxious to adopt a baby if its biological parents choose not to raise it. Adoption is, in fact, quite common. Sandra Pikujak Katsak, a 20-year-old woman from Pond Inlet, Nunavut, described her parents' reaction to her sister's pregnancy.

They never said anything about Allan, Mona's boyfriend, though—even when Mona got pregnant. I thought that my parents would get pissed off when she told them. Mona said it in a vague sort of way, "Oh, Mom, I've been missing my periods lately," that kind of thing. And my mom said, "Well, you must be pregnant." That was about it. My dad, he was in the washroom at the time. Mom told him when he came out. His face was hidden for a while, he was quiet, then he turned around and has a big smile on his face. That really shocked me. She was fourteen, fifteen, something like that. I thought he would start screaming and yelling. He was smiling pretty hard.[25]

Selecting Partners

Parents no longer choose marriage partners for the children, but this change occurred at different times in different regions. In the Inuvialuit community of Ulukhaktok, for example, young Inuit began arranging their own marriages only in the 1970s.

By the mid- to late 1970s, church weddings ceased to be a critical element in the pairbonding process [in Ulukhaktok], indicating a departure from the experience of the preceding generation. Not only were young people selecting partners on their own, but they were generally living together for several years and [would] have children long before the formal marriage ceremony. The typical pattern was as follows. A young couple would start to see one another on a regular basis. This frequently entailed sexual relations, but on an extremely clandestine basis. . . . Once the young couple decided upon their compatibility, they would get "shacked up" (to use the local expression). This entailed either the young man or the young woman moving into the other's bedroom in the parents' home. When a housing unit became available, the young couple would set up [an independent household]. Frequently—only after several years of marriage and at least one or two children—the couple would decide to have a formal church wedding. Prior to the formal ceremony the couple nevertheless considered themselves and were considered by others to be husband and wife.[26] [At present, Canadian law also considers them to be married in "common-law."]

Life in modern towns and villages along with the transition to a wage labor economy and formal schooling has contributed to Inuit marrying at later ages than previously. It has also made it possible for individuals to remain unmarried, willingly or not. Many of the smallest Inuit communities throughout the North have unbalanced sex ratios as women, especially, have migrated to larger towns and to southern cities, leaving men unable to find partners.

SEXUALITY

Although marriages were not established on the basis of romantic passion, there are many accounts that indicate that many long
marriages were characterized by love. But this was not always the
case, and as Apphia Awa's account of her own marriage shows,
women often had no knowledge of sex at the time they married and
their first sexual experiences would today be characterized as rape.
Women were also subjected to sexual violence in the form of abduc-
tion and forced marriage. Cape Dorset artist Napachie Pootoogook's
(1938–2002) drawing "Attachialuk Stealing the Women" depicts an
historical incident in which a man abducted several women after
killing their husbands. Rape and sexual violence is also a theme in a
number of traditional stories. This lack of women's power in sexual
relations contrasts markedly with the important role that women
played in subsistence work and cosmology and the two situations
are not easily reconciled. The status of women remains an important
issue in Inuit communities throughout the North where women are
frequent victims of sexual and domestic assault.

Spouse Exchange

While many married couples shared a deep affection for one another, traditional Inuit culture permitted, and even encouraged,
spouse exchange—short-term exchange of partners for the purpose
of sexual relations. It seems likely that most married couples participated in spouse exchange relationships at some point in their
marriages. In some parts of the Inuit North, spouse exchanges occurred as part of mid-winter festivals in which people born in winter were matched by a shaman with partners born in summer. This
level of formal organization, however, did not characterize all spouse
exchanges.

Traditionally, marriages were formed on the basis of social and
economic need. Spouse exchanges provided a legitimate outlet for
sexual relations based on infatuation and the exchanges were often
initiated by women. By providing a reciprocal and egalitarian ave-
nue for extramarital sex, Inuit were able to acknowledge and act upon
sexual infatuation without threatening the marriage bond. This is
not to suggest that sexual jealousy did not exist, but none of the historical accounts of Inuit social life indicate that it was associated with
spouse exchange. Not surprisingly, Christian missionaries found
spouse exchange an anathema, and according to Ulukhaktok elder

Albert Palvik, they succeeded in eliminating it as a legitimate institution. The end of spouse exchange did not end extramarital sexual relations, with the result, in Palvik's view, that missionaries caused
promiscuity.[27]

THE DAILY LIVES OF CHILDREN
AND ADOLESCENTS

The concentration of Inuit into permanent town and villages contributed to many changes in Inuit family life and has been an especially
significant source of change in the Inuit life course. Children growing up in hunting camps were rarely out of immediate sight of their
parents or other adult relatives, and may have had few other children to play with. While babies and small children were demanding
and greatly indulged, older children were not. Children as young
as four or five years of age, though clearly recognized as children,
would begin to comport themselves like adults, modulating their
emotions and avoiding making demands upon others. Describing
the children at the last hunting camp at Chantrey Inlet, Nunavut,
anthropologist Jean Briggs noted that, "the older Utku children *were*
usually gentle-mannered, even when they did not feel shy (*ilira*) and
afraid (*iqhi*). They were never chittery in the noisy manner of children
in my own world, never buzzed inside the tents and iglus with the
young restlessness that would have been so distracting in those close
confines; but normally there was a gaiety, a spontaneity—a childlike
aliveness—in their quietness."[28]

While children were allowed a great deal of autonomy in their daily
activities, girls, in particular, were often encouraged to take on tasks
such as making tea, scraping hides, sewing, or caring for younger
siblings. Because adults were always close at hand, children learned
by observing and through trial and error with the assumption that
children would, at their own pace, develop the competencies necessary to survive and to have successful lives. To a large extent, Inuit
have maintained their traditional childrearing practices in modern
communities.

Life in government-administered towns and villages was different
from camp life in many ways, but perhaps most important from the
perspectives of children and teens, was that living in towns permitted an expansion of their social worlds. The combination of population concentration, increased birth rates, and schooling fostered the
development of youth cultures and peer groups and extended the
period between childhood and adulthood. Whereas Inuit children

Ulukhaktok children playing at 3:00 A.M. during the summer of 1982.
(Photo by author)

in the past moved from childhood into their adult roles in their early
to mid-teens, Inuit today experience an extended period of adolescence. Despite these changes, the daily lives of Inuit children and
teens continue to revolve around their extended families. Children's
closest and most important social relationships are with parents,
grandparents, aunts and uncles, siblings and cousins.

Schooling, in particular, has been an important source of change
because it takes children out of the immediate environment of their
parents and introduces new values and expectations, many of which
cannot be met in Inuit communities where wage employment opportunities are extremely limited. One result is high levels of unemployment and underemployment and a further extension of the
adolescent period. In the Nuuk, the capital of Greenland, adolescents
and young adults have developed a subculture of music and graffiti
as an outlet for their frustrations; in the much smaller Canadian Inuit
community of Ulukhaktok, unemployed youth fill their time playing and watching hockey and other sports. Music and sports may be
productive responses to frustrated goals, but Inuit youth throughout
the North also have extremely high rates of suicide.

AGING

Traditional Inuit culture accorded authority on the basis of age, and in many cases elders continue to be held in high esteem as keepers of Inuit culture. Elders are often singled out for special distributions of country food and invited to share their knowledge. Until quite recently, elders continued to live with their offspring and were supported as they aged. As with other aspects of Inuit family life, care of the aged has also come to resemble the practices in the broader society. Even in small villages, where presumably people are able to continue to live according to traditional Inuit norms and values, the life course is experienced in ways common to urban non-Natives. For example, a 12-year-old girl from the East Greenland village of Ittoqqortoormiit (pop. 529) described the local nursing home. "In the old people's home [there] are many old people who do not have a home. But their home is the old people's community. They are sent from their children that are grown up children, because they are too busy."[29]

NOTES

1. Saladin d'Anglure, Bernard (1994) "From Foetus to Shaman: The Construction of an Inuit Third Sex," in *Amerindian Rebirth: Reincarnation Belief among North American Indians and Inuit,* Antonia Mills and Richard Slobodin, eds., Toronto: University of Toronto Press, 94.

2. Nuttall, Mark (1992) *Arctic Homeland: Kinship, Community and Development in Northwest Greenland,* London: Belhaven Press, 69.

3. Peter Irniq quoted in Alia, Valerie (2007) *Names and Nunavut: Culture and Identity in Arctic Canada,* New York: Berghahn Books, 28.

4. Angilirq, Paul Apak, Zacharias Kunuk, Herve´ Paniaq, and Pauloosie Quilitalik, Norman Cohn, and Bernard Saladin d'Anglure (2002) *Atanarjuat: The Fast Runner: Inspired by a Traditional Inuit Legend of Igloolik,* Toronto: Coach House Books and Isuma Publications, 67. This book was issued alongside the film and contains the film script.

5. Guemple, Lee (1988) "Teaching Social Relations to Inuit Children," in *Hunters and Gatherers: Vol. 2, Property, Power, Ideology,* Tim Ingold, David Riches, and James Woodburn, eds., Oxford: Berg, 135.

6. Rasmussen, Knud (1929) *Intellectual Culture of the Iglulik Eskimos, Report of the Fifth Thule Expedition (1921–24),* Vol. 7, No. 1, Copenhagen: Gyldendalske Boghandel, 58.

7. Søby, Regitze Margrethe (1997) "Naming and Christianity," *Etudes/Inuit/Studies* 21(1–2): 293–301.

8. Nuttall, *Arctic Homeland,* 88–89.

9. Quoted in Wachowich, Nancy, with Apphia Agalakti Awa, Rhoda Kaukjak Katsak, and Sandra Pikujak Katsak (1999) *Saqiyuq: Stories from the*

Lives of Three Inuit Women, Kingston and Montreal: McGill-Queens University Press, 65.

10. Scott, James C., John Tehranian, and Jeremy Mathias (2002) "The Production of Legal Identities Proper to States: The Case of the Permanent Family Surname," *Comparative Studies in Society and History* 44(1): 27.

11. Quoted in Wachowich, *Saqiyuq,* 132.

12. Searles, Edmund (2002) "Food and the Making of Modern Inuit Identities," *Food and Foodways* 10: 65.

13. Alia, Valerie (1994) "Inuit Women and the Politics of Naming in Nunavut," *Canadian Woman Studies* 14(4): 13.

14. Bodenhorn, Barbara (1990) "'I'm Not the Great Hunter, My Wife Is': Iñupiat and Anthropological Models of Gender," *Etudes/Inuit/Studies* 14(1–2): 65.

15. Rasmussen, Knud (1952) *Posthumous Notes on the Alaskan Eskimos, Report of the Fifth Thule Expedition (1921–24),* Vol. 10, Copenhagen: Gyldendalske Boghandel, 24.

16. Bodenhorn, " 'I'm Not the Great Hunter'," 63.

17. Saladin d'Anglure, "From Foetus to Shaman."

18. Briggs, Jean L. (1974) "Eskimo Women: Makers of Men," in *Many Sisters: Women in Cross-Cultural Perspective,* Caroline J. Matthiassson, ed., New York: Free Press, 297.

19. Saladin d'Anglure, "From Foetus to Shaman."

20. Quoted in Wachowich, *Saqiyuq,* 38–39.

21. Ibid., 40–41.

22. Quoted in Stern, Pamela R., and Richard G. Condon (1995) "A Good Spouse is Hard to Find: Marriage, Spouse Exchange and Infatuation among the Copper Inuit," in *Romantic Passion: A Human Universal?* William Jankowiak, ed., New York: Columbia University Press, 203.

23. Guemple, Lee (1986) "Men and Women, Husbands and Wives: The Role of Gender in Traditional Inuit Society," *Etudes/Inuit/Studies* 10(1–2): 9–24.

24. Condon, Richard G. (1987) *Inuit Youth: Growth and Change in the Canadian Arctic,* New Brunswick, NJ: Rutgers University Press, 148.

25. Quoted in Wachowich, *Saqiyuq,* 235.

26. Stern and Condon, "A Good Spouse," 212.

27. Ibid., 202.

28. Briggs, Jean L. (1970) *Never in Anger: Portrait of an Eskimo Family,* Cambridge, MA: Harvard University Press, 118.

29. Quoted in Rygaard, Jette (2008) "The City Life of Youths in Greenland," *Etudes/Inuit/Studies* 32(1): 41.

2

LANGUAGE AND INTELLECTUAL LIFE

The Inuit language is called *Inuktitut,* meaning "the Inuit way [of speaking]." Before contact with non-Natives, Inuktitut was not written. The fact that communication was exclusively oral and Inuit communities were widely dispersed helped foster regional variations in vocabulary, phonology, and grammar. Nonetheless, linguists consider Inuktitut to be a single language with many dialects. This means that with some bit of effort people who speak the Greenlandic dialect of Inuktitut, which is called *Kalaallisut,* can understand and be understood by people who speak one of the Canadian dialects of Inuktitut, or the dialect from North Alaska called *Inupiaq.*

Linguists classify Inuktitut as polysynthethic, meaning that words (and sentences) are created by adding multiple suffixes to a base or root word. The result is that a sentence or other complex phrase may consist of a single, long word made up of many short units of meaning. (See the discussion of *Inuit Qaujimajatuqangit* below for an example of the way Inuktitut combines units of meaning.) Inuktitut, like all languages, is dynamic. One bit of evidence of this is that young Inuit tend to attach fewer suffixes in forming words than older Inuit.

LANGUAGE SURVIVAL UNDER COLONIALISM

It is frequently the case that indigenous peoples lose their language and start speaking a national language under conditions of colonialism. For Inuit in Canada that means English or French; in Alaska, it is English. This language shift disrupts communication between generations, because children are usually the first to pick up the new language. While the shift is occurring people in different generations have very different language abilities, with children most likely to be monolingual in the national language and their grandparents to be monolingual in the indigenous language. For Inuit it is generally the case that as one moves across the Arctic from Greenland through Canada to Alaska, a smaller proportion of Inuit adults are able to speak their own language. There are Inuit communities, particularly in Alaska and in the western Canadian Arctic, but also in Labrador, where children no longer learn Inuktitut as their first language. In 2005, for example, there were almost no Inupiat (Alaskan Inuit) under the age of 45 whose first language was Inupiaq.[1]

In Nuuk, Greenland's capital city, many Inuit are bilingual in Kalaallisut and Danish, and significant numbers also speak English. Kalaallisut is the everyday vernacular. This is likely the result of support given to Kalaallisut, first from the Danish colonial government, and more recently, from the Home Rule government's policy of Greenlandization. English speakers in North America tend to regard learning a second or third language as unusual and difficult, but this is an example of where North Americans are contrary to historical and global norms. In the past, Inuit living near other language communities spoke the languages of their neighbors as well as their own language. This is not surprising given that Inuit, especially those in Alaska, had regular trading relationships with peoples on both sides of the Bering Strait (see Introduction). While many Inuit in Canada speak English, Inuktitut remains strong in most of Nunavut and Nunavik (Arctic Quebec), and the Nunavut territorial government has a policy to make Inuktitut the language of the workplace.

WRITING SYSTEMS

The first writing systems for Inuktitut were developed by Christian missionaries so that Inuit would be able to read the Bible and other religious literature. The first translation of the Bible into Inuktitut was completed in 1766. For the most part, the missionaries were not trained linguists, and the writing systems they created were idiosyncratic and thus, not well suited for use in developing a written Inuktitut literature. Beginning around 1850, however, two very different efforts at creating a written Inuktitut resulted in orthographies that Inuit both adopted and adapted to their own needs.

Samuel Kleinschmidt, a linguist and Moravian missionary in Greenland, produced a grammar and a dictionary. He also wrote articles for the first Greenlandic newspaper, *Atuagagdliutit*, which began publication in 1861 (see Chapter 9). The orthography that Kleinschmidt published in 1871, based on the dialect of Inuktitut spoken in West Greenland, became the standard for Kalaallisut. Kleinschmidt's orthography was used in newspapers and schoolbooks in Greenland until 1973 when it was revised and simplified. The writing system created by Kleinschmidt used the Roman alphabet, the same alphabet used to write most European languages.

Syllabics

During the same period a pair of Anglican missionaries in Nunavik, John Horden and E. A. Watkins, adapted a writing system

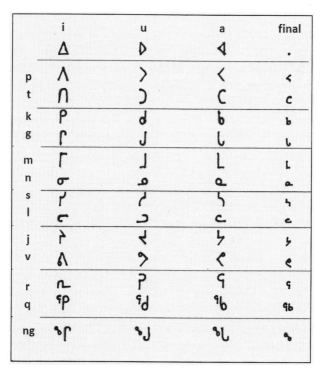

	i	u	a	final
	Δ	Ḋ	◁	·
p	Λ	>	<	‹
t	∩	⊃	⊂	c
k	ᑭ	ᑐ	ᑳ	ᑊ
g	ᒉ	ᒎ	ᒐ	ᒡ
m	ᒥ	ᒧ	ᒪ	ᒻ
n	ᓂ	ᓄ	ᓇ	ᓐ
s l	ᓯ	ᓱ	ᓴ	ᔅ
	ᔨ	ᔪ	ᑫ	ᔆ
j	ᔨ	ᔪ	ᔭ	ᔾ
v	ᕕ	ᕗ	ᕙ	ᕝ
r	ᕆ	ᕈ	ᕋ	ᕐ
q	ᖅᑭ	ᖅᑐ	ᖅᑳ	ᖅᒃ
ng	ᖏ	ᖑ	ᖓ	ᖕ

Inuktitut syllabics.

developed by another missionary for the Ojibwa and Cree languages to Inuktitut. This orthography, which is based on Pitman shorthand, is a syllabic system in which each symbol stands for a syllable consisting of a consonant-vowel combination. There are 14 consonant symbols written in 3 positions depending upon the vowel sound. A superscript version of each symbol is used to indicate a final consonant.

Inuktitut syllabics were popularized among Inuit in the eastern Canadian Arctic through the evangelical activities of the Reverend Edmund James Peck. Peck, who was called *Uqamaaq* ("the Great Speaker") by Inuit, proselytized to Inuit in northern Quebec and southern Baffin Island, eventually establishing a mission near Pangnirtung (1894–1904). Using the syllabic script, he produced a translation of the New Testament in 1876, and "insisted that Inuit to learn read syllabics in order to keep contact with the Scriptures."[2] Peck succeeded in his missionary work, in part, because Inuit converts worked to spread Christianity among other Inuit. He also used traders and Inuit travelers to distribute church literature. The result was that nearly all speakers of Inuktitut in Nunavut and Nunavik became literate in Inuktitut.

By the first decades of the 20th century most Inuit living in what is today Nunavut and Nunavik could read and write Inuktitut using syllabics, a somewhat remarkable fact given that there were no schools in the Canadian Arctic at the time. Instead, Inuit taught each other to read and write with syllabics and parents taught their children. Peter Pitseolak (1902–73) recorded that he had learned syllabics as a child, a fact that greatly surprised a Canadian government official.[3] Members of the Fifth Thule Expedition 1921–24 noted that the Inuit around Igloolik were writing letters to each other using syllabics and that paper and pencils were in great demand.[4] This is especially interesting because, despite this evidence to the contrary, Fifth Thule Expedition investigators and others regarded Igloolik Inuit as isolated and unaffected by contact with whalers and other non-Natives.

In Alaska, too, it fell to Christian missionaries to create writing systems for Inupiaq and other indigenous languages. In 1946 Inupiaq minister Roy Ahmaogak (d. 1968) worked with missionary and linguist Eugene Nida develop the orthography for Inupiaq that is still in use today. He also worked with Wycliffe Bible Translators to complete a translation of the New Testament. Non-Native missionaries and church officials in Alaska, however, tended to regard the use of indigenous languages as "a practical approach to the evangelization of Natives" but did not encourage the use of indigenous languages in schools or for other secular purposes.[5]

Existence of Multiple Writing Systems Presents a Challenge

Today, each region of the Inuit North uses a distinct writing system developed for that region, making it difficult for Inuit in one part of the Arctic to read literature produced by Inuit in another. Inuit in Greenland, Labrador, Alaska, and the western Canadian Arctic write their language using the several orthographies based on the Roman alphabet, while Inuit in Nunavik and most of Nunavut use syllabics for writing Inuktitut. Inuit across the North have proposed reforms that would establish a single writing system to be used by all Inuit, and in 1983 the Inuit Circumpolar Conference adopted a resolution calling for a single Inuktitut writing system. The resolution was not heeded because no Inuit group is willing to give up its own way of writing. Even within regions, some individual Inuit have rejected orthographic reforms meant to improve literacy. Outside of Greenland there is, in fact, very little reading material aside from a few bilingual newspapers and magazines as well as government documents produced in Canadian dialects of Inuktitut (see Chapter 9). In Labrador, in the western Canadian Arctic, and in Alaska, written Inuktitut remains almost exclusively a liturgical language.

ORAL TRADITIONS

Storytelling is an important medium for transmitting information in all cultures. Inuit, like all peoples, tell stories to entertain. But storytelling also creates a shared knowledge base about things like history, the nature of humans and animals, how people should act toward each other, how to avoid danger, and what happens to people who break the rules. Inuit told stories in intimate family settings such as in tents and snowhouses, but stories were also told in large public gatherings. Inuit continue to tell traditional stories, though today they sometimes do so in English or Danish as well as in Inuktitut.

There are two primary types of stories: *quliaqtuat* and *unipkaat* (in the Inupiaq dialect). *Quliaqtuat* are about events that occurred in the recent past. They could be about ordinary events or they may tell of unusual or extraordinary incidents. Very often quliaqtuat include events, such as people turning into animals or flying through the air, which could seem fantastical, but are regarded as true. For example, the following story told by Alec Millik from Point Hope, Alaska, is a quliaqtuaq (sing.) that includes a description of another quliaq-tuaq:

It was 1953, wintertime. My wife invited Masiiñ [a shaman] to supper. And after we had eaten, the old man told stories. Then he called me by name, and told us he'd been traveling last night. He'd been to Russia. And when he'd flown round for a while, he saw the Russian boss. "That's a bad man," said Masiiñ, "so I killed him." Next day at three o'clock—we had a bat-tery radio—I listened at my coffee break. The news announcers said Stalin was dead.[6]

All Stories Are Presumed to Be True

What makes a story a quliaqtuaq is that it is about people who are still living or who lived recently enough that it is possible to trace their connections to living people. There are no restrictions on the subject of a quliaqtuaq, but they are regarded as true stories. The ve-racity of the tale is judged by "the narrator's ability to relate his or her experiences in an immediate and vivid way."[7]

Unipkaat are stories about the distant past, a past so long ago that it is impossible to trace a direct connection to specific living people. Like quliaqtuat, unipkaat are also assumed to be true stories, but the events happened so far in the past that the storyteller is unable to personally vouch for the veracity of the story. Instead, the narra-tor begins an unipkaaq (sing.) by stating who he or she learned the story from. Unipkaat almost always contain fantastical events such as human-animal transformations or small people who live in the ground. Unipkaat often tell about the origins of phenomena like the sun and moon or how animals came to have particular character-istics. Quite a number of unipkaaq tell of misfortunes that befell people who violated taboos or that happened to children who dis-obeyed their parents, but they also describe the proper ways that people should treat each other or treat animals. According to film-maker Zacharias Kunuk, an Inuit story is "like a lesson on how you want to lead your life when you grow up. These stories were taught to us, they were like bedtime stories for us when we used to sleep side by side. Mothers would tell stories to put their kids to sleep and give lessons."[8] Inuit storytelling today is done through a variety of media including art (see Chapter 10) as well as music, films, and written literature (see Chapter 9).

INUIT EDUCATION

Inuit, traditionally, had no need for education specialists or formal schools. As a former teacher observed, "there were no places in traditional culture where children were herded together for a set number of hours a day to learn how to become functioning adults."[9] Instead, children learned from observing their parents and other adults and by trial and error and were usually allowed to mature at their own pace. Aside from storytelling, Inuit emphasized learning through nonverbal means, and children were discouraged from asking questions or demanding explanations. This is not to say that adults were not actively engaged in teaching children. They were, and there are numerous accounts of adults pushing children to master a task.[10] For example, girls learning to sew often had their seams ripped out and were told to start over. Adults also quizzed children and played verbal games with them, especially games that helped children develop understanding about how people are related (see Chapter 8). They responded to mistakes with laughter or teasing, teaching children to be careful in their judgments and to learn to laugh at their own mistakes. The key to Inuit ways of teaching is that "children are not separated from adult society in order to learn, but are included in it, and even more importantly, are expected to provide their own interpretations and to make their own decisions almost from the start."[11] This way of teaching and learning is very different from what children experience in school.

SCHOOLING

The earliest schools for Inuit were established by Christian churches. This was the case in Greenland, Alaska, Canada, and Labrador (which only became part of Canada in 1949), although the specific way that schooling was enacted differed in the four places. American educators tended to regard indigenous languages as inferior to English and believed that the retention of indigenous languages acted as a barrier to social advancement. This was true of church as well as of later Bureau of Indian Affairs educators. As a result Inupiaq children were educated in English almost exclusively until the 1970s. Inupiaq and other Alaska Native children "were slapped, beaten, ridiculed, punished for speaking their own languages in school."[12] The same hostility toward Inuktitut as a language of instruction was true in Canada where Inuit students were taught with a curriculum adopted from the province of Ontario.

Only in Greenland has Inuktitut always been the language of instruction. At present, Greenlanders themselves debate whether to intensify the teaching of Danish to give students more access to advanced education and employment.

Labrador

Inuit in Labrador, prior to 1949, were taught in Inuktitut. There, the schools were run by Moravian missionaries following the model of schools in Greenland. The first Moravian school opened in Nain in 1791. In 1914 there were eight schools, including one that served as a boarding school. The instruction was limited to subjects that the missionaries regarded as practical and necessary—reading, writing, basic arithmetic, geography and history, plus sewing, singing, carpentry, and the Bible—and was equivalent to approximately three years of elementary school education. When Labrador (along with Newfoundland) became Canada's 10th province in 1949, education of Inuit became a provincial matter. Immediately, English became the language of instruction, but the education level also increased so that Inuit students in Labrador can now obtain high school and postsecondary educations.

Canada

In the rest of Canada, the Catholic and Anglican churches created day schools for Inuit beginning in the 1920s, and each opened a boarding school in the Mackenzie Delta region of the western Canadian Arctic in 1929. Children at the boarding schools often spent up to nine months away from their families. While some Inuktitut was permitted at the day schools, it was not permitted in the boarding schools. It is likely that this discrimination against Inuktitut in the western Arctic contributed to the loss of fluency in Inuktitut among Inuit there.

The Canadian government replaced church-run schools with federal day schools in most Inuit communities between 1948 and 1963. Except in the largest communities, however, these did not offer education beyond elementary school. Students who wished to continue their educations were forced to attend a government boarding school. Canada opened a boarding school for Inuit high school students in Churchill, Manitoba, in 1964. Later, the government established boarding schools in Inuvik, Yellowknife, and Iqaluit. Inuit students suffered as a result of being separated from their families as well as from emotional, physical, and sexual abuse by residential school staff. At the same time the Inuit political leaders who fought for land claims settlements and other aboriginal rights have said that meeting young Inuit from other communities while at residential schools enabled them to recognize that they faced a number of common problems that could only be addressed through collective action (see Chapter 6).

Although Nunavik is part of the province of Quebec, the provincial government largely ignored that region, its resources, and its Inuit residents until the mid-1960s. But as Francophone nationalism grew in Quebec in the 1960s, provincial leaders began to take an interest in the North. One interesting consequence is that the provincial government opened schools that used Inuktitut as the language of instruction for the first two years and French for subsequent years. The federal government continued to operate schools where English was the language of instruction, and the two school systems competed for pupils until 1978 when the Inuit-run Kativik School Board assumed authority over Inuit education in Nunavik.

Inuit Control of Education

Inuit control of education was one of the provisions of the 1975 James Bay and Northern Quebec land claims agreement (see Chapter 6). While Inuit control of education is important for both practical and symbolic reasons, it has done little to change the language used in school in either Nunavik or Nunavut. In Nunavik, children learn in Inuktitut through Grade 2, but after that either English or French is the language of instruction. A similar situation exists in Nunavut, where Inuit also (by virtue of constituting 85% of the population) control education. While there is some instruction on Inuit cultural topics, English is the only language of instruction in the two westernmost communities, Kugluktuk and Cambridge Bay, where survival of Inuktitut is most at risk. In the rest of the territory, children are taught in Inuktitut from kindergarten through Grade 5 with a transition to English instruction beginning in Grade 4. Justice Thomas R. Berger, who was commissioned to review the implementation of the Nunavut land claims agreement, believes that the Inuit ability to govern the Nunavut Territory according to their cultural values is put at risk by the current educational practices. According to Justice Berger, the government of Nunavut needs to give much more attention to providing schoolchildren with a strong foundation in Inuktitut literacy as well as bilingual education if it is to reach its goal of having Inuit hold a share of government jobs equivalent to their proportion of the population.

While extraordinary efforts have been made—often successfully—to provide post-secondary courses in Nunavut, it is simply not possible to provide the full spectrum of required courses in place. Even where is it possible to bring courses to the communities, advanced education is of necessity in English. Nunavut needs a generation of executives and managers, computer software designers, architects, audiologists, nurses, doctors, lawyers, accountants, x-ray technicians, RCMP [police] members and, of course, teachers. It is likely that few of them will receive their post-secondary education in Inuktitut.[13]

Berger goes on to say that the evidence points to the fact that strong literacy skills in a first language are essential to development of competency in a second. Yet, employers in Nunavut "complain that many students who leave school in Grades 10, 11, or 12 to work do not have sufficient literacy skills in either [English or Inuktitut] to be effective employees."[14]

Alaska

After Alaska became a state in 1959, it took over control of education from the federal Bureau of Indian Affairs. It did not fund high schools in many rural villages where most Alaska Natives lived. As was true in Canada, most Inuit students who wished to attend high school had to go to a boarding school. In 1971, a plane carrying students to the Mount Edgecumbe School in Sitka, Alaska, crashed killing 11 Inupiaq students from the North Slope Borough. This and other events led Alaska Natives to push for the state to provide high schools in every village, eventually filing a lawsuit. The suit alleged that forcing rural students, who were overwhelmingly Native, to attend boarding schools constituted a pattern of discrimination against Native students. In 1976, the state settled the case by agreeing to provide public education through Grade 12 in every village regardless of the number of students.

Inuit control of education was a primary factor behind the Inupiat fight to form a municipal government, the North Slope Borough, in 1972. Eben Hopson (1922–80), who became the first mayor of the North Slope Borough, saw control of education as essential to Inupiat cultural survival. With the property taxes levied on the Prudhoe Bay oil installations, the North Slope Borough was able to establish its own public school authority.

Hopson's interest in education, and certainly his political aspirations, can be traced to his youth. As a teenager in Barrow, Alaska, Hopson protested to the Commissioner of Indian Affairs that Inupiaq students were required to provide unpaid labor on Bureau of Indian Affairs public works projects. The local principal in Barrow retaliated for Hopson's impertinence by denying him passage to boarding school, thus ending his formal education. In a 1975 speech, Hopson argued that Inupiat must have both political and professional control over education in order to transmit "Inupiat traditional values and ideals." He went on to explain:

We must have teachers who will reflect and transmit our ideals and values. We must have Inupiat-centered orientation in all areas of instruction. I do not want my children to learn that we were "discovered" by Columbus or Vitus Bering. I do not want to hear that we were barbaric or "uncivilized." I do not want our children to feel inferior because their language and culture are different from those of their teacher. I do not want to see school planning surveys which list hunting, fishing, whaling or trapping as a "social" or "recreational" activity.[15]

POSTSECONDARY INSTITUTIONS

The opportunities for Inuit to pursue postsecondary education in the North are extremely limited. Most Inuit students who seek vocational training or university degrees need to leave the North to do so. The University of Greenland/Ilisimatusarfik is the only four-year university in Inuit lands. A teacher training program has existed in Greenland since the mid-19th century, but until recently most Greenlanders who sought higher education traveled to Denmark. Ilisimatusarfik was established as a degree-granting institution in 1987. It grew out of a research center called the Inuit Institute. In 2008 it served about 500 graduate and undergraduate students in a newly constructed building. Most classes are taught in Danish.

In the Canadian Arctic, Aurora College and Nunavut Arctic College serve students seeking vocational and technical training in the Northwest Territories and in Nunavut, respectively. Both colleges are especially important in training Inuit to be teachers, nurses, translators, and court workers. Nunavut Arctic College opened in Iqaluit in 1984 and has branch campuses in Cambridge Bay and Rankin Inlet. Both colleges also offer certificate courses in other communities on an ad hoc basis. A particularly innovative program was the Akitsiraq Law Program offered in Iqaluit by the University of Victoria,

New campus buildings of the University of Greenland/Ilisimatusarfik, August 2008. (Photo by Peter V. Hall)

which trained a small cadre of Inuit to be lawyers. It graduated 11 students in 2005, most of whom have been called to the bar. It is not certain whether the program will be offered again.

Many Alaska Native university students attend one of the University of Alaska campuses, and the university has branch campuses in a number of rural villages including Kotzebue. In the 1970s, the state legislature directed the University of Alaska at Fairbanks to establish the Alaska Native Language Center to study indigenous languages and to improve literacy and teaching in Alaska Native languages. The center is responsible for training speakers of Inupiaq and other Alaska Native languages to work as teachers and teacher's aides.

Ilisagvik College, in Barrow, Alaska, offers two-year degrees. It is part of the North Slope Borough, but is affiliated for degree-granting purposes with the University of Alaska. Ilisagvik College grew out the North Slope Higher Education Center established in 1986. An earlier North Slope Borough postsecondary institution, the Inupiat University of the Arctic, was short-lived.

Finally, it is important to mention the University of the Arctic, which was established in 2001 as a collaborative effort between academic, research, and indigenous organizations with activities in the Circumpolar North. The University of the Arctic offers an interdisciplinary Bachelor of Circumpolar Studies and other programs primarily through online courses.

INUIT WAYS OF KNOWING: INUPIAQ ILITQUISIAT AND INUIT QAUJIMAJATUQANGIT

In recent years, through land claims and self-government agreements, Inuit have regained some control over educational and other institutions. Inuit recognize that both Inuit culture and the social, economic, and political worlds in which Inuit live are significantly different today than they were before the arrival of non-Natives. At the same time, Inuit remain distinct from the national cultures of Canada, Denmark, and the United States, prompting discussions and debates within Inuit communities about what it means to operate government (and to live) in an Inuit way or according to Inuit cultural values. *Inupiaq Ilitquisiat* and *Inuit Qaujimajatuqangit* are two social movements that have emerged from these discussions.

Inupiat Ilitquisiat, meaning the "wisdom and lessons of Inupiaq people," originated in Alaska's Northwest Arctic Borough. It emerged in the early 1980s as a movement to "assert and validate Iñupiat ethnic identity, reactivate and preserve Iñupiaq skills and solve pressing social problems" especially drug and alcohol abuse.[16] Inupiat Ilitquisiat came out of discussions among Inupiaq political leaders, and these same leaders have worked to integrate its principles into the public and Inupiaq institutions in the region. These principles include affirmation of idealized Inuit values such as sharing, cooperation, personal responsibility, conflict avoidance, and respect for others as well as reassertion of the value of the Inuit cultural practices of subsistence hunting, deference to elders, and speaking the Inupiaq language. There have been some concrete outcomes of the movement including establishment of a bilingual Inupiaq-English preschool, a spirit camp for youth, and the creation of advisory committees of elders.

Inuit Qaujimajatuqangit, like Inupiat Ilitqusiat, is an elite movement. Frequently referred to by the initials IQ, it has emerged as the way to discuss the insertion of Inuit cultural values into the institutions of governance in the Nunavut Territory. *Qaujimajatuqangit* is broken down as follows:

Qaujima is a verb, meaning "to know." Adding the suffix-*jaq* turns it into a noun, meaning "that which is known." The addition of the suffix-*tuqaq*, an adjective meaning "has existed for a while"—makes *qaujimajatuqaq*. It denotes "something that has been known for a long time." The final suffix-*ngit* is a third-person plural possessive. Thus, *Inuit Qaujimajatuqangit* means literally "the things that Inuit have known for a long time"—in other words, specifically Inuit ways of thinking, acting, and being.

Like Inupiat Ilitqusiat, IQ emphasizes the need for sharing information between youth and elders. This, in part, comes from the recognition that the previous colonial administration of Inuit communities disrupted the Inuit ways of teaching and learning. As a result, a number of workshops aimed at defining and identifying the principles of IQ have been convened and the various departments of the Nunavut Government have committed to integrating IQ into their practices. In these workshops, however, IQ defies any clear definition, and participants have repeatedly emphasized that IQ cannot not be codified into a simple list of Inuit values. It is too soon to know how IQ is being integrated into daily life in Nunavut. For the time being, though, IQ remains a dynamic concept that requires ongoing discussion and debate.

NOTES

1. Kaplan, Lawrence D. (2005) "Inupiaq Writing and International Inuit Relations," *Etudes/Inuit/Studies* 29(1–2): 234.

2. Dorais, Louis-Jacques (1990) "The Canadian Inuit and Their Language," in *Arctic Languages: An Awakening,* Dirmid R. F. Collis, ed., Paris: UNESCO, 236, retrieved June 1, 2009 from http://unesdoc.unesco.org/images/0008/000861/086162e.pdf.

3. Pitseolak, Peter, and Dorothy Eber (1975) *People from Our Side,* Edmonton: Hurtig (reprinted Montreal: McGill-Queens University Press, 1993).

4. Mathiassen, Therkel (1928) *Material Culture of the Iglulik Eskimos, Report of the Fifth Thule Expedition (1921–24),* Vol. 6, No. 1, Copenhagen: Gyldendalske Boghandel, Nordisk Forlag, 233.

5. Kaplan, Lawrence D. (1990) "The Language of the Alaskan Inuit," in *Arctic Languages: An Awakening,* Dirmid R. F. Collis, ed., Paris: UNESCO, 134, retrieved June 1, 2009 from http://unesdoc.unesco.org/images/0008/000861/086162e.pdf.

6. Quoted in Lowenstein, Tom (1992) *The Things That Were Said of Them: Shaman Stories and Oral Histories of the Tikigaq People,* Berkeley: University of California Press, 196.

7. Bodenhorn, Barbara (1997) "People Who Are like Our Books: Reading and Teaching on the North Slope of Alaska," *Arctic Anthropology* 34 (1): 126.

8. Quoted in Crouse, Richard (2003) *The 100 Best Movies You've Never Seen,* Toronto: ECW Press, 6.

9. Mallon, S. T. (1979) "How Can an Alien Bureaucracy Safeguard a Language?" in *Eskimo Languages: Their Present-Day Conditions,* Bjarne Basse and Kirsten Jensen, eds., Aarhus: Arkona Publishers, 66.

10. See, for example, Bodenhorn, "People Who Are like Our Books"; Briggs, Jean L. (1998) *Inuit Morality Play: The Emotional Education of a Three Year Old*, New Haven, CT: Yale University Press; and Stern, Pamela (1999) "Learning to Be Smart: An Exploration of the Culture of Intelligence in a Canadian Inuit Community," *American Anthropologist* 101(3): 502–14.

11. Bodenhorn, "People Who Are like Our Books," 127.

12. Krauss, Michael E. (1979) "The Eskimo Languages in Alaska, Yesterday and Today," in *Eskimo Languages: Their Present-Day Conditions*, Bjarne Basse and Kirsten Jensen, eds., Aarhus: Arkona Publishers, 42.

13. Berger, Thomas R. (2008) *The Implementation of the Nunavut Land Claims Agreement Annual Report 2004–2006*, Ottawa: Department of Indian Affairs and Northern Development, 31.

14. Ibid.

15. Hopson, Eben (1975) Mayor's Address on Education, televised speech given in Barrow on December 19, transcript retrieved June 2, 2009 from http://www.ebenhopson.com/archives/Education.html.

16. McNabb, Steven (1991) "Elders, Iñupiat Ilitquisiat, and Culture Goals in Northwest Arctic," *Arctic Anthropology* 28(2): 65.

3

ECONOMIC LIFE

Historically Inuit made their livelihoods from the materials available in their immediate environment. Far from being desolate, the Arctic ecosystem provided all of the nutritional and material needs of Inuit communities. Prior to their encounters with non-Native whalers, traders, and others, Inuit made use of marine and terrestrial mammals for food and fuel as well as for the materials for making tools and clothing and for constructing houses and boats. Inuit lifestyles changed considerably as a result of contact with non-Native whalers, traders, colonizers, and missionaries, yet Inuit are often mistakenly idealized as subsistence hunters; that is, they are idealized as a people whose livelihoods are based exclusively or primarily on the noncommercial use of natural resources. But even in the distant past Inuit communities were not isolated or self-contained. They had well-developed, long-distance trading networks for valuable materials such as soapstone, iron, and baleen. Trading fairs were regular, important social and economic events.

Inuit throughout the North continue to engage in subsistence harvesting, and value it for social and cultural as much as economic reasons. But like all other peoples in the world today, Inuit are part of the global economy. In order to further their efforts towards self-determination, Inuit communities, organizations, and governments must concern themselves with modern forms of economic development and investment. Subsistence harvesting is one component of the mix of economic activities in contemporary Inuit communities that also includes wage labor, the purchase of imported consumer goods, banking, taxes, and government services and transfers.

SUBSISTENCE AND SHARING

Inuit families and communities harvest renewable resources to provide high-quality nutrition as well as to reaffirm valued social relationships. Inuit subsistence harvesting is a social as well as an economic activity and "the arctic environment requires many resources if it is to be exploited for subsistence. Boats, snow machines, rifles, sleds, clothing, equipment, food, fuel, as well as detailed knowledge of the terrain, the weather and so forth, are all crucial to a hunter's survival. To be fully prepared, one must call upon friends and family for help."[1]

Modern Tools for Modern Subsistence Harvesting

The tools used for subsistence harvesting now include snowmobiles, outboard motors, canvas tents, and other items that must be purchased. Hunters need to have access to cash in order to engage in subsistence hunting. For some this cash comes from wage employment. In Inuit communities in Canada and Alaska, often the most active subsistence hunters are individuals with jobs. There are, however, severely limited employment opportunities in many Inuit communities, so that many people who need jobs are unable to find full-time or even permanent work. Subsistence hunting remains highly valued even by families who can afford to purchase a diet comprised solely of imported foods. People give many different reasons for engaging in subsistence hunting including obligations to elders, a taste preference for country foods, and the high cost of purchasing imported foods. A young hunter from Ulukhaktok in the Northwest Territories declared that "it must be real boring spending all your time in town and having people hunt for you. [Hunting is] the best part of life!"[2]

Hunter Support Programs

Hunter Support Programs in Nunavut and Nunavik are an institutional way that Inuit in those regions have affirmed the value of subsistence work. The Nunavik Hunter Support Program (HSP), which began in 1983, was established as a provision of the James Bay and Northern Quebec Agreement (see Chapter 6), and it is funded with revenues derived from the James Bay hydroelectric dams. Funds are allocated annually to each Nunavik community, which collectively determines the specific ways that the moneys will be used to support local subsistence harvesting. Individual communities may decide to purchase large equipment such as a boat that can be used for communal hunting, or to build a freezer, or to provide gasoline and other supplies to hunters whose catch will be distributed to community members, or to purchase meat and fish directly from hunters and then redistribute it free of charge to others in the community. The HSP serves the twin purposes of providing some financial support to subsistence hunters who lack other means to support hunting and of ameliorating community-wide and individual household food shortages, but the levels of support are relatively low. They do not fully compensate hunters for the costs they incur, much less constitute a wage for hunting. For example, in 1997, 28 hunters in Akulivik received an average of $735 each for meat purchased by the local HSP.[3]

Markets for Country Food

There is much greater economic specialization in Greenland in contrast to Inuit communities in Alaska and Canada. Since the late 19th century, Greenlandic hunters have sold part of their catch to other Greenlanders who work for wages. At present, approximately 2,500 Greenlanders, living mostly in small villages, are considered to be "commercial hunters"; that is, their income comes primarily from selling meat, skins, and ivory derived from subsistence hunting.[4] Royal Greenland, a trading company owned by the Home Rule government, is a primary purchaser, but there are also local markets, similar to farmer's markets in North America, called *kalaaliaraq*, where individual hunters may sell some of their catch to other Greenlanders who do not engage in subsistence hunting. This system of markets for country food provides a source of income for residents of villages where there are few wage jobs, but more important, it ensures a reliable source of quality, locally produced foods that would otherwise have to be imported at great cost. Contrary to what might be expected, selling subsistence products into the market has not substantially altered sharing networks or the kin-orientation of subsistence work.

For the most part, however, it is not possible to make clear distinctions between activities that belong in a cash economy and activities that are part of a subsistence or noncash economy. In the absence of other sources of income, the money earned by selling skins, ivory, and even meat from the animals that Inuit hunt for food provides the cash required to engage in subsistence harvesting. Without the ability to sell some products from the subsistence catch, many Inuit would be unable to hunt at all. Nonetheless, the fact that subsistence hunting has been monetized affects the way many non-Inuit regard it, and thus affects the way it is regulated.

Sharing Maintains Social Relationships

Subsistence harvesting is also valued by Inuit for the role it plays in maintaining social relationships through the institutionalized sharing of country food and other items. Some Inuit groups in the Central Canadian Arctic had very formalized sharing partnerships in the past. The unrestricted sharing of food and other items related to subsistence harvesting continues in Inuit communities in every region of the North. Most sharing occurs within extended families, but some large game animals are shared more widely. In general, sharing includes all kinds of food as well as tools, childcare, clothing, and advice. Sharing within extended families is an ordinary and everyday activity that binds people together through mutual aid. While country food is perhaps the most salient of the items that circulate through sharing, it is the act of sharing and the manner in which it is done that makes sharing culturally significant to Inuit. There is substantial prestige associated with sharing generously. Nonetheless, the need to maintain a respectful relationship with animals adds a moral dimension to the activity. "The sharing and distribution of meat is guided by an obligation to give which is central to the customary ideology of subsistence. Because animals are believed to give themselves up to hunters it is incumbent on the hunter to give them in return to other people."[5]

Subsistence hunting is more than an economic system; it "is a way of life based upon the harvesting of renewable resources."[6] Inuit sharing of meat and other resources serves to unite people and animals in a complex web of social relationships. Despite concerns expressed by many non-Native wildlife managers, environmental conservationists, and regulatory agencies, sharing of meat and other essential items persists even where portions of the harvest are sold. It is difficult to overestimate the importance of subsistence work to Inuit. This is not simply because of the high nutritional value of Inuit foods (see Chapter 11), but more important, it is because subsistence hunting and fishing are tightly interwoven with kinship and local social relations. While other resources are also shared, many Inuit continue to place tremendous value on sharing and consuming country foods. Thus, the activities associated with "procuring, processing, preparing, and sharing [Inuit] foods help bind families and communities together."[7]

WHALING

Inuit culture is a hunting culture, and hunting marine mammals was likely one of the most important factors in the development and long-term success of Inuit communities. Marine mammals, such as whales, seals, and walruses, provide reliable food security, and the fat was a valuable fuel used for heating. Paleoeskimos hunted seals and small whales at least 5,500 years ago, and archeological evidence suggests that the ancestors of contemporary Inuit in the Bering Strait region began hunting large whales such as bowheads (*Balaena mysticetus*) about 2,000 years ago. The tools and techniques as well as knowledge of whale behavior were well developed by 1000 c.e. and, thus, Thule Inuit carried them east into Arctic Canada and Greenland.

Bowheads are slow-swimming whales that prefer swimming along ice edges. They are extremely long-lived and can grow to 12 to 18 meters in length. An adult bowhead weighs between 75 and 100 metric tons. The thick layer of fat, which the animal uses for protection from the cold, also provides buoyancy, so that it usually floats for a while after it is killed. Colder temperatures after 1400 c.e. limited the migratory range of the whales so that the Inuit communities in the Central Canadian Arctic ceased hunting these large whales and switched their attention to smaller whales such as belugas and narwhals and to seals and walruses. Bowheads did continue to migrate through the Bering Strait and into the Chukchi and Bering Seas in the west and into Davis Strait and Hudson Bay in the east. In these regions, Inuit hunted whales collaboratively from small boats, harpooning them to attach floats and then using a lance to kill them. It is estimated that Inupiat took between 45 and 60 bowhead whales annually and that smaller communities of Inuit living near Pangnirtung had yearly catches of between 8 and 12 animals.[8]

Commercial Arctic Whaling

Dutch whalers were present in Greenlandic waters as early as 1614, and Denmark employed Greenlanders in shore-based whaling from the late 18th to the mid-19th century, but it was not until the mid-19th century that Inuit in Canada and Alaska were affected by the activities of commercial whalers. Scottish and American commercial whaling vessels entered Inuit regions of Canada and Alaska after 1840 and continued fishing until the first decade of the 20th century when the combination of overfishing and the development of petroleum replacements for whale oil made commercial whaling in the Arctic unprofitable.

Commercial whalers introduced infectious diseases to Inuit and disrupted Inuit communities in other ways; nonetheless, many Inuit experienced the commercial whaling era as a positive time. Inuit developed valuable economic and social relationships with whalers. In the Canadian Arctic and North Alaska, in particular, Inuit men obtained employment as part of whaling crews. Others hunted and provided meat for the whalers; women produced clothing worn by whalers. This work provided Inuit with access to desired metal tools and utensils, cloth, tobacco, rifles, and many other manufactured goods, and Inuit adopted many new tools and techniques learned from commercial whalers. For example, Inupiat replaced hand-thrown harpoons with darting guns for attaching a line and float to the whale as well as exploding grenades fired from a shoulder gun. Despite technological changes, Inupiat continue many traditional aspects of the whale hunt including the use of skin-covered boats (*umiat*), sharing, and whaling festivals and rituals.

Contemporary Inuit Whaling

In recent years, Inuit in Canada have taken a small number of bowhead whales. Inuvialuit hunted whales in the Beaufort Sea in 1991 and 1996. Nunavut Inuit resumed hunting bowhead whales in 1994, taking one whale every two or three years. In 2009, the Nunavut Wildlife Management Board and the Canadian Department of Fisheries and Oceans agreed on an annual quota of three whales. Since the late 1940s, some Greenlanders have engaged in community-based hunting of minke (*Balaenoptera acutorostrata*) and fin whales (*Balaenoptera physalus*).

Bowhead whaling is a major social, cultural, and economic activity in several of Alaska's Inupiat communities, involving most members of the community and year-round preparations. Inupiat in Barrow, the largest community of the North Slope Borough, engage primarily in spring whaling when the bowheads are migrating north and east through openings or leads in the pack ice.[9] The actual business of hunting whales is carried out by whaling crews made up primarily, but not exclusively, of men. Crews tend to endure over time, though an individual may change crews or may be a member of more than one crew. The whaling crew is under the leadership of a married whaling couple. An unmarried man cannot become a whaling captain (*umialik*) for two reasons. First, the organization and work involved in outfitting a crew and managing a successful hunt is extremely demanding and requires both male and female labor. Second, Inupiat regard it as a fact that the whale gives itself, not to the whaling captain or crew, but to the wife of the umialik, who through her thoughtful and respectful actions reveals herself to be a good host.

Preparations for the next whaling season get underway as soon as the celebrations of the current season, signified by Nalukataq, come to a close. Beginning in June, under the direction of the umialik, men hunt bearded seals (*Erignathus barbatus*) and walruses (*Odobenus rosmarus*) that will be used during the whaling season. Walrus is considered to be an especially warming food to eat and thus is desirable nourishment for the whaling crews. Bearded seal is also eaten, but more important, the skins are used as *umiaq* covers. Boats and motors used for hunting must be maintained and repaired along with other hunting equipment. The umialik's wife, assisted by other women, purchases and prepares food and other supplies for the hunting trips. When the hunters return, the animals must be butchered, preserved, and stored.

In fall time, caribou (*Rangifer tarandus*) are hunted for meat, for skins to be used as mattresses, and for their sinew, which will be used for sewing the bearded sealskin covers on the umiat (pl.)

Winter is when the clothing and equipment used for whaling are prepared. These include fur parkas, socks, and *kamiks* (skin boots). Also, if necessary, boat frames are built or repaired.

As spring comes, the bearded sealskins are thawed, sewn together, and used to cover the umiaq. This needs to be done every other year. New white snow shirts are made for the whaling crew every year. As well, the ice cellar is cleaned and all remaining whale meat and *maktak* (the skin and layer of attached fat) are given away as gifts. This is done to provide a welcoming space for the whale. The umialik and other men make ice trails from the shore across the ocean ice to the open lead. This is a difficult and sometimes dangerous task.

The geography of Barrow causes the ice there to be rough and uneven with pressure ridges, making it extremely difficult to traverse. A good ice road is necessary, not only to transport the umiat and other equipment to the camping/hunting site, but in the event that the ice begins to break up suddenly, the crews need to be able to depart swiftly and safely.

Whaling begins in April and continues for about a month. Crews camp at the open lead and wait for whales. Those who have jobs in town may travel back and forth, commuting to work each day. When a whale is sighted, the crews follow in their skin boats and attempt to capture it by attaching floats shot from a dart gun and killing it with an exploding charge. While individual crews compete to see which will capture a whale, when a whale is struck, they work together to tow the whale to the ice edge. A block and tackle is used to pull it onto the ice to be butchered.

The umialik, the harpooner, and the harpoon owner each take specifically designated shares of the whale, while everyone else who helps with whaling earns an equal share. The captain distributes part of his share to others who helped directly and indirectly and is also responsible for providing distributions of whale meat and maktak. Hospitality is extended to the whale through acts of generosity and hospitality to the wider community, which begins with the successful landing of the whale and continues through a number of whaling feasts and festivals as well as community feasts at Thanksgiving and Christmas.

As the whale is being butchered, women crew members prepare pots of fresh, boiled *maktak* and serve them with hot coffee to people helping on the ice. Simultaneously sled-loads of meat are taken to town so that other women can start preparing a meal at the captain's house, boiling huge portions of every part of the whale: meat, *maktak,* heart, lungs, tongue, kidney, etc. When it is ready, the crew's flag goes up over the house and the entire community is invited in for a meal.[10]

Hunting bowhead whales is demanding in terms of time, organizational skills, and finances. Nonetheless, Inupiat regard it as essential for its contribution to nutrition and for the maintenance of Inupiat cultural and social values.

FUR TRADING

With the end of commercial whaling, Inuit had to develop new ways to obtain the imported goods that they had become dependent upon. In the Canadian Arctic fur trading became an important economic activity, but one that was organized quite differently from whaling. Whereas whalers paid Inuit for their labor directly regardless of how many whales were caught, the financial arrangements surrounding fur trading were based upon the number and quality of the furs, mostly Arctic fox (*Alopex lagopus*), obtained. Traders extended credit in the form of traps, ammunition, and other supplies, which they expected to be paid back at the end of the trapping season, thus tying Inuit to particular traders. In many regions a single trading company operated as a monopoly, giving traders almost total control over the supply of manufactured goods. Inuit, who had come to depend on these goods in order to engage in subsistence harvesting, had no choice except to comply with traders' demands. Further, prices paid for furs depended upon global markets and fluctuated wildly. The 1920s was a period when fox fur prices were rising, and some Inuit were able to earn substantial amounts of money trapping and were able to capitalize their subsistence harvesting activities. Some Inuvialuit in the Mackenzie Delta region of Canada, for example, "were able to purchase their own schooners and load them down with supplies."[11] This situation did not last, however. Commodity prices for furs fell during the Great Depression and again following World War II, causing extreme economic difficulty for those who had come to depend upon trapping. Still, the activity of

Arctic fox (*Alopex lagopus*) pelts drying outside an Ulukhaktok home. (Richard G. Condon photo collection)

trapping was compatible with subsistence hunting, and there were almost no other means for Canadian Inuit to earn money for ammunition and firearms, and later for the snowmobiles, gasoline, and other supplies that had become necessary to engage in subsistence harvesting. This changed with the development of a commercially viable process for tanning sealskins in 1961. Ringed seal (*Phoca hispida*), long an important food resource for people and dogs, became an important cash resource until the 1980s. For example, in the early 1970s, subsistence hunters in Clyde River, Nunavut, earned three-quarters of the cash required to support their harvesting by selling sealskins, narwhal ivory, polar bear hides, and Arctic fox pelts. Of these sealskins provided the most important and most stable source of income available to Inuit from renewable resources.

ENVIRONMENTALISTS' ATTACKS ON INUIT SUBSISTENCE HARVESTING

The rise of the environmental movement in the 1970s and 1980s had unintended negative consequences for Inuit subsistence harvesting. Whale and seal hunting, in particular, came under attacks from environmental and animal rights organizations such as Greenpeace and the International Fund for Animal Welfare. These organizations engaged in a direct and active campaign against a non-Native hunt, the annual harvest of immature harp seals (*Phoca greenlandicus*) in the Gulf of St. Lawrence and off the coast of Newfoundland. At first the animal rights organizations wrongly claimed that harp seals were endangered, but later focused on what they perceived as "inhumane" methods of killing. While Inuit seal hunting was not the original target of the "Save the Seals" campaign, many animal rights activists argued against Inuit hunting because Inuit employ rifles, snowmobiles, and other modern tools. The international "Save the Seals" campaign contributed to the 1972 passage in the United States of the Marine Mammals Protection Act. The Act severely restricted the hunting of all marine mammals in the United States. Exceptions were made for subsistence hunting by Alaska Natives, but the Act prohibited importation to the United States of all products derived from marine mammals including byproducts of subsistence hunting by Canadian and Greenlandic Inuit.

Europe Bans Seal Imports

In 1982, the European Economic Community (now the European Union or EU) imposed a voluntary ban on the importation of seal products. This had a direct and drastic effect on the economies in Inuit communities. The antisealing campaign and the EU ban eroded the market for sealskins and other seal products. Prior to the EU action, Inuit hunters in the Northwest Territories (including Nunavut) received an average of $21.54 for each sealskin sold. The year after the ban, the average price per sealskin dropped to only $9. Baffin Island hunters, including those from Clyde River, saw their revenues from the sale of sealskins fall by 92 percent from what they had earned in the period immediately prior to the EU ban. The value of the market for Baffin Island sealskins was halved again the following year, forcing a number of Inuit subsistence hunters to turn to welfare for the first time.[12]

The EU action also adversely affected subsistence hunting in Greenland. The Home Rule government has subsidized hunting since the original EU ban, reasoning that "harvesting provides the basic food supply in most communities. If harvesting were to decline as the major source of food, traditional food would have to be replaced by expensive imported food; this could actually result in higher levels of subsidies to support the nutritional needs of the people."[13]

The world market for sealskin began to recover in the late 1990s, but this situation was temporary. In 2008 and 2009, the EU reaffirmed the opposition of European consumers to the hunting of seals by banning the importation of seal products from countries that allow "inhumane" forms of hunting. While this is specifically aimed at harp seal hunting in Canada's Atlantic provinces and the legislation makes an exception for seal products derived from aboriginal subsistence hunting, the effect has been an almost complete erosion of the market for all seal products regardless of their origin.

Challenges to Subsistence Whaling

European and North American animal rights organizations have also opposed all forms of whale hunting, leading the International Whaling Commission (IWC) to begin regulating aboriginal subsistence whaling. One of its first acts was to attempt to impose a moratorium on subsistence whaling by Yupik and Inupiat in Alaska in 1977.

The IWC was established by the 1946 International Convention for the Regulation of Whaling. The IWC is a management agency that was created to regulate commercial whaling in order to protect the livelihoods of commercial whalers. In the absence of regulation, commercial whalers had no incentives to limit their catches, and thus engaged in overfishing. One species of whale, the Atlantic Gray, is thought to have become extinct as a result. Other species, including those hunted by Inuit, were severely depleted by commercial whalers at the end of the 19th century. Not all commercial whaling nations participate in the IWC, and others, including Iceland and Norway, have failed to comply with the quotas and moratoriums imposed by the regulatory body. At the same time, nations that do not engage in whaling but whose citizens oppose whaling have joined the IWC. While the IWC was not established to regulate small-scale aboriginal and subsistence whaling, as it lost its ability to regulate commercial whaling activities, it extended its authority over Inuit and other aboriginal whaling.[14]

Several events, including settlement of Alaska Native land claims, development of the Prudhoe Bay oil fields, and establishment of the North Slope Borough, led to greatly improved economic conditions in Inupiat communities in the 1970s. Rising individual incomes seems to have led to an increase in the number of whaling crews and increased bowhead whaling activity, and consequently drew the attention of the IWC. Members of the IWC expressed concern that Inupiat were harvesting whales at unsustainable levels and that too many whales were being struck, and were injured and possibly killed, but not landed.

Inupiat Fight Back

In 1977, despite inadequate scientific data regarding the population of bowhead whales, the IWC announced that it would impose a complete moratorium on bowhead whaling for the following year. Inupiat and Yupik from whaling communities responded by establishing the Alaska Eskimo Whaling Commission (AEWC) to fight the ban on their subsistence whaling. The IWC eventually agreed to a quota of 12 whales landed or 18 struck to be shared by 7 Inupiaq and 2 Yupik whaling communities. The North Slope Borough Department of Wildlife initiated a research program aimed at documenting the size and health of the whale population.

Inupiaq whaling remains subject to quotas set by the IWC on the basis of the nutritional and cultural needs of the whaling communities and on the documented size and health of the whale population. Each year the quota of struck and landed whales has been raised, and beginning in 1981, the IWC issued multiyear quotas. The Alaska Eskimo Whaling Commission determines how to allocate the quota among the various whaling communities. For example, in

1993, Alaskan whaling communities were permitted to land 41 or strike 54 whales. A third of the strikes were initially allocated to the community of Barrow, the largest of the whaling communities. The remaining strikes were divided among the other eight communities.

Restrictions on Subsistence Hunting

In all parts of the North today, hunting and fishing are subject to strict regulation concerning where, when, and how animals may be harvested. In many parts of the North, Inuit participate in managing wildlife through co-management agreements where users and academically trained wildlife experts collaborate in determining hunting quotas and other wildlife management issues. This is not universal, however. For example, Inuit in Nunavik are subject to quotas on their beluga whale hunting that they regard as inappropriately low.[15]

In Alaska, indigenous rights to pursue subsistence harvesting on public lands are protected by the Alaska National Interest Lands Conservation Act (ANILCA) enacted by Congress in 1980. As discussed in Chapter 6, the 1971 Alaska Native Claims Settlement Act (ANCSA) did not make any provisions for subsistence activities and does not protect Alaska Natives' lands from alienation. In fact, the ANCSA incorrectly presumed that subsistence harvesting was part of an older, premodern way of life that Alaska Natives were happy to abandon. The primary purpose of the ANILCA was to balance the interests of environmentalists who wanted to prevent resource development on public lands in Alaska and development agents who wished to extract mineral and timber resources from those lands. However, it also included a provision that accorded priority to "nonwasteful subsistence uses" of fish and wildlife over commercial and recreational hunting and fishing. The Act defines subsistence uses as "the customary and traditional uses by rural Alaska residents of wild renewable resources for direct personal or family consumption." The lawmakers who drafted the ANILCA gave preference to rural users in order to provide for the subsistence needs of Alaska Natives who make up the majority of rural Alaskans. But they erred in assuming that subsistence harvesting is exclusively an economic activity. As noted above subsistence harvesting is an important social and cultural activity for Inuit and other Native peoples. ANILCA, as written, does not protect the rights of growing numbers of urban Alaska Natives to engage in subsistence harvesting.

Externally imposed definitions of aboriginal subsistence harvesting, such as those created by the International Whaling Commission or the Alaska National Interest Lands Conservation Act, are meant to protect the subsistence activities of Inuit and other indigenous peoples. But they do so at the cost to Inuit of restricting them to externally imposed interpretations of what constitutes authentic Inuit culture. The inability of Inuit to sell subsistence products into the market limits Inuit from developing their resources in ways that they feel are appropriate and meet their particular cultural and economic needs.

NONRENEWABLE RESOURCE DEVELOPMENT

Though there is no doubt that subsistence harvesting is socially, culturally, and nutritionally important to contemporary Inuit communities, it no longer can serve as the economic basis of self-governing Inuit societies. Many Inuit expect to and desire to work in modern wage labor occupations and Inuit self-determination requires that Inuit rather than non-Natives hold the public sector and administrative jobs in their communities.

Given the restrictions on commercializing the products of subsistence hunting and the lack of markets outside of the North for subsistence products, it simply is not possible for Inuit to participate in the global economy without other sources of revenues. Tourism, art, and commercial fishing offer some opportunities for economic development, but to date, aside from a few localized successes, these have not proven to be engines of sustainable economic growth. Greenland, for example, has a commercial fishing industry that brings in significant revenues, but these are not sufficient to support the Home Rule government, and thus Greenland also relies on an annual subsidy from Denmark that is currently around 3.5 billion Danish kroner (approx. US$670 million or 470 million Euros) or almost US$12,000 for each Greenlander.

To address economic development issues and advance self-determination, Inuit in every region are turning to the development of nonrenewable resources such as oil and gas and mining. In fact, the self-governance arrangement that Greenland implemented on June 21, 2009 (see Chapter 6) provides for Greenland to gradually replace the Danish subsidy with revenues from oil and mineral extraction. The Nunavut Land Claims Agreement provides for Inuit there to collect royalties on minerals extracted from public lands. Several mines are in the planning stages or have recently opened in Green-

Loading Greenland shrimp for export, Nuuk, Greenland. (Photo by Peter V. Hall)

land and Nunavut and there is ongoing exploration for offshore oil and gas in Greenland.

As discussed in Chapter 6, the development of the Prudhoe Bay oil fields enabled the economic and political development of Inupiat communities. Much of the property tax revenues that support the North Slope Borough are derived from assessments on oil installations and half of the $1 billion cash settlement in the Alaska Native Claims Settlement Act came directly from oil revenues. Similarly, the Northwest Arctic Borough levies property taxes on the Red Dog zinc mine. While these extractive industries are a source of direct employment for some Inupiat and other Alaska Natives, several Native corporations have also invested in catering and other companies that service the oil industry.

The economic lives of Inuit continue to include a mix of commercial and noncommercial activities and forms of income and exchange. In the past, Inuit relied heavily on subsistence hunting, but were involved in trade even before colonial settlement. While Inuit are no longer fully dependent on hunting and collection of wild foods, subsistence harvesting continues to be a highly valued activity, but one that requires a cash income. So instead of jobs in the formal economy and government welfare transfers displacing hunting entirely, the one activity often supports the other.

NOTES

1. Bodenhorn, Barbara (2005) "Sharing Costs: An Exploration of Personal and Individual Property, Equalities and Differentiation," in *Property and Equality: Ritualisation, Sharing, Egalitarianism,* Thomas Widlok and Wolde Gossa Tadesse, eds., New York: Berghahn Books, 82–83.

2. Quoted in Condon, Richard G., Peter Collings, and George Wenzel (1995) "The Best Part of Life: Subsistence Hunting, Ethnicity, and Economic Adaptation among Young Adult Inuit Males," *Arctic* 48(1): 37.

3. Kishigami, Nobuhiro (2000) "Contemporary Inuit Food Sharing and Hunter Support Program of Nunavik, Canada," in *The Social Economy of Sharing: Resource Allocation and Modern Hunter-Gatherers,* George W. Wenzel, Grete Hovelsrud-Broda, and Nobuhiro Kishigami, eds., Osaka, Japan: National Museum of Ethnology, Senri Ethnological Studies 53, 184.

4. Greenland Home Rule (2006) *Management and Utilization of Seals in Greenland,* Report by the Department of Fisheries, Hunting and Agriculture, November, retrieved July 28, 2009 from http://www.ambottawa.um.dk.

5. Nuttall, Mark (2005) *Protecting the Arctic: Indigenous Peoples and Cultural Survival,* London: Routledge (originally published 1998), 111.

6. Ibid., 104.

7. Caulfield, Richard A. (1997) *Greenlanders, Whales, and Whaling: Sustainability and Self-Determination in the Arctic,* Hanover, NH: University Press of New England, 69.

8. Freeman, Milton M. R., Lyudmila Bogoslovskaya, Richard A. Caulfield, Ingmar Egede, Igor I. Krupnik, and Marc G. Stevenson (1998) *Inuit, Whaling, and Sustainability,* Walnut Creek, CA: AltaMira Press.

9. The description here is based primarily on the descriptions of contemporary whaling preparations in Barrow, Alaska, by Ahmaogak, Maggie (2002) "The Alaska Eskimo Whaling Commission: Overview and Current Concerns," *Traditional Whaling in the Western Arctic,* retrieved July 27, 2009 from http://www.uark.edu/misc/jcdixon/Historic_Whaling/AEWC/aewc_maggie%20presentation.htm; Bodenhorn, Barbara (2003) "Fall Whaling in Barrow, Alaska: A Consideration of Strategic Decision-Making," in *Indigenous Ways to the Present: Native Whaling in the Western Arctic,* Allen P. McCartney, ed., Edmonton: Canadian Circumpolar Institute Press, 277–306; and Bodenhorn, "Sharing Costs."

10. Bodenhorn, "Sharing Costs," 83–84.

11. Condon, Richard G. (1994) "East Meets West: Fort Collinson, the Fur Trade, and the Economic Acculturation of the Northern Copper Inuit, 1928–1939," *Etudes/Inuit/Studies* 18(1–2): 118.

12. Wenzel, George (1989) "Sealing at Clyde River, N.W.T.: A Discussion of Inuit Economy," *Etudes/Inuit/Studies* 13(1): 3–22; Wenzel, George (1991) *Animal Rights, Human Rights: Ecology, Economy and Ideology in the Canadian Arctic,* Toronto: University of Toronto Press.

13. Greenland Home Rule, *Management and Utilization of Seals in Greenland,* 10.

14. Nuttall, *Protecting the Arctic,* 104.

15. Tyrrell, Martina (2007) "Sentient Beings and Wildlife Resources: Inuit, Beluga Whales and Management Regimes in the Canadian Arctic," *Human Ecology* 35: 575–86.

4

COMMUNITY LIFE

Today, more than half of the world's people live in cities. Inuit towns and villages, however, are remarkably tiny, ranging in size from around 25 people in Bathurst Inlet, Nunavut, to approximately 15,000 people in Nuuk, the capital of Greenland. While there are several Inuit towns with populations numbering a few thousand, most are much smaller, with populations in the hundreds. Growing numbers of Inuit also make their homes in cities outside of the Arctic. According to the 2006 Canadian census of population, about 17 percent of the 50,485 Inuit in Canada live in urban centers outside the Arctic, and the proportion of Alaskan Inuit (Inupiat) in cities is probably similar.

INUIT COMMUNITIES

Aside from the Inupiat in North Alaska, before the establishment of government-administered towns and villages in the 19th and 20th centuries, Inuit did not live in permanent settlements. Even without permanent settlements, however, Inuit did create stable communities that were associated with specific regions.

Inuit communities were organized primarily around kinship, and usually consisted of two or more extended families joined together through marriages. There were no formal leadership positions, and no individuals had authority over others (see Chapter 6). Rather, the continuity of communities depended upon voluntary participation and mutual support. Families living in a particular region were part of the same community. They referred to themselves and were referred to by the name of their region plus the suffix-*miut*, meaning "the people of." In this way, the residents of Tikigaq, near present-day Point Hope, Alaska, were the Tikigaqmiut and people from Ulukhaktok in the Inuvialuit Settlement Region of Canada are Ulukhaktokmiut. While people could move from one region to another they were unlikely to do so unless they had relatives in the new community. This was because social and economic relationships were organized primarily along family lines. Inuit communities consolidated or dispersed following a regular annual cycle that brought people together when food resources were abundant and spread them out at the times of the year when resources were scarce. Evidence suggests that, except for in Alaska, the largest communities usually consisted of about 50 people.

In comparison to the Canadian Arctic, North Alaska is a biologically rich environment with seals, whales, waterfowl, land mammals, and many species of fish. Consequently, Inupiat were able to establish large permanent villages, some with as many as 500 people from several extended families. Most Inupiat, however, did not live year-round in the villages. Instead they dispersed as independent family-based groups to seasonal camps for hunting and fishing, coming together only a few times a year. This flexible organization with economically and politically self-sufficient families allowed Inupiat to maintain a very affluent lifestyle.

Traditional Leadership

The major social institutions in Inupiat villages were *qargit* (sing. *qargi*). These are sometimes described as men's houses, but it is more appropriate to think of them as clubs or community centers. Most villages had two or more qargit comprising members of a whaling crew under the leadership of an *umialik* (boat owner/whaling captain). While most qargit had structures, a qargi was the organization rather than the building, and groups sometimes used an *umiak* (boat) turned on its side to provide a windbreak. Men and older boys spent a good deal of their time in the qargit repairing tools, discussing issues, and telling stories. Women and girls visited to bring meals to men, but they also participated in the social life of the qargit, attending dances, festivals, and storytelling sessions.

Colonialism Unites Communities

After 1867, when the United States took control of Alaska, Inupiat were encouraged by Christian missionaries and government officials to make the villages their year-round homes. At the same time missionaries worked to end use of the qargi structures and many of them fell into disrepair (see Chapter 7). In the process Inupiat came to see themselves as a single people rather than separate regional groups.

Danish officials in Greenland established permanent settlements for Inuit around churches and trading posts beginning around 1800. By 1850, all Greenlanders lived in permanent towns and villages, and began to think of themselves as Greenlanders. In contrast, Canadian officials actively discouraged Inuit from settling around missions and trading posts until after World War II. As a result, both sedentization and creation of a shared Inuit ethnic identity occurred much later in Canada than in Alaska or Greenland.

THE SOCIAL LIFE OF CONTEMPORARY INUIT COMMUNITIES

Most of the currently existing Canadian Inuit towns and villages were constructed in the 1950s and 1960s when the Canadian federal government reversed its long-held policy of dispersing Inuit and, instead, began actively encouraging them to move into permanent settlements. The major way that the government encouraged Inuit to take up residence in the towns was by providing subsidized housing. It also began providing day schools and health care services for Inuit citizens.

Movement from camps into permanent villages was a dramatic change for most people, and transformed economic, social, and domestic life. For one thing, where camps had been made up of one or two extended families, the towns comprised many unrelated people. These included large numbers of children and teenagers who developed a distinct social identity and youth subculture.

There were few wage employment opportunities in the new towns at first and hunting and trapping remained an important occupation, but it was one that men tended to engage in alone while women and children remained in the town. This has had important consequences for family life and has helped to disrupt the transmission of hunting and other subsistence skills from adults to generations of children raised exclusively in permanent settlements. Schooling, television, and other imported technologies have had both positive

Ulukhaktok in the Inuvialuit Settlement Region. (Photo by author)

and negative consequences for Inuit communities. On the positive side, Inuit are better able to advocate for more local control of decision making. But schooling has also prepared young Inuit to expect wage employment. At present there are many more wage labor jobs than existed during the first few decades of sedentization, but there are far fewer jobs than there are people who want them. This has contributed to economic disparities within communities and fuels social problems such as alcohol abuse.

Modernization

In the post–World War II era, the Danish administration in Greenland modernized the country by transforming the economy from subsistence hunting by individual producers to industrialized fishing. It also worked to improve housing, education, and health care. Population concentration was a key feature of this modernization. Up until this time, most Greenlanders lived in small, kin-oriented villages. Families were large and households were interdependent. The men and women in an extended family worked together to provide most of their own food, clothing, and shelter; men primarily engaged in hunting and women were primarily concerned with processing the catch. Hunters earned modest incomes by selling skins and surplus meat and fish to the government trading company.

The economy of Greenland was industrialized during the 1950s, 1960s, and 1970s. As part of this, Danish administrators encouraged Greenlanders to abandon small villages and relocate to larger towns. It was extremely successful in this effort. In 1950 more than half of Greenlanders lived in villages. By 1960 almost 57 percent of Greenlanders lived in towns; in 1980 more than three-quarters of the population lived in these larger communities.[1] By 2005, only 18 percent of Greenlanders lived in villages. The Danish authorities made towns more attractive places to live than villages by providing jobs, modern housing, schools, and hospitals in the former. At the same time they began to withdraw services from villages, closing schools and stores and allowing conditions to deteriorate.[2]

Greenlanders found the way of life in towns very different from what they had experienced in their villages. For one thing, houses in villages were detached, single-family structures, but the new housing in towns was mostly apartments. These were too small for the large or extended families that had shared accommodations in the villages. Importantly, also, apartments did not afford space to store hunting equipment or to process meat and skins. Photographs of Nuuk apartment complexes taken in the 1960s show seal and polar bear skins hung from balcony railings to dry. Those same apartment complexes are showing their age today, but are still occupied. The exteriors, however, no longer display as much evidence that the occupants are involved in subsistence hunting. As Dybbroe has observed, in Greenland as well as in the Canadian Arctic, the modern settlements created for Inuit in the 1950s and 1960s were built without consultation with the intended residents and were "intended as solutions to the administrative and economic problems" rather than to address resident needs.[3]

The move from villages to towns made Greenlanders much more dependent upon cash to pay rent and to purchase the food and clothing that people had largely provided for themselves previously. With men working in the fishing industry rather than engaged in subsistence hunting, women's traditional tasks also became obsolete. Rural-urban migration also fragmented the kinds of kin-based social relationships that were characteristic of life in the small villages. Many women who remained in villages felt a loss of purpose as well as a loss of social support. This further encouraged migration to larger centers, especially by young women seeking education and employment. The population remaining in Greenlandic villages today is, thus, aging and predominantly male.

Maniitsoq (pop. 3,000), on the west coast of Greenland, is one of the towns that grew as a result of the industrialization of fishing, but

Mix of structures in Nuuk, Greenland, August 2008. (Photo by Peter V. Hall)

also suffered with more recent changes in the fishing industry. It is typical of contemporary Greenlandic towns in its blending of local and global styles.

Maniitsoq is a bustling town with people moving around at all hours of the day by car, skidoo, bicycle, or foot. In spring and summer, groups of children skateboard or roller-skate on the concrete roads connecting the quite far-flung built-up areas. On a good day weather-wise, you may hear through open windows music that tells you this is a place in close contact with the rest of the world. Walking along a street, you will notice the affluence, the smartness of dress. Just around the corner, the visitor's eye meets another sight, *kalaalimineerniarfik*—an outside place, often just a board or piece of plywood, set up to display hunting products for sale.[4]

The policies that caused Inuit to move from camps into permanent settlements and from villages to larger towns were enacted without consulting the intended new residents, and new towns were often organized in ways that interfered with subsistence activities and family life. Nonetheless, the relocations discussed above were more or less voluntary, and most government administrators acted with the intent to improve living conditions. Sadly, there are a number of examples where Inuit were involuntarily moved for reasons that had nothing to do with them or their needs.

FORCED RELOCATIONS

Cold War tensions between the Western nations and the Soviet Union had real consequences for many Inuit communities. Beginning in the late 1940s, the United States and its NATO allies began construction of the Distant Early Warning (DEW line) radar network across the North American Arctic, Greenland, and northwestern Europe. In the process, Inuit in several communities were evicted from their homes and told to relocate. Even Inuit communities that were not moved had to put up with the noise, social disruption, and environmental degradation inherent in military activity. In Alaska, the U.S. military appropriated the site of the village of Kaktovik to build an airstrip and radar station in 1951. In 1953, the Air Force gave residents almost no notice that they had to relocate. Using bulldozers, the military dismantled houses and ice cellars of the Kaktovik Inupiat and moved the remnants to a new site up the beach.

During the same period the U.S. military was also responsible for the forced relocation of 27 families from Uummannaq in northwest Greenland to Qaanaaq 150 kilometers to the north. This was done so that the Air Force could expand Thule Air Force Base. Former residents of Uummannaq and their descendents were only compensated financially for the loss of their homes in 1999, four and half decades after their evictions.

Canada also relocated Inuit involuntarily, sometimes with little or no advance warning. This occurred in Killiniq, a village in Nunavut, just across the border from both Nunavik (Quebec), and Labrador. Following signing of the James Bay and Northern Quebec land claims agreement in 1975, the federal government of Canada began withdrawing medical, education, and other services from the settlement as it regarded the Inuit residents as parties to the land claims agreement. As a result, about half of the residents left to live in other settlements. On February 8, 1978, the remaining residents were notified that they were being evacuated immediately and that the town would be closed. Within a few hours planes arrived. The Killiniq families were forced to leave many of their possessions behind. Killiniq residents were transported to five separate Nunavik communities that were also given no notice to expect arrivals. Even more disruptive, extended families were separated with some members left in one community and other members left in others.

The relocation of Killiniq residents bears some similarity to a better known (because of its tragic consequences) relocation of Inuit in the late 1950s from an area west of Hudson Bay. In both cases the Canadian government displaced Inuit communities out of administrative expediency combined with an apparent desire to avoid the cost of providing health and welfare services to Inuit. In the earlier incident, the government repeatedly removed people living around Ennadai Lake and Garry Lake because administrators believed the Inuit there had become dependent upon personnel at a nearby radar station and on the Catholic mission, respectively. These dislocations unfortunately coincided with a change in the annual migration route of the barren ground caribou, and led to several deaths by starvation among the Inuit during the winter of 1957–58. Government officials had moved Inuit and had ignored requests for help, at least in part, because they mistakenly believed that the calls for help were motivated by laziness and dependency rather than genuine need.

Government concern about Inuit dependency is a common theme in the history of Canadian administration of Inuit territories, but a relocation of Inuit from Nunavik to the High Arctic in the 1950s may involve an additional motive—territorial sovereignty—as well.

International law requires countries to physically occupy the lands they claim as part of their national territories, and although Canada had possession of the Arctic Archipelago beginning in 1880, the northernmost islands were unoccupied and Canada had done little to assert its ownership of those lands. While no other nation seriously threatened Canada's sovereignty over the Arctic islands, it is possible that some in the government felt the need to shore up Canada's territorial claim to that land. This may have been because of United States' assertions then (and now) that the Arctic Ocean is an international waterway as well as the fact that, at the time, the United States had military bases in the Canadian Arctic.

In 1953 and 1955, the government moved a combined total of 11 families from Inukjuak in northern Quebec 2,000 kilometers to the north to what eventually became the towns of Grise Fjord and Resolute. A few families from north Baffin Island were also relocated, ostensibly to assist with the adjustment of the families from the southern region. Canadian government officials claimed that the relocation was voluntary and necessary to prevent overhunting in northern Quebec. They also painted a rosy picture of Inuit responses to the relocation. Evidence today, however, is that the Nunavik Inuit were coerced into moving and were repeatedly refused permission to return to Nunavik. In the late 1970s Inuit political organizations, particularly Inuit Tapiriit Kanatami and Makivik Corporation, took up the cause of the "High Arctic Exiles," as the Nunavik relocates have become known, winning relocation assistance in 1987 for those who wished it, and financial compensation for all of them 10 years later.

CALENDARS AND TIME RECKONING

Part of what unites a community is a common understanding of time. People who live together develop shared perceptions about many phenomena and these include beliefs about when particular activities are appropriate (or inappropriate) as well as knowledge about how to reckon the passage of time. Geographically, the Arctic is noted for its extreme seasonal variation in temperature and the number of hours of daylight or photoperiod. During the winter, depending upon latitude, the sun may not rise above the horizon for several weeks or even months. Spring and summer, in contrast, are periods of continuous sunlight. But despite the extreme changes in photoperiod over the course of the year, Inuit have no trouble using stars or other natural phenomena to separate each 24-hour period into episodes of night and day.

As is true of all human societies, Inuit activities differ according to the season. Even though there are significant seasonal differences in the environment, "seasonal variation in human activities was due less to changes in temperature and light, as such, than it was to seasonal variation in the abundance and distribution of the animal and plant species on which [Inuit] economies were based."[5] Inuit communities today observe the same Gregorian calendar as others in their nations, but also continue to time some activities according to traditional or local patterns.

Inuit Calendars

In the past, Inuit used a combination of lunar, solar, and environmental phenomena to reckon the passage of time. Inuit throughout the North recognized a 13-month lunar calendar, with the months named after phenomena in the natural world such as the birth of seal pups or the thickening of caribou hair. Specific month names differed from community to community, chiefly because of variation in the timing of animal cycles across the North. In each area, however, people kept the lunar calendar synchronized with the natural phenomena for which the months were named by occasionally omitting the lunar month that occurred at the winter solstice. As one

Iglulingmiut man told explorer/anthropologist Knud Rasmussen, the lunar months in December and January did not need any special designation because "they are dark, cold, and hunting in them is difficult."[6]

Seasons were determined according to the state of the landfast ice that was critical for hunting and travel. Communities grew or contracted, in large part, on the basis of the availability of resources. Not surprisingly, population came together during periods when collaboration in subsistence was necessary and dispersed when it was not. For Inuit in much of the Canadian Arctic, this period of population concentration occurred in late winter when people built large snowhouse communities on the ocean ice and cooperated in hunting seals at their breathing holes. As the year progressed, people dispersed into smaller groups to pursue land-based resources, but might come together briefly in larger groups to cooperate in fishing or caribou hunting.

Festivals and Trade Fairs

All across the North, Inuit gathered in large groups for several weeks during winter. According to the explorer/anthropologist Vilhjalmur Stefansson, these gatherings occurred around the winter solstice, the coldest, darkest period of winter. The weather made this a difficult time for hunting, so when possible, Inuit cached enough food to be able to relax, and make long journeys to visit friends.[7] Other observers place these gatherings a bit later, around the time of the return of the sun above the horizon, which according to Rasmussen was regarded as the start of the new year.[8] Some Inuit communities celebrated the return of the sun above the horizon with a ritual in which all of the lamps (*qullit*) were extinguished and then relit from a single source.

In summer, Inupiat gathered for trading fairs. One at Sisualik, north of present-day Kotzebue, regularly drew 2,000 people from both sides of the Bering Strait. In both seasons, gatherings were extended periods of trading, feasting, dancing, competitive games, and socializing. They were opportunities for old friends to meet, share news, and arrange marriages. These large celebrations continue today, though they follow somewhat different patterns than in the past. Inupiat whaling communities continue to celebrate *Nalukatuq*, a one- to three-day festival with feasting and competitive games, as well as American holidays such as Thanksgiving, while Canadian Inuit communities organize contests and dances at Christmas and Easter (see Chapter 8).

URBAN INUIT LIFE

Inuit across the North participate in global networks that emanate from urban centers, but there is only one Inuit city: Nuuk, the capital of Greenland. Nuuk (pop. 15,000), however, is no bigger than a small town in North America. Yet, it truly is an urban center. It has a variety of public spaces: schools, a university, museums, cafes, a microbrewery, discotheques, theaters, cinemas, parks, recreation centers, and retail outlets. And "in Nuuk, as in any other urban centre, a modicum of anonymity is also possible."[9] Nuuk also has urban problems such as poverty, violence, social isolation, and decaying infrastructure.

Commercial plaza in downtown Nuuk, Greenland, August 2008. (Photo by Peter V. Hall)

Greenlanders express somewhat contradictory feelings about urban life. On the one hand, lyrics of popular songs, many of which detail the social disorder of contemporary life, suggest that Greenlanders experience their capital as dangerous, unfriendly, and dirty. On the other hand, migration of Greenlanders from outlying regions to Nuuk has not slowed, and despite an active homebuilding program, there is a 20-year-long waiting list for an apartment. Continued willingness to put one's name on that waiting list is one indication that "everybody wants to live there."[10]

The number of Inuit living in cities outside the Arctic has been growing since the 1980s. Canadian cities with significant Inuit populations include Ottawa, Yellowknife, Edmonton, Montreal, and Winnipeg. Greenlanders migrate to Copenhagen, while Alaskan Inuit are in Anchorage and Fairbanks.

The reasons Inuit migrate to cities are varied. Many leave the North for medical treatment or schooling and end up staying longer than initially anticipated. Some Inuit move to cities for employment or because of the lack of employment opportunities in the North. Inuit organizations, including Inuit Tapiriit Kanatami (ITK) and several land claims corporations, have chosen to locate their headquarters in cities outside the Arctic. These organizations are important employers of Inuit. Marriage to someone who is not Inuit may also lead to outmigration. Finally, some Inuit, especially women, leave northern villages in order to escape difficult family situations including domestic violence.

Experiences with Racism

Outside the North, Inuit and other indigenous peoples often experience racism or other forms of discrimination. Inupiat mothers living in Anchorage in the late 1980s ran into problems with non-Native social workers and school counselors who tended to view the Inupiaq hands-off style of parenting as "negligent" and indicative of household dysfunction.[11] Homeless Inuit in Montreal told anthropologist Nobuhiro Kishigami that they avoid using homeless shelters because the shelter staff *and* other homeless people "often say: 'the Inuit smell,' 'the Inuit are noisy,' 'the Inuit have fleas and lice.'"[12] Regardless of their economic circumstances, urban Inuit may feel subtle or overt pressure to live in a particular district of a city where Native people are concentrated. Inuit in Canadian cities are a disparate group, and those who are employed, nonetheless, do not feel that they have much in common with those who are homeless or substance abusing.

Urban Inuit, however, do seek out ways to interact with other Inuit. In 2000 a group of employed Montreal Inuit established the Association of Montreal Inuit to hold monthly dinners of Inuit foods and to encourage other expressions of Inuitness, but have struggled to maintain the association. Several Inuit raising children in Ottawa told Donna Patrick and Julie-Ann Tomiak that they appreciate opportunities for their children to learn Inuktitut and other Inuit cultural practices, but that they find this to be a struggle in the city.[13]

It seems likely that more and more Inuit will move both to cities outside the Arctic and to the larger towns in the Arctic over the next several years. As this occurs, Inuit urban residents will create new social and cultural institutions associated with life in urban centers.

NOTES

1. Petersen, Marie-Louise Deth (1986) "The Impact of Public Planning on Ethnic Culture: Aspects of Danish Resettlement Policies in Greenland after World War II," *Arctic Anthropology* 23(1–2): 273.

2. Ibid., 272.

3. Dybbroe, Susanne (2008) "Is the Arctic *Really* Urbanising?" *Etudes/Inuit/Studies* 32(1): 26.

4. Ibid., 18.

5. Burch, Ernest S., Jr. (2006) *Social Life in Northwest Alaska: The Structure of Iñupiaq Eskimo Nations,* Fairbanks: University of Alaska Press, 32.

6. Aua quoted in Rasmussen, Knud (1930) *Iglulik and Caribou Eskimo Texts, Report of the Fifth Thule Expedition (1921–24),* Vol. 7, No. 3, Copenhagen: Gyldendalske Boghandel, Nordisk Forlag, 63.

7. Stefansson, Vilhjalmur (1944) *The Friendly Arctic: The Story of Five Years in the Polar Regions,* New York: MacMillan, 24.

8. Rasmussen, *Iglulik and Caribou Eskimo Texts,* 63.

9. Rygaard, Jette (2008) "The City Life of Youths in Greenland," *Etudes/Inuit/Studies* 32(1): 44.

10. Ibid., 43.

11. Fogel-Chance, Nancy (1993) "Living in Both Worlds: 'Modernity' and 'Tradition' among North Slope Inupiaq Women in Anchorage," *Arctic Anthropology* 30(1): 98.

12. Kishigami, Nobuhiro (2008) "Homeless Inuit in Montreal," *Etudes/Inuit/Studies* 32(1): 77–78.

13. Patrick, Donna, and Julie-Ann Tomiak (2008) "Language, Culture, and Community among Urban Inuit in Ottawa," *Etudes/Inuit/Studies* 32(1): 55–72.

5

MATERIAL LIFE

Non-Native visitors to the Arctic were often astounded that Inuit could make a secure and comfortable living in what seemed to the visitors to be a harsh and barren environment. One should not mistake the technologies that Inuit developed for hunting, for making shelter, for traveling, for making clothing, or for preparing nutritious food as the essential features of Inuit culture. Certainly, values, beliefs, and patterns of social interaction are more important to a uniquely Inuit way of life. Nonetheless, it is important to note that it was precisely because ancient Inuit developed technologies that made use of the unique physical properties of locally available materials including snow, ice, and permafrost that they were able to colonize and live successfully in the Arctic environment.

As discussed in the introductory chapter, prehistoric Inuit communities also engaged in regional and long-distance trade for exotic luxury materials and the mundane necessities of everyday life. In terms of day-to-day necessities Inuit living in coastal regions had access to marine resources, especially marine mammals, that were important nutritionally and as a fuel source. Inuit living inland, on the other hand were able to procure caribou which, while eaten, also provided an essential material for the clothing that enabled Inuit to survive in the Arctic in winter. Inuit easily incorporated Norse and later visitors to the Arctic into their trading networks, and very quickly the materials that these outsiders had to offer—metal, wood, cloth, sugar, flour, and tea—became essential bits of Inuit material culture. While many Inuit have retained some traditional items of local manufacture, albeit in modified forms, over the past 300 years Inuit communities have become tightly integrated into the modern global economy. Not surprisingly, the same types of consumer goods that are available in Los Angeles, Copenhagen, and Toronto can be found in Inuit communities today.

The Arctic environment poses significant challenges to its residents. The weather is extreme and often treacherous, the landscape can be quite difficult to navigate, and the animals upon which people depended for food, clothing, fuel, and shelter are mobile and thus, sometimes difficult to find. Consequently, "life in an Inuit hunting camp, though often experienced as pleasurable and comfortable, was at the same time a life of unbuffered risk, in which the alternative to correct action might be death."[1] A willingness to adopt new materials and to adapt old materials to new purposes is one way that Inuit historically learned to cope with "dangerous uncertainty" in their environment. As Briggs observes, Inuit culture encourages people to study and carefully observe the physical world and individual objects in order to understand the multiple uses to which an object may be put. Objects intended for one purpose are often refashioned, if necessary, to meet another purpose. In fact, creativity and innovation are among the most valued cognitive abilities in many Inuit communities. Inuit have long engaged in the kinds of material transformations that are currently celebrated in North America as DIY (do-it-yourself) culture, and what Inupiaq chronicler William A. Oquilluk referred to as the need to "work in their minds to stay alive."[2] For example,

An *ulu*, a woman's semilunar knife, is made out of an old saw, a pipe out of a discarded flashlight battery or thimble, a barbed fishhook out of a large nail. Scavenging is a favorite activity, both in abandoned Inuit campsites and in Euro-Canadian dumps, and the most unlikely and bedraggled object can take on new life in the hands of an inventive Inuk. New store-bought goods, too, may be reshaped to make them more useful—sometimes for purposes altogether unimagined by the manufacturer. The cutting edge of an ice chisel may be restyled; a butcher knife may have its handle removed and a bone handle twice as long substituted to convert it into a snow knife. In other words, the world of objects can be imaginatively reshaped at a moment's notice, and any materials available, traditional or modern, can be incorporated and utilized to serve present needs in the most practical way, without regard for tradition, ritual, authority, or possible future needs.[3]

While Inuit across the North had the same basic needs and made use of many of the same raw materials to meet those needs, they developed regional stylistic variations in traditional material culture. The descriptions below focus on two broad areas of Inuit material culture: architecture and clothing.

ARCHITECTURE

Inuit traditional architecture was perfectly suited to both the environment and the social needs of Inuit communities. In other words, Inuit built structures that used locally available materials to provide safety and security against the elements, allowed for seasonal mobility, and provided adequate space for domestic and communal activities.

Domestic Structures

In the past, Inuit lived in permanent or semipermanent structures in the winter and in tents in the summer. Though domed snowhouses are often assumed to have been the most common form of Inuit housing, in fact, their use was restricted seasonally to winter and early spring and geographically to the Central Canadian Arctic where other building materials were scarce. Snowhouses were most commonly constructed on the ocean ice in places that were convenient for seal hunting. Like sod houses described below, snowhouses contained downward-sloping entrance passages that served as cold traps. The main chamber also was sunk below the snow's surface and was constructed of blocks of snow cut from what then became the interior of the snowhouse. Only certain types of snow were suitable for building a snowhouse. The best snow was firm, of even consistency, and came from wind-packed drifts. The blocks were positioned in an inward sloping spiral in order to create a domed structure. The structural integrity of the building was produced by applying two sharp blows as each block was set in place.

Snowhouses that were meant to be occupied for a period of time might contain a window made of ice. The back portion of the structure consisted of a sleeping/living platform of snow that had been left uncut. This was covered with caribou or muskox skins for warmth. Heat and light came from a *qulliq*, or stone lamp, in which seal or walrus fat was burned. The only other furnishings might be a rack for drying clothes positioned over the qulliq. Small storage porches might be added off the entrance passage. And frequently, closely related families connected their snowhouses with tunnels or passages. Far from being unpleasant, the living/sleeping region of the snowhouse was both warm and comfortable. Tents were sometimes erected inside to provide additional insulation or to extend the season in which the snowhouse could be used.

In other regions of the North Inuit winter houses were fairly substantial, usually semisubterranean sod houses. Whale bone or driftwood, depending upon local availability, provided the support framework. Inuit living in the Mackenzie River Delta made substantial use of the wood that floated down river each spring to build their domestic structures. In the late 19th century Inupiaq near present-day Barrow, Alaska, constructed small, rectangular houses "framed with planks hewn from driftwood. Each was entered through a long underground tunnel framed with whales' bones, and off to one side of the tunnel was a kitchen."[4] The entrance tunnel, which was below the level of the house floor, served as a trap for cold air. A long, low bench provided a sleeping and working space. Seal oil lamps provided heat and light. Elevated structures behind the house were built to keep kayaks, tools, and other equipment away from dogs, and meat was stored in "freezers" excavated into the permafrost and lined with whale bones or wood.

The *qarmaq*, or stone house, built by Inuit in the eastern Canadian Arctic, is a variation on the sod houses constructed by Inuit in both North Alaska and Greenland. These were chinked with sod and employed driftwood or whale bone to support a roof made of skin or canvas. The addition of a porch constructed of newly formed sheets of ice provided a secure place to store meat, seal oil, and other supplies. Qarmat (*pl.*) were used as primary housing into the 1950s and are still used sometimes as camps today.

Contemporary Housing

In the early decades of the 20th century, Christian missionaries encouraged Inupiat in North Alaska to abandon their semisubterranean sod houses for above-ground frame houses so that by the 1950s there were few, if any, Inupiaq families living in the traditional style of house. New above-ground wooden houses with separate living and sleeping areas more closely suited the missionaries' ideas about appropriate households comprising nuclear families and of the physical seclusion of marital sexual activity. Many Inuit in Alaska (and in Canada, as well) accepted this new form of housing, in part, be-

Family of Joseph Idlout (left) inside their qarmaq, 1953. (Wilkinson/NWT Archives/N-1979-051: 0158)

cause the new houses seemed modern and prestigious. For example, in the 1930s, two Canadian Inuit, Ikey Bolt and Angulakik, who operated as traders for the CanAlaska Trading Company, each imported wooden kit houses for their own use.[5] These two Canadian men may have been exceptions. Although they integrated new materials into their constructions, most Canadian Inuit continued to live in tents, snowhouses, and qarmat of their own design and manufacture until the 1950s.

After several decades of preventing Inuit from settling permanently at trading posts and mission stations, in 1953 the Canadian government reversed its policy and began encouraging Inuit to move into new government-administered towns and villages. The Canadian government accomplished this policy shift partly through the provision of housing; though there was considerable debate within the government as to whether housing for Inuit should be market-based or social housing, delaying the actual delivery of housing to the late 1950s and early 1960s. In the interim, Inuit built their own houses in towns and villages out of castoff packing crates and other scavenged materials. These "shack houses," as they are referred to, were crowded and poorly insulated and contributed to the poor health of many Inuit.

New Houses

Eventually, the proponents of social housing prevailed, and throughout the 1950s and 1960s, the Canadian government delivered prefabricated frame housing units to Inuit communities and provided these at greatly subsidized and sliding-scale rents. The houses, however, were designed by non-Native architects and anticipated the kinds of activities and family structures that prevailed in non-Native homes in southern Canada. Like the public housing provided to Greenlanders discussed in the previous chapter, the new houses did not contain spaces for processing game or for repairing hunting equipment, and some northern administrators became distressed when Inuit used their new homes for these culturally important domestic activities. In response, the Canadian government produced a booklet illustrated with line drawings to explain to Inuit how to conduct family life in the new houses. The booklet, entitled *Living in the New Houses,* consisted of unnecessary and paternalistic instructions. One page, for example, showed a drawing of a boy holding a garbage can bearing the single line, "Garbage ready for pickup." Another illustration shows a woman standing at a kitchen sink while an older girl sweeps the floor. The text reads, "A tidy kitchen." While the educational value of this simplistic kind of training is doubtful, the choice of illustrations presumed that Inuit should also adopt the same gendered domestic roles and nuclear family forms that were idealized for Euro-Canadian households. Traditional Inuit houses had consisted of a single room without interior walls fostering intimacy and easy nonverbal communication among household members and across generations. Modern frame houses, on the other hand, have multiple rooms, disrupting multigenerational interactions.

At present in the Canadian North, in addition to social housing, there are a number of programs intended to enable Inuit with secure incomes to become homeowners. Most Canadian Inuit, however, continue to live in social housing where the rent is determined by a formula that considers documented income (usually from a wage labor job) and household size. The formula does not consider financial obligations that Inuit may have to family members outside their immediate household. This practice incorrectly assumes that the economic obligations of Inuit to relatives, like Euro-Canadians, rarely extend beyond the nuclear family. There are, however, severe housing shortages in many communities, particularly in Nunavut. This housing shortage causes overcrowding, which in turn contributes to numerous health and social problems.

Communal Structures

Traditionally Inuit also built large communal structures. In Inupiaq North Alaska, these were called *qargi* (pl. *qargit*) and provided a space where men and boys who were part of the same whaling crew met to converse, repair tools, plan activities, and discuss issues of concern. Usually qargit were above ground, but might be banked with snow or sod in winter. Entrance was through an underground passage. Dances, shamanic séances, and other events in which women and girls also participated were often held in the evenings. Technically, the term qargi refers to the association rather than to the building. The qargit served as the focal point for religious feasts and festivals such as the Messenger Feast (see Chapter 7).

Inuit in the Central Canadian Arctic held *qaggiq* celebrations. These often occurred in large snowhouses that were built with benches along the wall for sitting rather than a sleeping platform. Qaggiq celebrations included drum singing and dancing, traditional games, storytelling, shamanic séances, and sometimes Christian religious services.

Like non-Native communities, contemporary Inuit communities contain multiple single-purpose structures. These include schools,

Drum singing and dancing at Christmastime inside a qaggiq at Pelly Bay, Nunavut, 1961. (Wilkinson/NWT Archives/N-1979-051: 0823S)

shops, churches, municipal buildings, offices, health centers, and so forth. In recent years it has become more common for these to be designed in ways that express Inuit culture. For example, the new campus of Ilimatusarfik, the University of Greenland (pictured in Chapter 2), was designed to blend into the surrounding tundra. Likewise, the Nunavut Legislative Assembly building (pictured in Chapter 6) is meant to evoke the image of a qaggiq.

CLOTHING

Traditionally Inuit used materials from many different animals for clothing. These materials included the skin and feathers of birds, the intestines of walruses and seals, and the pelts of polar bears, seals, muskoxen, foxes, and wolves. Caribou skins, which are lightweight and provide superior insulation, however, were probably the most important material for Inuit winter clothing, but the dehaired skins of seals and walruses were used when waterproof material was needed. Sinew was used for thread.

In the coldest seasons two layers of caribou skin clothing were worn. The garment closest to the body was worn with the hair side against the body, while the outer layer was worn with the hair side out. Although functionality was critical, Inuit also cared about the workmanship and the aesthetic qualities of clothing. Clothing style and design was one way the Inuit in the past (and still today) recognize and reinforce their own regional differences. Designs have changed over time, but there continue to be distinctive regional styles of parkas and *kamiit* (boots).

A national costume, based on traditional garments, is one of the symbols created specifically to express Greenlanders' sense of national identity as Kalaalliit. The Greenlandic national costume for men is relatively simple, consisting of a white anorak, black pants, and black sealskin boots. The women's costume consists of a blouse with a long beaded collar, decorated seal fur pants, and long boots made of sealskin that has been dyed white. Greenlanders wear manufactured clothing for everyday wear, but may don the national costume for special occasions such as Christmas worship services, Greenland's National Day (June 21), or cultural performances. In East Greenland, many children are given their first national costume around the age of six, and may wear them on important personal occasions such as their first day of school.

Inuit clothing also identifies the gender and age of the wearer. Women's parkas, called *amautit,* in addition to being longer than

Musical performers in the Greenlandic national costume at the University of Greenland. (Photo by Peter V. Hall)

men's, usually include an expandable pouch at the back for carrying a baby.

With the arrival of non-Natives in the North, Inuit added new materials such as cloth and beads to their clothing designs. Inuit throughout the North now wear manufactured clothing for most purposes, and young Inuit pay careful attention the latest global styles. Also, jackets and T-shirts that express participation on a sports team, membership in a work group, or residence in a community are popular throughout the North.

Traditional and locally produced designs are still desirable for parkas and boots, especially on special occasions. In most circumstances it is considered too costly and impractical to use animal skins for entire garments, but most traditional garments retain some fur elements such as a ruff worn around the face. New parkas, parka covers, or kamiit are gifts women make for their families. Young women, just learning to sew, might make mitts for their loved ones. In Ulukhaktok, for example,

[M]any women continue to sew new parka covers for their families at Easter and Christmas. The new garments are admired by others who take note of the workmanship of the garment and the artistry of the decoration and trim. One 27-year-old mother of four told me that she despises sewing, but that she always makes new parka covers at both holidays "because I want my family to have nice things" (Stern field journal, 1993). Her ability to make those nice things for her family permits her to demonstrate her maturity as well as her skill and, thus, enhances her status in the community.[6]

WHAT MAKES A TECHNOLOGY INUIT?

With the encouragement of government administrators, traders, and Christian missionaries, Inuit readily adopted new technologies and became enmeshed in expanded global exchange networks. Inuit communities today are awash with the same technologies enjoyed by people around the world. These include televisions, digital video cameras, the Internet, airplanes, and consumer goods as well as snowmobiles, rifles, and global positioning systems. Ironically, outsiders have sometimes challenged the rights of Inuit to engage in activities that involve imported technologies on the claim that somehow adopting a new technology makes the activity no longer authentically Inuit. This has been particularly the case with respect to Inuit hunting. For example, in the 1940 and 1950s, Canadian game managers severely restricted the numbers of caribou that Inuit were allowed to take for food and, more important, for clothing. The game managers claimed that Inuit using rifles were overhunting and endangering the caribou, but there was no evidence that Inuit hunters were taking more animals than necessary or that Inuit hunting was harmful to the health of the caribou population.[7] The hunting restrictions, however, caused real hardship for Inuit who were living on the land. In the 1950s, there were not any adequate substitutes for caribou skin parkas; nor did most Canadian Inuit have the ability to purchase imported outerwear if it had been available. The hardship was compounded by the fact that until the late 1950s the Canadian government prevented most Inuit from settling at mission stations and trading posts.

More recently, animal rights activists challenged the rights of Inuit using snowmobiles, rifles, and steel traps to participate in the fur trade. One of the claims the activists made is that Inuit using imported technologies or living in modern frame houses were not "real Inuit." Animal rights activists have used these technological changes to question the morality of Inuit participation in the fur trade. As discussed in Chapter 3, the activities of animal rights organizations and supporters contributed to the collapse of a market for Inuit-produced fur and produced severe economic hardship in some Inuit communities.

Questions of technology have also vexed Inupiaq whalers. For example, the International Whaling Commission insists that in order to qualify as indigenous, and therefore be permissible under international rules, Inupiaq whalers must continue to use the darting and killing technologies they adopted from 19th century commercial whalers rather than more modern, efficient, and possibly more humane methods. This is because the IWC regards the technology rather than the sharing of labor, meat, and *maktak* as the attributes that makes Inupiaq whaling "traditional." Many Inupiat disagree.

Neither antiquity nor "new-ness" is automatically thought to be valuable in itself. An *umipiaq*, or skin boat, may be used in the spring because one can navigate it through the spring ice more easily than an aluminum boat. The heavy autumn seas, on the other hand, are much more safely negotiated in a sturdier boat with an outboard motor. Gortex may produce excellent rain gear; however, skin parkas continue to provide the warmest possible protection for winter hunting. The best equipment is neither valued because it represents powerful "Western" knowledge, nor preferred because it expresses "traditional Inupiaq values." Instead in an echo of Oquilluk's story, people "work in their minds to stay alive," making, trading, buying, or adapting useful things. Iñupiat were doing this long before Europeans showed up in the 19th century, and they have continued to experiment with other's knowledge into the present day.[8]

Rather, what is important to Inupiaq whalers, and to Inuit generally, in assuring the Inuitness of a practice, are the social relationships fostered and maintained by participating in collective activities such as whaling. For example, does the practice advance Inuit interpretations of appropriate relationships among people and between people and animals? And as noted above, Inuit also value creative and clever adaptations of materials.

CLIMATE CHANGE AND TECHNOLOGIES

The technologies (both traditional and modern) in place in Inuit communities today were designed for a climate that was colder and weather that was more predictable. Unstable ice, thawing permafrost, and increased ferocity of winter storms threaten to wreak havoc on the infrastructure of Inuit communities and the material culture of Inuit lives. The structural integrity of modern Arctic buildings, roads, and airport runways requires that the permafrost remain frozen. Several Inupiaq communities in northwest Alaska are already threatened with erosion now that landfast ice no longer forms to protect the coastline from winter storms. The movements of animals that Inuit continue to use for food are in the process of change, and are no longer as predictable as they once were. And the sea ice that Inuit have long used as an extension of land is disappearing. Inuit culture adapted to dramatic climate change in the distant past, and it is likely that Inuit will also adapt to the current climate change. A warming Arctic may offer new opportunities to Inuit and other Arctic residents, but it is not yet clear exactly what those opportunities are.

NOTES

1. Briggs, Jean L. (1991) "Expecting the Unexpected: Canadian Inuit Training for an Experimental Lifestyle," *Ethos* 19(3): 259–60.

2. Oquilluk, William A., with Laurel L. Bland (1973) *People of Kauwerak: Legends of the Northern Eskimo*, Anchorage: Alaska Methodist University Press, 1.

3. Briggs, "Expecting the Unexpected," 263–64.

4. Oswalt, Wendell H. (1999) *Eskimos and Explorers*, 2nd ed. Lincoln: University of Nebraska Press, 208.

5. Tester, Frank James (2006) *Iglutaq (In My Room): The Implications of Homelessness for Inuit*, report prepared for the Harvest Society, Kinngait, Nunavut, 232, retrieved September 20, 2009 from http://www.socialwork. ubc.ca/fileadmin/template/main/images/departments/social_work/ faculty/IGLUTAQ__in_my_room_.pdf.

6. Stern, Pamela (1999) "Learning to Be Smart: An Exploration of the Culture of Intelligence in a Canadian Inuit Community," *American Anthropologist* 101(3): 508.

7. Kulchyski, Peter, and Frank James Tester (2007) *Kiumajut (Talking Back): Game Management and Inuit Rights, 1900–70*, Vancouver: University of British Columbia Press.

8. Bodenhorn, Barbara (2003) "Fall Whaling in Barrow, Alaska: A Consideration of Strategic Decision-Making," in *Indigenous Ways to the Present: Native Whaling in the Western Arctic*, Allen P. McCartney, ed., Edmonton: Canadian Circumpolar Institute Press, 301.

6

POLITICAL LIFE

Today all Inuit live in modern nation-states and have the same legal rights, privileges, and responsibilities as other citizens of those nations. In contrast to the experience of First Nations or Indians in other parts of North America, no Inuit group was forced to sign a treaty ceding their land or was consigned to a reservation. At the same time, Inuit were not asked or even consulted when European, Canadian, and American governments drew national borders and made claims of ownership of Inuit lands. This was the true, for example, when the United States purchased Alaska from Russia for $7.2 million in 1867. It was also the case in 1953 when Denmark ended its formal colonization of Greenland by making Greenland a province of the Danish Kingdom. National governments still exercise ultimate control over the administration of Inuit lands, but since the 1970s, Inuit have increasingly participated in decision making about their lives and lands and, in several parts of the North, Inuit have achieved a measure of indigenous self-government.

TRADITIONAL POLITICAL AUTHORITY

Prior to European (including Canadian and American) colonization of Inuit lands, Inuit lived in dispersed self-governing communities that were independent, but part of extended trade and social networks. Local political life was organized around kinship with leadership usually vested in a senior male. Leaders had no formal authority to require people to accept their decisions. The leader's authority derived from his position within the family and from the experience that came with age. Older people, both men and women, were respected for having developed more knowledge and experience over the course of a long life. Still, a leader had to continually demonstrate his wisdom in order to maintain his authority. One way he did this was to share generously the proceeds of the hunt. Another was to maintain a calm and even temperament. Any leader whose actions led to uncertainty or insecurity might find that his group splintered.

The traditional political unit was a group of people associated with place or region. Many of these local groups were quite small, usually consisting of as few as 25–50 related people. But there were some Inuit groups, especially in Alaska, comprising several hundred people. The size of the population in any given place was related to the availability of food and, especially, fuel resources; thus, it fluctuated seasonally. Inuit in the Central Canadian Arctic formed large snowhouse communities on the ocean ice during late winter when seals, which were both food and fuel, could be hunted at their breathing holes. These gatherings provided opportunities to share news, to trade, to socialize and renew friendships, and to work cooperatively.

The largest permanent Inuit communities were in north and northwest Alaska where people had consistent access to an abundant variety of fish, as well as to land and marine mammals. Bowhead whales (*Balaena mysticetus*) were an especially important resource and the logistical problem of storage alone would have encouraged Inupiat to establish permanent villages. Not only did a single whale provide a significant amount of meat and *maktak* (skin and outer layer of fat), but whale bone was used as structural supports for building, the flexible baleen had many uses, and the fat or blubber was an important source of light and heat. The difficulty of hunting, landing, and butchering a 75- to 100-ton sea mammal using small boats is considerable, and thus, individuals who could organize and direct the necessary labor to hunt, land, butcher, and distribute this valuable resource would have had their political power elevated.

Political Power and Responsibility

Although Inuit societies are often described as egalitarian, meaning that no individual had preferential access to productive resources, there is substantial archeological evidence to indicate that within Thule period settlements some individuals and households did possess more wealth and social status than others. These status differentials continued into historic times in Inupiaq north and northwest Alaska, with high status and political authority being accorded to *umialiit* (sing. *umialik*) or whaling captains and their wives. The term, umialiit, refers to their status as boat owners, but their role as whaling captains concerned not only providing the skin boat but also food and gear for a 6- to 8-person whaling crew; managing all aspects of the whale hunt, including preparatory feasts, butchering, and distribution of meat and *maktak*; and generous contributions to celebrations and ceremonies throughout the year. These were tasks that the umialik shared with his wife. It is critical to bear in mind that the responsibility for organizing and maintaining a whaling crew was and remains a task for married couples, and women also have political power. Umialiit wives are often described as being quite outspoken. In the 18th and 19th centuries, and probably earlier, an umialik also maintained wealth and status by organizing long-distance trading fairs. The umialik and his wife had substantial authority within a community, but it was authority that came with considerable responsibility for ensuring the security of the community. In contemporary Inupiaq towns and villages, political leaders are still frequently leaders of whaling crews.

The umialik's authority extended only to those who were members of his *qargi* (pl. *qargit*). The qargi is sometimes called a "men's house," but it is more appropriate to think of it as a community center where men and women collaborated, socialized, and discussed matters of importance. Most qargit were "founded by an *umialik* as a place where he and his male relatives could visit, work, and pass the time. Over the years, other people would be invited (or would request) to join."[1] But membership was not permanent. Those who "became dissatisfied, for whatever reason, with the situation in the *qargi* to which they belonged could establish a new one."[2] Most Inupiaq communities had more than one qargi, and these could, and sometimes did, become separate political factions.

Managing Conflict

Inuit used a variety of methods to maintain social order within their communities. First and foremost was the value that Inuit placed on conflict avoidance. Overt interpersonal conflicts were (and to a large extent, still are) avoided by cultural practices such as expressing desires indirectly, noninterference in the affairs of others, and emotional restraint.

Within a community, individuals who violated norms or whose behavior was disruptive or dangerous could be dealt with in a number of ways. These included humor and joking, but gossip, ostracism, confrontation, and threats of banishment were also used to control offenders. In her book *Never in Anger,* anthropologist Jean Briggs describes how her adoptive family at Chantry Inlet ostracized her after she reacted angrily to a group of non-Native sports fishermen who had damaged the family's equipment. In extreme cases, mentally ill individuals who threatened the safety of others could be killed with the consent of the community, but this was rare. According to elders interviewed by students from Nunavut Arctic College, law breakers should be made to realize and allowed to correct their misdeeds. The first step in dealing with an offender was private counseling by elders. According to one elder, "If offenders were not made to feel embarrassed, and they understood what was said to them, there would be more of a chance to improve that person's behavior."[3] According to another elder, if repeated attempts at counseling failed,

then the person was told to live on his own if he didn't want to abide by the rules of the community. Later he would realize that he did have something to contribute and when he started thinking about this, he would want to go back to the community. That's part of being wise. All of us here have a mind. They wanted him to be part of the community. . . .

In my community a person was not literally banished. Maybe they used to do that in other regions but in my community, I have never heard of this happening. I have never seen a person banished from the community. What happened was he would not be allowed to be involved with the community for a while. The offender would do what he wanted to do, but he would have to do it by himself.[4]

Managing Conflict between Communities

Archeological and ethnohistorical data indicate that conflict between communities was fairly common and "relations with people from distant areas in particular could be characterized by mutual distrust and contain the seeds of animosity."[5] This animosity could erupt into warfare from time to time. Fear of violence often served to keep groups apart, but complete avoidance was not always possible or necessarily desirable. Where avoidance could not be maintained, both contests and hospitality worked to smooth relations between groups. In north and northwest Alaska, these frequently occurred in the context of feasts and trading fairs and included both Inupiat from many communities as well as other peoples. People traveled from significant distances to participate in these annual events. Dance, song, and strength competitions during festivals, much like modern Olympics, provided a formal, ritualized way to express competitive and even hostile feelings (see Chapter 8), but they also provided a forum for real and potential enemies to be turned into allies. Trade was an important component of feasts and fairs, but they were also venues for arranging marriages, showing hospitality, and engaging in diplomacy. Diplomacy sometimes failed; oral histories and several 19th-century ivory engravings record stories in which hostile groups took advantage of the fact that people were preoccupied with the festival in order to mount a raid and massacre the participants.[6]

One form of conflict management deserves special mention: song duels. Inuit used satirical songs to air grievances (see Chapter 8), though the institution of the song duel, like trade fairs, disappeared under colonization. These most commonly occurred between antagonists from different communities, but there are reports of song duels between people in the same community. Song duels often occurred within the context of trade fairs or other celebrations, but they could also occur outside of those special occasions. It appears that an individual with a complaint against someone in a neighboring group would compose songs of derision, and then go with an entourage to confront his or her adversary. The person challenged was expected to respond with his or her own mocking lyrics. Winning or losing resulted from the way the antagonists comported themselves during the contest, rather than the wittiness of the lyrics. A loser was someone who became flustered, tongue-tied, or forgot the words. Despite whatever feelings of resentment and hostility they might hold, the combatants in a song duel "were expected to act smiling and unconcerned. The fact that a specific formal code of behavior had to be followed made it easier to play this ambivalent role, [reducing] the risk that other weapons than words might be used."[7]

POLITICAL LIFE TODAY

Although they all are wealthy Western democracies, Denmark, Canada, and the United States have distinct political institutions, political histories, and political cultures. Each nation took a different approach, based on its own laws and cultural practices, to administering Inuit communities, and these historical variations in colonization account for much of the diversity found in Inuit self-governance today. Greenlanders are moving toward political independence from Denmark, creating what will be the first independent Inuit state. Greenlanders have been able to achieve self-government without making specific claims of aboriginal rights or title to land. In contrast, in both Canada and the United States, Inuit asserted aboriginal title to their traditional lands as a way to pursue aboriginal rights to self-determination. Land claims agreements have proven to be a valuable mechanism for political development and have been integral to Inuit efforts to achieve a measure of self-government. What Inuit in each country are hoping to achieve is the ability to create laws and governance structures that reflect their unique cultural values and sensibilities. This is an ongoing process and the exact nature and form of Inuit political development is likely to continue to vary across the North.

KALAALLIIT NUNAAT/GREENLAND

Politically, Greenland has been part of the Kingdom of Denmark since 1721 when Danish-Norwegian priest Hans Egede established a colony near present-day Nuuk. An early attempt to privatize trade was unsuccessful because the private trading companies were unable to make a profit. Consequently, trade with Greenlanders remained a government function. Unlike most colonial situations in modern history, the Danish crown administered Greenland as a closed-colony, severely restricting the manufactured goods and the persons who could visit the island. This situation continued until World War II.

The lives of Greenlanders changed with Danish colonial rule, but most Greenlanders continued to live in small, kin-oriented communities, supporting themselves by hunting and fishing, and exchanging some of their harvest for manufactured goods. A minority, many of whom were descended from Danish traders, missionaries, and other officials, lived mostly in larger towns and worked as teachers, catechists, and in public administration. The town-dwellers formed a social and intellectual elite within Greenland society. Widespread literacy, enabled by development of a standard orthography for Kalaallisut and publication outlets for local writing, helped Greenlanders to come to think of themselves as a single people distinct from Danes. As early as the 1880s ordinary Greenlanders debated in print whether their identity as a distinct people derived from their ties to traditional hunting culture or from their shared language, history, and love of country (see Chapter 9).

Denmark was occupied by Nazi Germany during World War II, temporarily severing its ties to Greenland. The U.S. military, however, used Greenland as a North Atlantic base of operations, and in the interim, the U.S. government administered the Danish colony, shattering the economic and cultural isolation of the island. Greenlanders had access to American music, films, and commercial goods. After the war, Denmark could not impose the same isolation that had prevailed previously. As a result, in 1953, Denmark amended its constitution to formally end Greenland's colonial status and make it a province of Denmark. Greenlanders received two seats in the 179-member Danish Parliament; they retain these today.

Although Greenland was no longer formally a colony, it continued to be one in practice because Greenlanders did not control the economic or political development of the island. Denmark made major investments in health, education, housing, and the economy, significantly improving the standard of living. But the decision making about these economic and social development activities remained in the hands of Danish administrators. Significantly, the number of Danes in Greenland jumped from less than 5 percent of the population in 1950 to almost 20 percent in 1975.[8] Danes rather than Greenlanders were hired both as construction workers and to manage the new public services and economic enterprises. Particularly galling to Greenlanders was a law enacted in 1964 that awarded a higher rate of pay to workers who had been born in Denmark. This, perhaps more than any other aspect of Danish administration, created a collective resentment of Danish control. This internal colonialism made Greenlanders Danish citizens and proclaimed Greenlanders and Danes to be equal, but then relegated Greenlanders to a second-class citizenship. As only nominally equal citizens in Denmark, Greenlanders had no possibility to insert their values or distinct circumstances into social programs or legislation. For example, in a 1972 national referendum on Danish membership in the European Community (EC), 70.2 percent of Greenlanders, concerned about Europeans fishing in Greenland waters, voted against joining. The majority in much more populous Denmark, however, voted in favor, and Greenland was forced to join the EC along with Denmark. It was able to withdraw only in 1985. A de facto policy of "Danification" that began in 1953 presumed that Greenlanders would conform to Danish values, norms of behavior, and laws rather than contribute their values to

Danish society. The cumulative effect of discrimination and brushing aside the wishes and cultural values of Greenlanders led to a growing sense of ethnic nationalism, particularly among the best-educated Greenlanders.

The Home Rule movement began primarily among Greenlandic students in Denmark in the 1960s, part of that era's global movements of mass student protests and opposition to colonialism. Founders of the Home Rule movement included Jonathan Motzfeldt, Greenland's first prime minister; Lars Emil Johansen; and Moses Olsen (1938–2008). Olsen's election to a seat in the Danish Parliament in 1972 helped set the stage for the establishment of Home Rule. The Danish Parliament was evenly divided between Liberals on one side and Social Democrats and Socialists on the other. Olsen held the tie-breaking seat that determined which party or parties would form the government. He used his swing vote as leverage to force Denmark to accede to Home Rule for Greenland.

Home Rule took effect on May 1, 1979. Greenland officially took the name *Kalaalliit Nunaat* (Land of the Greenlanders). Denmark retained authority over foreign policy, defense, justice, and the currency. Decisions about the development of mineral resources were shared by Denmark and Greenland. All other governmental functions were transferred to the Home Rule government in stages between 1979 and 1992 with authority over education being one of the first to be conveyed. With Home Rule, both Kalaallisut (Greenlandic) and Danish became official languages.

Greenlanders remain Danish citizens, and all Danish citizens who have lived in Greenland for 6 months or more, regardless of ethnicity, may vote in Greenland's elections. Greenland has a parliamentary-style government with 31 members selected through a combination of constituency-based seats and proportional representation. The political party with the most seats forms the Home Rule government.

There are three major political parties and several minor parties in Greenland. *Siumut,* meaning "Forward," began as a political movement in the early 1970s and became a political party in 1977. Politically, Siumut is left-of-center, with policies similar to European social democrats or Canada's New Democratic Party. Siumut was the governing party from the start of Home Rule until June 2009, but mostly in coalition with either of the other two major parties.

Atassut, meaning "Togetherness," was formed in 1978 as a more conservative alternative to Siumut. It advocates for maintaining strong ties with Denmark and for greater international interactions including participation in NATO and the European Union, the name of the EC since 1992. Atassut opposed Greenland's withdrawal from the EC in 1985. It also supports privatization of public enterprises. In general, Atassut is a centrist party comparable to the Canadian Liberal Party and the Democratic Party in the United States.

Inuit Ataqatigiit (IA), meaning "Human Fellowship," also formed in 1978. It is a radical socialist party, and has advocated collective ownership of Greenland's productive resources. It stresses pan-Inuit solidarity and is a strong advocate of the Inuit Circumpolar Council (ICC) (see Chapter 12). In the 1970s IA campaigned against Greenlandic Home Rule because, it argued, Home Rule would legitimize and perpetuate Danish control of the island. Instead it advocates for full independence from Denmark. Nonetheless, IA joined with Siumut to form the first coalition Home Rule government in 1979. The party has grown in electoral popularity since its founding, while Siumut and Atassut have lost ground. IA won the 2009 parliamentary election and formed a government in coalition with two smaller parties.

In November 2008, Greenlanders voted overwhelmingly to replace Home Rule with Self Rule. Under Self Rule, which took effect on June 21, 2009, Greenland will remain within the Danish realm, but will assume authority over nearly all of the remaining governmental functions. Of particular concern to Greenlanders is ownership and control of mineral resources. For the time being, Denmark continues to provide a substantial subsidy to Greenland and maintain shared control over resource extraction. Mineral exploitation appears to be the most likely route for Greenland to replace the Danish subsidy and gain full independence. To develop its mineral resources, however, Greenland would have to open itself to multinational mining corporations (see Chapter 3). It may gain its political independence from Denmark, but at the same time lose its economic independence to those global corporations.

SELF-DETERMINATION IN ALASKA AND CANADA

Like Denmark, both the United States and Canada enacted policies aimed at assimilating Inuit (and other indigenous peoples) to national norms. In both places, as in Greenland, Inuit have struggled to regain local autonomy and to develop forms of governance suitable to their own cultural values and norms of behavior within the legal frameworks provided by each nation. There are three separate but related areas in which Inuit in Canada and Alaska have advanced their goal of self-determination. These are land claims, co-management of natural resources, and self-government.

Land Claims Agreements

When Great Britain first colonized the lands that became the United States and Canada, it regarded the Native peoples as nations similar to European nations, with governments and national territories. In order to establish colonies in North America, Britain signed treaties, which are agreements between nations, with various Native American tribes and communities. This policy was formalized in law by the Royal Proclamation of October 7, 1763, in which King George III declared that Native lands "not having been ceded to or purchased by Us, are reserved to [Native peoples]" and that only the government could purchase Native land. Britain, and later the United States and Canada, often violated the terms agreed to in treaties, but by signing treaties and establishing government-to-government relationships with Native peoples, it established the legal basis for modern assertions of aboriginal title that were repeated in subsequent legislation enacted by Canada and affirmed by courts there. In the United States the courts have been less consistent. Aboriginal title, as interpreted by the courts, consists solely of the right to exclusive occupancy; it does not allow Native peoples to make decisions about that land or to sell it.

As in Greenland, the political struggle for Inuit indigenous rights in Canada and Alaska was led by young Inuit, many of whom had met each other at residential schools and discovered that they shared many of the same concerns about the colonization of their lands. In particular they were concerned about usurpation of Inuit lands for resource extraction. In Alaska, the Inupiat case for aboriginal title to land was first articulated in a university term paper written by future Inupiaq leader, Willie Hensley, in 1966. Hensley drew on a passage in the 1884 Organic Act, which established the territorial government of Alaska. This passage affirmed that Alaska Natives "shall not be disturbed in the possession of any lands actually in their use or occupation or now claimed by them, but the terms under which such persons may acquire title to such lands is reserved for future legislation by Congress."[9] With a few exceptions, no one other than Inuit paid much attention to or took any great interest in Inuit lands prior to the middle of the 20th century. But by the 1950s both government and private interests began encroaching on Inuit lands to build military bases and to extract oil, gas, and other minerals. For example, in the

late 1950s and early 1960s, the U.S. Atomic Energy Commission proposed using a nuclear explosion to gouge a harbor at Cape Thompson, an important food harvesting site for the Inupiat communities
in northwest Alaska. Although Project Chariot, as the scheme was
known, was eventually scrapped, planning for it was well underway
before Inupiat in the affected communities were even notified about
the project. In response, the Inupiat formed *Inupiat Paitot* (People's
Heritage) to press for their civil and aboriginal rights. They wrote a
letter of protest to President John F. Kennedy. At the same time they
established the first statewide Native newspaper, the *Tundra Times*,
to be a communication vehicle among Alaska's indigenous peoples
(see Chapter 9).

Alaska statehood in 1959 had substantial consequences for the land
rights of Inupiat and other Alaska Natives individually and collectively. Even though, legally, only Congress could extinguish Native
land rights, the Alaska Statehood Act allowed the state to take title to
Native lands and to collect royalties on the extraction of nonrenewable resources such as oil and gas and minerals. Congress granted
the state the right to select 105 million acres of federally owned land,
land on which aboriginal title had never been extinguished. Almost
immediately, the state began selecting land that Alaska Natives regarded as theirs. This had consequences for where Inupiat could
hunt, build their homes, and travel.

Alaska Natives protested the state's land selections and filed com-
peting claims, so that by the mid-1960s the amount of land claimed
exceeded the total available. Inupiat on Alaska's North Slope formed
the Arctic Slope Native Association to represent the interests of Inupiat living north of the Brooks Range. The Inupiat north of the
Seward Peninsula established the Northwest Arctic Native Association. Both organizations, along with the statewide Alaska Federation of Natives, petitioned the United States Secretary of the Interior,
Stewart Udall, for a halt to all land transfers. In 1966 Secretary Udall
suspended transfers of disputed land until Congress could resolve
the issue of Alaska Native claims to land, but it was the discovery of
a massive deposit of oil at Prudhoe Bay in December 1967 that finally
forced Congress to act.

Although the Prudhoe Bay oil field sat on uncontested state land,
the only practical way to remove the oil at the time was to build a 700-
mile-long pipeline from Prudhoe Bay to the ice-free port at Valdez.
The pipeline route would cross lands claimed by Alaska Natives and
thus could not be built without either settling Native claims or risk-
ing lawsuits.

Alaska Native protestors outside Sidney Laurence Auditorium in Anchorage oppose the sale of state oil leases. (Ward Wells, Ward Wells Collection, Anchorage Museum, B83.91.S4794.15)

Congress enacted the Alaska Native Claims Settlement Act (ANCSA), and President Richard Nixon signed it into law in December 1971. ANCSA (pronounced ānk-suh), which the Alaska Federation of Natives participated in writing, differed substantially from all previous Indian treaties and became the model for subsequent aboriginal land claims agreements in Canada.

ANCSA extinguished or ended the aboriginal title to land of Alaska Natives in exchange for ordinary title (called fee simple), including both surface and subsurface rights to 44 million acres (approx. 12% of the state) and $962.5 million in cash. Half of the money was to come from revenues from federal and state oil revenues, the other half from annual appropriations from Congress. The unique feature of ANCSA and of the more recent land claims agreements in Canada was the establishment of Native corporations.

Native Corporations

ANCSA mandated the creation of 12 for-profit regional corporations (and a 13th for Alaska Natives living outside of the state) and approximately 200 village corporations that received the money and the lands. Every Alaska Native alive on the date that the Act became law received 100 shares of stock in a regional corporation. The idea to create corporations is said to have originated with the state of Alaska's Land Claims Task Force, which was chaired by Inupiaq Willie Hensley. The primary rationale was to put modern financial structures and economic development institutions in the hands of indigenous peoples who had been left out of the mainstream economy. Surprising as it may seem, this plan was not controversial at the time. This was, in large part, because the specifics were vague and allowed different factions to envision distinct outcomes. Alaska Native communities were deeply impoverished and ANCSA seemed to offer a solution to Native poverty. "Assimilationists saw in corporations business dealings and modern capitalism. Tribalists saw more real autonomy . . . [and] new Native political leaders saw the opportunity for economic and political self-determination, not to mention the promise of management positions for themselves."[10]

As the Native corporations came into being, several problems became apparent. The first had to do with the matter of children born after December 18, 1971. The Act did not provide any mechanism for them to become shareholders except through inheritance. Second, Congress prevented any Alaska Native from selling his or her shares for 20 years, but there was genuine concern that, after 1991, non-Natives could gain control of the Native corporations. Because the corporations held the land title, it was also feared that if a corporation filed for bankruptcy it could be forced to sell land. Or individual Alaska Natives in need of cash might sell their shares and thus allow non-Natives to gain control of the land. This was a concern because of the continuing social and economic importance of subsistence hunting, something that was not anticipated in ANCSA. Amendments to ANCSA in 1987 allowed individual Native corporations to decide if and how to correct these issues.

More intractable issues have to do with running the corporations in ways that are both profitable and responsive to shareholders' needs. Many of the corporations found it difficult to juggle the mandate to make a profit and pay dividends with the mandate to create employment and economic development in their communities. The remoteness of most Alaska Native communities limits the local investment opportunities, while investing in profitable ventures outside the North limits the employment of shareholders. Further, the accounting and fiscal reporting responsibilities of corporations were financially burdensome and generally required the corporations to hire non-Native professionals. During the 1980s and 1990s, many of the Native corporations teetered on bankruptcy, but their financial situations have improved in recent years. Native corporations, nonetheless, have become important institutions of Native self-determination and have fundamentally changed the social and economic conditions for Alaska Natives. One outcome has been the creation of well-paid jobs for a small number of Alaska Natives, but the creation of Native corporations has not solved more widespread problems of unemployment and poverty, with the result of increased economic disparity.

Land Claims in Canada

Despite the shortcomings of ANCSA, it became the model for each of the land claims agreements signed in Canada. What Canadian land claims agreements borrowed from ANCSA were the principle of extinguishment of aboriginal title to all traditional lands in exchange for fee simple title to a portion of those lands, plus cash compensation and the establishment of Native corporations to invest the cash. Unlike ANCSA, Inuit Native corporations in Canada continuously enroll new beneficiaries as they become adults. The Canadian agreements also contain provisions for Inuit to participate in the management of natural resources on ceded land. Five land claims agreements been made with four Canadian Inuit groups: Inuit of northern Quebec signed the James Bay and Northern Quebec Agreement in 1975 and the Nunavik Inuit Land Claims Agreement in 2006; Inuvialuit in the western Canadian Arctic signed the Inuvialuit Final Agreement in 1984; the Nunavut Land Claims Agreement signed in 1993 settled the land claims of the Inuit in what is now the Nunavut Territory; and Labrador Inuit concluded the Labrador Inuit Land Claims Agreement in 2005. All of the land claims agreements have the legal status of treaties and are thus constitutionally protected and cannot be easily amended.

James Bay and Northern Quebec Agreement

As with ANCSA, a large energy project was the catalyst for the first Canadian land claims agreement. In 1971, the province of Quebec began work on a massive hydroelectric dam complex on the La

Grande and nearby rivers that empty into James Bay. It is one of the largest hydroelectric projects ever built and it was undertaken without any consultation with the aboriginal people who lived on and supported themselves from that land. Nunavik Inuit and Cree sought a court injunction to stop the megaproject. After nearly a year of testimony, a Quebec court issued the injunction, but it was overturned on appeal a week later. Nonetheless, in the interim, the Quebec premier, Robert Bourassa, agreed to negotiate Inuit and Cree land claims. The result was the James Bay and Northern Quebec Agreement (JBNQA) signed in 1975 by the Northern Quebec Inuit Association, the Grand Council of the Cree, Hydro-Québec, and the governments of Quebec and Canada.

Key aims of the Inuit and Cree included protection and support for the subsistence economy and the establishment of local self-government. One of the ways that the JBNQA addressed the first of these was through the establishment of a hunter support program that pays individual hunters to provide fish and game for a community pantry (see Chapter 3). The second aim, self-governance, was addressed by the creation of several entities: the Kativik Regional Government, the Kativik School Board, and the Nunavik Board of Health and Social Services. The nonprofit Makivik Corporation, successor to the Northern Quebec Inuit Association, was established to manage the cash payout, to invest in the regional economy, and to represent the political and economic interests of Inuit of Nunavik. Not all Nunavik Inuit accepted the land claims settlement. Inuit in Puvirnituq and Ivujivik opposed the extinguishment of aboriginal title and formed a dissident organization called *Inuit Tungavingat Nunamini* (The Inuit Foundation in Their Own Land).

The JBNQA agreement was negotiated very quickly and under pressure of development, and as a consequence, had weaknesses from the perspective of many Nunavik Inuit. For one, Inuit did not gain control of any mineral resources or of offshore areas. Further, the monitoring and enforcement mechanisms in the agreement were weak. The 2006 Nunavik Inuit Land Claims Agreement is meant to address these concerns. With regard to self-governance, Makivik Corporation has advocated and negotiated with the government of Quebec for a more consolidated form of regional governance that would include a legislative body that could make laws concerning "Inuit language and culture, and [have] substantive and effective (shared) powers in other areas such as education, health, environment, and land and resources," particularly over the development of natural resources.[11]

Nunavut Land Claims Agreement

In contrast with the JBNQA that was negotiated in less than two years, the Nunavut Land Claims Agreement took 17 years to settle. Like all of the other land claims agreements, Inuit in Nunavut exchanged their aboriginal title to their traditional lands for monetary compensation and fee simple title to 18 percent of the territory. They hold subsurface rights to about 10 percent of that as well as a share of royalties from any mineral development on public lands. The issue that proved almost insurmountable was the Inuit demand that the land claim include provision for self-government in the form of a new territory. Eventually compromise was reached to form a public government. Election of a majority of aboriginal members in 1979 made division of the Northwest Territories more palatable to its Legislative Assembly. Also, Nunavut Inuit agreed to negotiate creation of a Nunavut Territory separately from the land claim. The Nunavut Land Claims Agreement was signed into law on July 9, 1993. The Nunavut Territory came into being on April 1, 1999.

Self-Government—Nunavut Territory

The Nunavut Territory comprises an area that is one-fifth of the Canadian landmass with only about 30,000 people living in 26 dispersed towns and villages. It was created through division of the already existing Northwest Territories.

Like the other two territories in Canada, Nunavut has province-like powers over most governmental functions such as education, health care, and municipal services. The primary difference between a province and a territory, at present, is that a territory does not own or control the land or the natural resources contained on the land. Those are owned by the federal government (with the exception, in Nunavut, of the portion of resources that Inuit retained through the land claims settlement), and the federal government collects the royalties on any resources extracted.

Nunavut has a 19-member parliament, referred to as the Legislative Assembly. There are no political parties. The members of the assembly elect the premier who then chooses the Cabinet from the members of the Assembly. Any Canadian citizen residing in Nunavut may vote in territorial elections regardless of ethnicity, but because 85 percent of Nunavummiut (people of Nunavut) are Inuit, there is a unique opportunity to enact government policies that conform to Inuit cultural values. That is, indeed, the expectation for the Government of Nunavut (GN). The GN has adopted several policies intended to conform to Inuit needs and expectations. They include operating the Legislative Assembly on a consensus basis rather than the party discipline that prevails in most parliamentary systems, decentralizing the bureaucracy to several regional centers, and using *Inuit Qaujimajatuqangit* (IQ) (see Chapter 2) to inform policy making in all government departments. The intent to make a government that reflects Inuit sensibilities was described in a statement of priorities, the Bathurst Mandate, produced by the first Cabinet.

Gender Parity Proposal

In planning for the establishment of the Nunavut Territory, the Nunavut Implementation Commission (NIC), along with *Pauktuutit* (the Inuit Women of Canada) and several other organizations, proposed that each of the 19 electoral districts, called ridings in Canada, in the Nunavut Legislative Assembly be represented by two legislators: a man and a woman. Proponents of the measure felt that this first-of-its-kind measure was one way to advance the Inuit character of the new legislature in a region where men and women historically had distinct but complementary and interdependent roles that had been altered by years of Canadian colonial administration. Opponents, however, argued that gender parity was an imported idea that both threatened the Inuit family and advanced the political careers of unqualified women. The leading voice in the opposition was a female member of the Nunavut Caucus in the Northwest Territories' Legislative Assembly, Manitok Thompson. In May 1997, the gender parity proposal was put to a public referendum where it earned only 43 percent of the vote in a low turnout.[12] There was a much higher voter turnout (88.6%) for the selection of the territory's first Legislative Assembly in February 1999. Eighteen men and one woman, Manitok Thompson, were elected. The third Nunavut government, elected in 2008, also has only a single female member of the legislative assembly (MLA), Eva Aariak. MLA Aariak, however, was selected to serve as premier.

Inuit Values in Action

At first glance the Nunavut Legislative Assembly appears to operate no differently than other legislatures in Canada or other Westminster-style parliaments around the world, save for the facts that there are no political parties and the MLAs sit in a circle. The rules of procedure are formally prescribed. Each sitting of the assembly

Nunavut Legislative Assembly building. (Photos by Peter V. Hall)

opens with a prayer. This is followed by personal statements from cabinet ministers and ordinary members. Visitors to the gallery are recognized. Then the assembly gets down to work. MLAs direct questions to various cabinet ministers, committee reports are presented, documents are tabled, and bills are debated and voted on. Nunavut MLAs conduct business in both English and Inuktitut, both of which are simultaneously translated for members and visitors. And all members use a very formal and ritualized style of speech to conduct assembly business just as in other Canadian parliaments. For example, MLAs address all of their statements in the legislative chamber to the Speaker of the Assembly and begin them with the phrase, "Mr. Speaker, I rise today to . . ."[13]

The absence of political parties, referred to as "consensus government" is unique to Nunavut and the Northwest Territories, both of which have substantial Aboriginal populations. It is meant to avoid the rancor that comes with the establishment of a governing party and an opposition party, and thus, consensus government is sometimes described as being in concert with Aboriginal forms of decision making. The existence of consensus government should not be taken to mean that MLAs do not have substantial political differences and disagreements. In the Nunavut Legislative Assembly, however, disagreements are often expressed in culturally Inuit ways. For example, an MLA who is planning to aggressively challenge a cabinet minister may use his member's statement to make a humorous or self-deprecating remark. By doing this, he uses a traditional Inuit way to signal that his seemingly hostile questions to come are not personally directed and that he is not dangerous. As with the song contests that Inuit used in the past to resolve disputes, this humor, as well as the ritual language and form used in the Legislative Assembly, is meant to keep contemporary disputes from spiraling out of control.

Nunavut has not been a panacea for Inuit self-determination. The serious economic and social problems that were present before establishment of the Nunavut Territory continue to exist. In comparison to Canada as a whole Nunavummuit experience low educational attainment, high unemployment, and inadequate and seriously overcrowded housing (see Table 6.1). These issues contribute to the ongoing problems of economic disparity, domestic violence, poor public health, youth suicide, and alcohol and drug abuse. There are also serious obstacles to the goals to making Inuktitut the working language of government and to have a bureaucracy that is representative of the population. In the matter of public service employment, the aim is for 85 percent Inuit staff, since that is the proportion of the

Table 6.1
Social and economic indicators, Nunavut 2006

Indicator	Nunavut	Canada
Population	29, 474	31,612,897
Overcrowded dwellings	18%	1.5%
Completion of high school and/or postsecondary education (age 15 and older)	42.7%	76.2%
Unemployment rate	15.6%	6.6%

Source: Census 2006, Statistics Canada, Community Profiles.

Nunavut population that is Inuit. Thus far, this has not been attained. In fact, the percentage of Inuit public service workers has fallen since the inauguration of the Government of Nunavut, with administrative support employees as the only category of public service worker that is representative of the population.[14] Even though the Legislative Assembly operates, in some respects, in an culturally Inuit manner, without Inuit in the higher levels of the bureaucracy, it will be difficult, if not impossible, to establish policies that closely conform to Inuit norms and values.

Self-Government—North Slope Borough, Alaska

American law provides for a dizzying array of local governance arrangements for Alaska Native communities, and it is not uncommon to find multiple forms of local government operating in a single place. These include municipal governments chartered under the state of Alaska, traditional tribal governments recognized by the Bureau of Indian Affairs, and IRA tribal governments chartered under the federal Indian Reorganization Act extended to Alaska in 1936. To a certain extent these reflect distinct approaches to governance and different political factions within communities, but they also reflect the efforts of economically disadvantaged peoples to maximize opportunities and have access to as many federal and state funding programs as possible. For example, to be eligible for benefits under federal Native programs an individual must be a member of a federally recognized tribal entity. For many Alaska Natives the recognized entity is a Native corporation established by ANCSA. It is quite possible, given the way ANCSA was set up, that an individual born after 1971 is not a shareholder in a Native corporation. In those cases an IRA tribal government functions as the recognized tribal entity of record.

In 1972 the Inupiat in the region of Alaska lying north of the Brooks Range established the North Slope Borough (NSB), a regional municipal form of government chartered under the state of Alaska. The NSB comprises eight towns and villages in an area of 89,000 square miles. The boundaries of the NSB are contiguous with the land claims region the Arctic Slope Regional Corporation created under ANCSA. The population is approximately 7,300 with more than half living in Barrow. Almost three-quarters of NSB residents are Inupiat.

A primary architect of the NSB and its first mayor was Eben Hopson (1922–80). Hopson, along with Tlingit attorney Fred Paul, pushed for the establishment of the North Slope Borough as a route to Inupiaq self-government that would complement the economic potential of ANCSA. By incorporating, the NSB became able to levy property taxes on the oil installations at Prudhoe Bay. It uses those revenues to support a full array of municipal services including education (see Chapter 2), public housing, and public safety. Not surprisingly, the establishment of the North Slope Borough was opposed by the oil companies whose properties would be subject to property taxes, and they filed suit to prevent the borough's establishment. The court, however, ruled in favor of incorporation of the North Slope Borough.

Borough activities, particularly in the areas of housing and municipal services, greatly improved the standard of living for North Slope residents. The borough also operates a department of wildlife management. Although wildlife management might be considered out of the normal scope of activities for a municipality, it fits within the North Slope Inupiat's understanding of their cultural needs and values. The NSB Department of Wildlife Management has an active research program covering all areas of natural resource management including whaling, climate change, and other topics of concern to subsistence harvesters (see Chapter 3).

Inuit communities today are working to fully participate in the legal and political institutions of modern, democratic nation-states while at the same time maintaining (and creating new) institutions rooted in their unique cultural values. This is a difficult process. Land claims and other agreements cannot turn back the clock to a world in which Inuit communities were politically autonomous, but they have permitted Inuit to stop unwanted development. Importantly, in recent years, Inuit have begun to promote development on their terms. To succeed, however, they will need to develop institutions that are fiscally stable, flexible, and are able to deal with the attention that the Arctic is getting from mineral exploration and associated transportation and other development activities.

NOTES

1. Burch, Ernest S., Jr. (2006) *Social Life in Northwest Alaska: The Structure of Iñupiaq Eskimo Nations,* Fairbanks: University of Alaska Press, 105.

2. Ibid.

3. Akisu quoted in Oosten, J.G., Frederic Laugrand, and Nunavut Arctic College (1999) *Interviewing Inuit Elders: Vol. 2, Perspectives on Traditional Law,* Iqaluit, Nunavut: Language and Culture Program of Nunavut Arctic College, 46.

4. Imaruittuq quoted in Oosten et al., *Interviewing Inuit Elders: Vol. 2,* 40.

5. Kleivan, Inge (1971) "Song Duels in West Greenland—Joking Relationships and Avoidance," *Folk* 13: 13.

6. Fair, Susan W. (2001) "The Inupiaq Eskimo Messenger Feast: Celebration, Demise, and Possibility," *Journal of American Folklore* 113(450): 471.

7. Kleivan, "Song Duels in West Greenland," 17.

8. Dahl, Jens (1986) "Greenland: Political Structure of Self-Government," *Arctic Anthropology* 23(1–2): 317.

9. Act of May 17, 1884, ch. 53, 23 Stat. 24, sec 8.

10. Colt, Stephen G., and Michael Pretes (2005) "Alaska Native Claims Settlement Act (ANCSA)," in *Encyclopedia of the Arctic,* Vol. 1, Mark Nuttall, ed., New York: Routledge, 36.

11. Wilson, Gary N. (2008) "Nested Federalism in Northern Quebec: A Comparative Perspective," *Canadian Journal of Political Science* 41(10): 80.

12. Steele, Jackie, and Manon Tremblay (2005) "Paradise Lost? The Gender Parity Plebiscite in Nunavut," *Canadian Parliamentary Review,* Spring: 35.

13. Examples of the ritualized language used by Nunavut MLAs can be found in *Hansard,* the transcript of parliamentary debate. These are archived at http://www.assembly.nu.ca/english/debates/index.html.

14. Timpson, Annis May (2006) "Stretching the Concept of Representative Bureaucracy: The Case of Nunavut," *International Review of Administrative Sciences* 72(4): 523.

7

RELIGIOUS LIFE

The film *The Journals of Knud Rasmussen*[1] presents the story of a clash between two religious traditions—the Inuit religion and Christianity. At the end of the film, as in history, the adherents to Christianity prevail and the Inuit traditional religion fades. Though the Inuit filmmakers offer an explanation of why their ancestors chose Christianity over their earlier beliefs, as discussed below, theirs is only one of the many theories that have been proposed. In all likelihood there is no single explanation. Further, while it is the case that most contemporary Inuit are at least nominally Christian, it is a mistake to think that Inuit, even devoutly Christian ones, have abandoned all traditional Inuit religious beliefs.

The traditional Inuit cosmology conceived of a natural world that included multiple *tuurngait* or spirits (sing. *tuurngaq*). Prior to conversion to Christianity, many Inuit interactions with the spirit world were mediated by shamans called *angakkuit* (sing. *angakkuq*) who developed relationships with particular tuurngait. The tuurngait became the shamans' helpers. The natural world was densely populated by tuurngait and other, sometimes frightening, beings. Tuurngait included the souls of the deceased, mythical figures, heavenly bodies, land forms, and animals. They, and other mythical beings, could shape-shift, taking many different forms unrelated to the form they were associated with. These included dwarves and giants and composites of animals and humans. They could make themselves invisible to ordinary folk. They could also change their forms.

BECOMING A SHAMAN

Shamans were both male and female, and while there were some angakkuit who were considered more powerful than others, it is likely that most adults had some helping spirits and engaged in some forms of shamanic activity. Anthropologist Edith Turner speculates that most women performed as shamans in the ordinary course of attending to the health needs of their households.[2] The most powerful shamans, who were able to call on a large number of helping spirits, usually underwent a period of training from an experienced shaman. This usually began in adolescence.

The first objective [of shamanic training] was initiation into the language of the spirits and into the conduct of rituals—both private and public. Then came the acquisition of clairvoyance, *qaumaniq*, which showed itself in a clear, brilliant aura visible to animals, spirits, and shamans. To acquire a strong *qaumaniq*, long periods of isolation and abstinence were needed. Some candidates never managed to acquire it.[3]

SHAMANIC HEALING

A primary task of an angakkuq was to heal the ill. This was done through a number of divining techniques, in which the angakkuq consulted with spirits to determine the cause of a patient's illness. For the most part, illnesses, misfortunes, and even a failure to capture game were attributed to a violation of one or several taboos. A cure could be brought about only if the patient or other guilty person publically confessed his or her violations. Part of the shaman's role was to force a confession of broken taboos.

While there were some general and widespread taboos, such as avoiding intercourse during menstrual bleeding or not sewing caribou skin clothing while living in winter snowhouses on the ocean ice, shamans frequently decreed taboos on individuals or families. From an outsider's perspective, many of the taboos appear to be unreasonable, arbitrary, and capriciously imposed. For example, a woman whose curing ceremony was witnessed by members of the Fifth Thule Expedition 1921–24 was discovered to have been made ill by violating numerous taboos over a period of several years. Her violations included combing her hair soon after giving birth, smoking tobacco mixed with local plant leaves, eating a piece of frozen caribou and a bit of bone marrow when they had been forbidden, touching a harpoon head while she was menstruating, sewing at the wrong time of year, scraping a seal skin while it was taboo for her, eating fresh caribou while it was taboo, preparing caribou skins while sharing a house with a menstruating woman, wearing the wrong clothing to gather moss, and most serious of all, hiding a miscarriage. Her husband had handled a walrus skull while he had been ill, and this too was said to contribute to the wife's illness.

Rejecting the Taboos

The frequent and unpredictable nature of the imposition of taboos may be one explanation for Inuit acceptance of Christianity. According to Igloolik elder, Noah Piugaatuk, Inuit turned to Christianity because the expectations and commandments were constant. "They found that it was much easier for them to observe [this] one day. So on that account they fully respected Sunday."[4] Similarly, Nunavut elders discussing health matters with students at Nunavut Arctic College described some of the taboos imposed by angakkuit as not only bothersome, but potentially harmful.

In the past a pregnant woman was not allowed to eat raw meat [even though it would be healthy]. She was only allowed to eat boiled meat, but it didn't have to be well done. She was not allowed to eat animals from the land and animals from the sea on the same day. It had to be decided at the beginning of the day whether it was going to be a land animal or a sea animal that was going to be eaten. . . . they had to abide by the rules. My mother did not practice that, but my grandmother had to. . . . When ministers arrived, this practice was stopped. Thanks to that, we can now eat anything.[5]

Shamanic Flight

All shamans were said to be capable of healing through divination. The most powerful shamans, however, were also able to engage in soul flight, in which they (or possibly their spirit helpers) traveled to distant places to look for game, to check on the well-being of relatives in other camps, to intercede with Nuliajuk (see Chapter 1) to ask her to release the sea mammals, or to visit the heavens to seek other favors for the living. A shaman would engage in soul flight at the request of an individual or a group of people.

In the Iglulik area, a skin curtain, a *taluaq*, would hide the angakkuq from view during the performance. The procedure was to tie the shaman down so that he could no longer make any movement. His two big toes were attached to each other, as were his two thumbs. His hands and arms were firmly tied behind his back. A loop thong stuck out between the top of his back and the nape of his neck. With the loop, the helping spirit would be able to pull him up and away from the *iglu*. . . . As the *angakkuit* floated away into the air, his voice would trail off gradually. Some witnesses said that only his *tarniq* [soul] flew away. Others said that his body travelled as well.

The spectators remained in the *iglu* after the shaman had flown away. They would then see a thong fall down the chimney, the same thong that had previously been firmly wrapped around his body. It now had the very recognizable shape of the helping spirit.[6]

Not all angakkuit used their powers for good. Contemporary Inuit speak of two different kinds of shamans. Good shamans used their abilities to heal illnesses, find lost objects, and locate game. Some shamans, however, were considered to be "evil" or to have malicious helping spirits (*tupilait*). Those angakkuit used their shamanic powers and people's fear of them to demand sexual favors, to threaten, and even to kill others. Some scholars have suggested that Inuit turned to Christianity in order to counter the power of evil shamans. Inuit discussing these matters today often say that shamans who used their power to harm tended to suffer misfortunes themselves, and that these misfortunes can continue into subsequent generations and the present time.

ARRIVAL OF CHRISTIAN MISSIONARIES

Christian missionaries were some of the earliest non-Natives to live among Inuit and in many cases served as colonial administrators in addition to their missionary activities. In this respect, the early missionaries had considerable power over the day-to-day lives of Inuit. In some places missionaries withheld medical care from those who also sought help from shamans. Many also forbade Inuit to hunt or do other work on Sundays, to perform traditional drum songs and dances, or to engage in song duels.

The first Danish colony in Greenland was established by Hans Egede, a Lutheran missionary who had hoped to minister to the long-separated Norse colonies. Egede arrived in West Greenland, at a place near present-day Nuuk, in 1721, but after finding no remaining Norse, he turned his attention to converting the Inuit. Within a few years the Danish crown established an administrative structure for the new colony. Unlike other European New World colonies, Greenland was not open for European settlement. Rather it was managed as a trading colony in which the Lutheran Church remained integral, particularly in the area of education. In addition to the Lutherans, German-speaking Moravians also established several missions in West Greenland, and it was a Moravian missionary, Samuel Kleinschmidt, who developed the first functional orthography for Kalaallisut (see Chapter 2).

In Inupiat regions of Alaska, Christian missionaries became active only in the last decades of the 19th century. In 1885, the U.S. Department of the Interior appointed a Presbyterian missionary, Dr. Sheldon Jackson, to be the General Agent of Education in Alaska. Jackson divvied up the Alaska territory and its peoples among several Protestant denominations. Episcopalians were assigned to Point Hope, Presbyterians to Wainwright, Barrow, and Kaktovik. The Evangelical Friends Church (also known as California Quakers) was allowed to set up missions in several communities in what is now the Northwest Arctic Borough. Jackson's decision to establish different churches in different regions eliminated the sectarian rivalry that existed between Catholic and Anglican (Episcopal) missionaries in the Canadian Arctic. There, the two churches maintained a somewhat hostile competition for the souls of Inuit parishioners. Today, the rivalry between churches is much less overt. Most Inuit communities in Alaska and in the Canadian Arctic have several Christian churches including the Pentecostal Assembly of God Church. And as in many non-Native communities in North America, the existence of different churches reflects social as much as, or more than, spiritual divisions within the community. Many northern congregations are now led by ordained and lay Inuit ministers.

Missionaries versus Shamans

Early Christian missionaries worked extremely hard to combat Inuit religious practices, especially shamanism, which they regarded as satanic. As discussed in Chapter 11, the missionaries' efforts to convert Inuit to Christianity were aided by the demographic, economic, and spiritual crises Inuit suffered as a result of introduced epidemic diseases. A number of missionaries openly and directly challenged shamans, calling them frauds and charlatans, and won converts, in part, because the healing techniques employed by shamans proved ineffective against the new diseases. Seeing shamans fail in their efforts to cure illnesses encouraged some Inuit, including shamans, to follow the missionaries. In fact, in several parts of the Inuit North, shamans were among the first converts, perhaps viewing the new religion as a way to maintain their authority over spiritual matters.

In nearly every region of the Inuit North, early Inuit converts to Christianity were important in proselytizing to other Inuit. There are many examples where Inuit succeeded in making converts before the arrival of missionaries. In Nunavut and Nunavik, much of the work of conversion was carried out by Inuit associated with the Anglican missionary, the Reverend Edmund James Peck. Peck was instrumental in introducing the syllabic writing system for Inuktitut (see Chapter 2) as a way to spread Christian teachings. His followers carried Bibles and other religious materials written in syllabics on their ordinary travels to other Inuit camps in the eastern Canadian Arctic.

In Greenland, as well, Inuit were active in spreading Christianity to the distant regions of the island. West Greenlander Hans Hendrik (1834–89) is thought to have preached Christianity to the Inughuit

Fusion of Inuit and Danish religious motifs and symbols inside a Greenlandic church. (Photo by Peter V. Hall)

of northwest Greenland when he lived among them in the 1850s. Poet and painter Henrik Lund (1875–1948), also a West Greenlander, spent the first decade of the 20th century as a missionary to Inuit in East Greenland.

In Alaska a number of Inupiat and Yupik also worked to spread Christianity. One Inupiaq woman, Ruth Koaliruq Egaq (c. 1876–45), is said to have converted to Christianity after being accused of causing the death of her shaman father when she violated a taboo. Her family abandoned her, and without protectors, she was a target of repeated sexual assault. She ultimately married and after a stormy period, she and her husband became members of the Evangelical Friends Church. Ruth became a missionary-teacher and with her daughter, Lily Savok, is remembered for having created a picture writing system for Inupiaq.

One of the most fascinating individuals in the history of Inuit religious change was Maniilaq (c. 1800–c. 1890), an Inupiaq from the upper Kobuk River area of northwest Alaska. Maniilaq was not a Christian; he lived most of his life prior to the arrival of Christian missionaries in northwest Alaska, but traveled widely and likely became aware of non-Native religious practices during his travels. Maniilaq is remembered in oral histories as a spiritual leader who ignored taboos imposed by shamans and had prophetic visions of the future. He is credited with having predicted many things that came to pass including the arrival of non-Natives and Christianity, the invention of airplanes, and the adoption of new time-saving technologies. Interest in Maniilaq and his teachings was revived in the 1970s, and incorporated into the spirit movement known as *Inupiaq Ilitquisiat* (see Chapter 2). Inupiaq Ilitquisiat blends Christianity with traditional Inupiat values of community support, respect for elders, and continuation of subsistence hunting. According to leaders in the spirit movement, "Our land is the physical symbol of the Inupiat Spirit. . . . By staying close to the land, we will stay close to God."[7]

SHAMANISM TODAY?

Contemporary Inuit no longer practice shamanism or perform shamanic rituals, but many Inuit continue to feel the presence of tuurngait or the power of past shamans in their lives. Further, many Inuit are certain that the angakkuit of the past had real power to fly through the air and under the sea, to read people's thoughts, to heal, or to cause harm. For example, Nunavut elder, Mariano Aupilaarjuk, described an event to students at Nunavut Arctic College in which he had left an offering near the grave of a long-dead shaman.

> Not long ago, I was travelling alone and I was near [the shaman's] grave. I knew he had been a heavy smoker. I gave him a cigarette and asked him to turn the bad weather into good weather. His grave was way up high, and I gave him an offering from way down below. Later on, I looked up into the sky and it seemed like it had split in the centre and the weather was becoming nice again. I was very happy. I knew it was because of the *angakkuq*.[8]

Several of the Nunavut Arctic College students who participated in the course that produced the book *Interviewing Inuit Elders: Cosmology and Shamanism* reported that they experienced fear and anxiety in the course of learning about Inuit shamanism, tuurngait, and other elements of Inuit cosmology. Several had nightmares or other unusual experiences that they related to the existence of tuurngait and other spiritual beings known to Inuit in the past. Despite being frightened, several of the students came to idealize shamanism and one student expressed the "hope that *angakkuit* will come back. There are many problems [such as suicide, alcohol abuse, and spousal assault] facing Inuit society that as of yet have no solutions. Maybe, maybe with a shaman . . ."[9]

While the young students at Nunavut Arctic College, who have never known a world in which angakkuit were powerful, might regard a return of shamanism as a form of Inuit self-determination and an Inuit-made solution for the ills of contemporary society, many of their elders are quite opposed. In part, this is a generational shift, with young Inuit interested in recovering knowledge about past Inuit beliefs and practices and older Inuit opposed to activities they regard as dangerous and potentially sinful.

It is important to note that most Christian missionaries did not require Inuit converts to disavow the existence of tuurngait and other spiritual entities or the abilities of angakkuit to interact with them. Rather, the missionaries, like Inuit, assumed that these spirits were real. They required simply that converts cease incorporating belief in the existence of tuurngait or the power of angakkuit into their spiritual practices. Many contemporary Inuit object to talk about shamanism and see it as anti-Christian (and the elders who participated in the course on cosmology and shamanism at Nunavut Arctic College repeatedly avowed their adherence to Christianity and to Christian practice). Others express the concern that shamanistic knowledge and skills will be abused similar to the way that drugs and alcohol are abused. In Alaska, several Inupiaq communities have revived some of the traditional festivals that were once associated with shamanism, but have blended the older rituals into the practice of Christianity.

The Inuit who produced *The Journals of Knud Rasmussen* relate the loss of shamanic power to the more general loss of Inuit autonomy that occurred under colonialism. With the arrival of Europeans as evidenced by members of Rasmussen's Fifth Thule Expedition 1921–24, multiple disasters befall the shaman, Aua, and his family. Most serious of all is the failure to find game, while other Inuit who have become Christians have no shortage of food. The Christians, however, will not share their food with heathens. Thus, at the end of the fictionalized *Journals,* the real shaman, Aua, with no choice but to accept Christianity or allow his family to starve, forcefully and tearfully sends his helping spirits away.

RITUALS

Prior to conversion to Christianity Inuit did not make distinctions between sacred and secular activities. Because the natural world was replete with helpful and dangerous spirits all thoughts and actions contained cosmological significance. Special events, however, also called for special rituals. One such special event was the Inupiaq Messenger Feast (*Kivgiaq*), which was part trade fair, part feast, part athletic contest, and part religious pageant. The demands on the hosts were such that Messenger Feasts occurred only once every several years. The festival, however, is named for the messengers who were sent to a neighboring village to issue invitations for the guests to bring gifts to the hosts. A highlight of the Kivgiaq was a performance of the masked Eagle-Wolf Dance in which performers ritually enacted the Inupiaq creation story. The last traditional Messenger Feast on Alaska's North Slope occurred in 1914. In 1988 Inupiat from the North Slope Borough revived the Messenger Feast as a way to affirm pride in being Inupiat.[10]

In the Igloolik region of Nunavut Inuit marked the annual return of the sun in late January with a ritual extinguishment and relighting of lamps. In the ideal all the lamps in the encampment were relit from a single source.

During the time when taboos were strictly adhered to [prior to conversion to Christianity], the first day that the Sun came out was marked by the belief that the whole community must start a new life, so the children of the camp would go to each household to blow out the flames of the *qulliq* [lamp]. After the lamps had been extinguished the old wicks were removed and a new wick set in place and then the lamp would be relit. In order to begin life anew, the children of the camp including myself, would run to each of the dwellings hoping that we would be the first to blow out the lamps before the others did. So this was how the first day of the Sun was observed.[11]

The ritual celebration of the return of the sun also had a sexual element that involved both masked cross-dressing and an exchange of sexual partners.[12] The latter may have occurred under the direction of shamans and was targeted by Christian missionaries for elimination. Inuit in some communities, however, retained elements of the cross-dressing, and incorporated it into Christmas festivities.[13]

In contrast to the family-based observance of Christmas in most Canadian, American, and European communities, among Inuit Christmas is largely a community celebration. Gift-giving is also largely symbolic. In the Canadian North, the week between Christmas and New Year's is filled with games and dances that begin late in the evening and extend to dawn the next day. As schools and most workplaces are closed for the week, it is common for people to get "turned around" so that they sleep during the day and then rise in the evening to once again join the celebration.

In Barrow, Alaska, Christmas is also a time for community activities. The celebration begins with a Christmas Eve church service and Christmas pageant. Christmas Day includes a feast hosted by church deacons, but with food provided by the whaling captains and prepared by their crews. After the feast people gather in the community center for drumming and dancing, and while some dances are performed by "experts" such as the Barrow Dancers, others are joined by any and all. Dancing is followed by competitive games. As in the Canadian Arctic, the "games continue every night until the early hours of the morning. People drift in and out during the course of the evening, but there is a certain amount of feeling that it is not 'right' not to come every day."[14] There is another church service on New Year's Eve and the festival concludes on New Year's Day with a 24-hour marathon of dancing and game playing.

Contemporary Inupiat also observe a number of rituals associated with whaling. The best known of these is the Nalukataq Festival, which occurs at the end of the whaling season. Each successful crew hosts a feast that also includes games, dancing, and gift-giving. The contemporary name of the festival, Nalukataq, is actually the name of the blanket toss, which is an iconic element of the celebra-

Nalukataq celebration at Barrow, Alaska, June 1987. (Richard G. Condon photo collection)

tion. While Nalukataq and other whaling rituals were once integral to Inupiaq religious observance, whaling rituals today usually begin with Christian prayers and blessings of thanksgiving. Just as Christmas and other Christian festivals have been indigenized, a number of Inuit traditions have incorporated Christian themes and rituals. It is not surprising that as Christianity spread across the North American Arctic, it blended with and incorporated traditional Inuit rituals. In each place that Christianity has spread around the world, it has incorporated local elements. Among Europeans and their descendents in North America the celebration of Christmas includes elements that were once regarded as pagan. The Christmas tree and mistletoe, for example, were incorporated as Christianity spread across northern Europe in the first centuries of the Common Era.

NOTES

1. Igloolik Isuma Productions (2006) *The Journals of Knud Rasmussen*, Igloolik, Nunavut: Igloolik Isuma Productions.
2. Turner, Edith (1989) "From Shamans to Healers: The Survival of an Inupiaq Eskimo Skill," *Anthropologica* 31: 3–24.

3. Aupilaarjuk, Mariano, Tulimaaq Aupilaarjuk, Lucassie Nutaraa-kuk, Rose Iqallijuq, Johanasi Ujarak, Isidore Ijituuq, and Michel Kupaaq (2001) *Interviewing Inuit Elders: Cosmology and Shamanism*, Bernard Saladin d'Anglure, ed., Iqaluit: Nunavut Arctic College, 33.

4. Quoted in MacDonald, John (1998) *The Arctic Sky: Inuit Astronomy, Star Lore, and Legend*, Toronto: Royal Ontario Museum, 204.

5. Elisapee Ootoova quoted in Joamie, Alacie, Akisu Joamie, Jayko Pit-seolak, Malaya Papatsie, Elisapee Ootoova, and Tirisi Attagutsiak (2001) *Interviewing Inuit Elders: Perspectives on Traditional Health*, Frederic Laugrand and Michelle Therrien, eds., Iqaluit: Nunavut Arctic College, 20.

6. Aupilaarjuk et al., *Interviewing Inuit Elders: Cosmology and Shamanism*, 149.

7. Quoted in Beach, Hugh (1984) "Developing Spirit in Northwest Alaska," *Ethnos* 3-4: 292.

8. Aupilaarjuk quoted in Aupilaarjuk et al., *Interviewing Inuit Elders*, 14–15.

9. Aupilaarjuk et al., *Interviewing Inuit Elders: Cosmology and Shamanism*, 228.

10. Riccio, Thomas (1993) "A Message from Eagle Mother: The Messenger's Feast of the Inupiat Eskimo," *The Drama Review* 37(1): 115–46.

11. Noah Piugaattuk quoted in MacDonald, *The Arctic Sky*, 109.

12. Laugrand, Frédéric, and Jarich Oosten (2002) "*Quviasukivik:* The Celebration of an Inuit Winter Feast in the Central Arctic," *Journal de la société des américanistes* 88, retrieved July 3, 2009 from http://jsa.revues.org/index2772.html.

13. Nelleman, George (1960) "Mitârtut: A West Greenland Winter Ceremony," *Folk* 2: 99–113.

14. Bodenhorn, Barbara (1993) "Christmas Present: Christmas Public," in *Unwrapping Christmas*, Daniel Miller, ed., Oxford: Clarendon Press, 208.

8

SPORTS AND RECREATION

Games are important to social life in all cultures in the world, providing a venue where children and young adults can learn, practice, and display culturally valued skills and attitudes. For Inuit in the past, games were often built from the physical skills that were critical to life on the land and from the social skills that were critical to life in small, close knit communities. Important physical skills included balance, agility, hand-eye coordination, strength, pain tolerance, and endurance, while independence, creativity, modesty, patience, humor, and cooperation were highly valued social attributes.

Specific games varied from place to place. A fairly exhaustive list of games is compiled in a booklet produced by the Keewatin Inuit Association.[1] One widely played game is known as the "Two Foot High Kick," in which a player starts from a standing position and holding both feet together, attempts to kick a hanging target. After each round, the target is raised. In another game, referred to as the "Head Push," two players stand on their hands and knees with their foreheads pressed together. Using their head and neck strength each tries to push the other out of a circle drawn around the pair. A game that is now called "Airplane" involves a team of four players. The primary competitor lies rigid on his or her stomach with legs and feet together and arms stretched out perpendicular to the body. Three assistants lift the competitor at the ankles and wrists and carry him

or her across the room as far as possible until the body sags. The
winner is the one who is able to travel the farthest distance without
sagging. And in Greenland, and perhaps elsewhere, men competed
to show their speed and agility in kayaks. Games include rolling the
kayak, racing, and riding the crests of waves.

In many traditional Inuit games individual competitors faced off in
these and similar displays of strength and endurance, with the winner of each contest taking on a new challenger. Eventually, a strong
competitor would become exhausted and could be successfully challenged by a weaker player. While it would be clear to spectators who
were the strongest and most skilled athletes, the practice promoted
an egalitarian ethos among competitors.

Games and contests were an important component of gatherings
and festivals that took place throughout the year. The timing of these
events varied from region to region depending upon the subsistence
cycle. In the Igloolik region of Nunavut one annual gathering took
place in the late winter and early spring. Inuit there held *qaggiq* (dance
house) celebrations that included dancing, singing, and game playing with increasing frequency as the days lengthened in the springtime. In nice weather, games were also played out-of-doors.

They would hold games with teams made up of *Aggiarjuit* [old squaw
ducks—Clangula hyemal] for those who were born in tents, and of *Aqiggiit*
[ptarmigan—Lagopus mutus] for those who were born in igloos. The idea
was to outdo each other in any games that may require some competition
when the temperatures were comfortable enough for people to stay out-
doors. These games would include a tug-of-war using leather thongs. . . .
All this would be done with the *Aggiarjuit* on one side and the *Aqiggiit* on
the other side trying to outdo each other. In addition they would hold a
Qaggiq to entertain themselves. . . . A *Qaggiq* was usually held early in the
evening. The men would take turns to dance while the women sat on the
bed platform singing aya-ja songs that had been composed by the dancer.
When the dancer stopped he would put down the drum and another man
would take it up and start to dance, meanwhile the women sang to him.
It sounded wonderful as all the women participated in the song. This was
the most enjoyable time![2]

In other parts of the Inuit North, intercommunity festivities were
held in conjunction with subsistence or other events. For example,
Inupiat in northwest Alaska held a Messenger Feast (*Kivgiaq*) (see
Chapter 7), while those on Alaska's North Slope held several festivals related to whaling. The most elaborate of these was *Nalukataq* at
the conclusion of the whaling season. Although the festivals were

religious or spiritual at their heart, they were also opportunities for trading, for making marriage commitments, for dancing, and for playing games. In fact, the name, *Nalukataq*, refers to one of the games—the blanket toss—played at the festival. In this game, individuals take turns being tossed into the air and caught on a "blanket" made of walrus skin. The Nalukataq Festival remains a major annual event in the whaling communities of Alaska's North Slope Borough. In recent years it has become common for female jumpers to throw gifts to the assembled crowd who scramble to retrieve them; though in the past gifts were thrown by male jumpers. In 1997, gifts at Point Hope "included bedding, candy, shower curtains, towels, and fur for parka ruffs. The competition was fierce."[3] It is also common to restrict eligibility to receive the tossed gifts. In the case of the housewares given away at Point Hope, only older women were allowed to compete to catch the prizes.[4]

In the Canadian North, in the decades just prior to the establishment of permanent government-administered towns and villages, Christmas and Easter were times when Inuit were encouraged to gather at missions and fur trading posts. In addition to trading and praying, these gatherings were a time for dancing and playing competitive games, some of which were organized by the trader who provided prizes. The practice of holiday game playing and dancing continues today in many Inuit communities throughout the North. In Barrow, Alaska, for example, dancing together at Christmas is one way Inupiat there express their social connections to other members of the community. In some communities Christmas festivities last the entire week between Christmas and New Year's Day and are played through the night, ending at dawn and beginning again the next evening. Some are variations on traditional Inuit games, while others are new inventions. Airplane, described above, may be a relatively new game or it may simply have a relatively new name. Easter games differ from those at Christmas only in the fact that the warmer weather and sunlight lend themselves to outdoor events such as snowmobile and dogsled races, snowhouse building contests, and rifle shooting.

For the most part, today, traditional games of strength and endurance are played only during special events such as holiday celebrations or at one of the several organized Olympic-type competitions. The first World Eskimo Olympics was held in Fairbanks, Alaska, in 1961. It was organized by non-Native employees of Wein Airways, based on Christmas games one of them had seen played in Point Hope several years earlier. In 1970, the *Tundra Times*, the first statewide

Native newspaper in Alaska, took over sponsorship of the games, changing the name to the World Eskimo and Indian Olympics in 1973 to reflect the fact that Indians were also participants.

Like the World Eskimo and Indian Olympics, the Arctic Winter Games were created by non-Natives—the Commissioners of the Northwest Territories and the Yukon Territory in Canada and the Governor of Alaska—in response to the poor showing of northern athletes at the 1967 Canada Winter Games. The first Arctic Winter Games opened in Yellowknife, Northwest Territories, in 1970 with teams from the three founding regions. Teams from Greenland and Nunavik participated sporadically in the next several years, but more recently the games have included athletes from the northern regions of the Canadian provinces and from Siberia, Greenland, and the Scandinavian countries. In 2002 Nuuk, Greenland, co-hosted the Arctic Winter Games with Iqaluit, Nunavut.

While both Inuit and Dene traditional games are now part of the Arctic Winter Games, they are not the primary focus. Rather the games are dominated by nonindigenous events such as Alpine skiing, badminton, speed and figure skating, curling, and basketball. Inuvialuit and others protested the exclusion of indigenous contests from the first Arctic Winter Games and organized an alternative event, the Northern Games, featuring traditional Inuvialuit and Dene games, traditional skills demonstrations, and fiddling contests. The first Northern Games were held in Inuvik in July 1970 and were organized as a centennial project of the Northwest Territories. One hundred seventy-five people from 12 communities in the Northwest Territories, Yukon Territory, and Alaska participated.[5]

Both the Northern Games and the Arctic Winter Games have continued as separate events, but the Northern Games have not benefited from the same level of funding or institutional support as the Arctic Winter Games. In part this stems from the fact that Canadian government funders have regarded the Northern Games as a cultural rather than a sporting event, a designation that the organizers of the Northern Games dispute. "It seems that some outsiders view Northern Games only as a cultural organization. It is a cultural event of the best kind, but its focus is on games and sport. Sports in the south are also cultural events with a different purpose (i.e., a winning purpose in a win-oriented culture). Must we buy that ethic to be funded?"[6]

Contemporary sporting events, like song contests discussed below, provide an opportunity to be playful and inventive. For example, at the 1989 Eskimo-Indian Olympics in Fairbanks, a dance group from Anaktuvuk Pass performed a masked dance wearing caribou-skin masks created solely as tourist art (see Chapter 10).

SONG CONTESTS

A number of early observers of Inuit described song contests in which members of different communities hurled insults at each other through satirical songs. Song contests were found in many widely dispersed Inuit communities and varied somewhat from region to region. In West Greenland the song contests that occurred were, in many ways, comparable to contemporary sports rivalries. In a song contest an individual or group challenged members of a rival community as a way to air grievances. Contestants prepared and practiced for the song contests. Though the goal was to take one's opponent by surprise, this was not always possible. The contest began with a song from the challenger. The opponent could then respond and the two would alternate taking turns singing against one another. In the ideal, singers should remain calm and avoid reacting to the insulting lyrics or to the derision hurled by the spectators. "The victim had to listen patiently as long as his opponent cared to continue, without interrupting. He should pretend indifference, while his assailant hurled diverse direct and indirect insults at him."[7] The contest ended with the departure of the challengers, either victorious or vanquished. Both men and women participated in song contests, with men singing against other men and women singing against women. Under most circumstances Inuit regard it as improper either to brag about one's own abilities or to belittle the inadequacies of another person, yet jealousies are normal and, without an appropriate outlet, can erupt in violence or other disruptive behavior. For Inuit in the past, song contests provided an acceptable formal forum for deriding another person or boasting about one's own abilities. Song duels may have had a cathartic effect by permitting people to express otherwise unacceptable sentiments.

GAMES AND CHILD DEVELOPMENT

Games and play are critical to child development as they allow children to practice culturally appropriate emotional responses to situations that they will encounter in life. Inuit used verbal games with young children in order to help them recognize their connections to others, to overcome their emotional conflicts, to learn emotional restraint, and to "cause thought." One way Inuit did this was

to present them with emotionally powerful problems that the children could not ignore. Often this was done by asking a question that was potentially dangerous for the child being questioned and dramatizing the consequences of various answers: "Why don't you kill your baby brother?" "Why don't you die so I can have your nice new shirt?" "Your mother's going to die—look, she's cut her finger—do you want to come live with me?"[8]

These verbal "games" were done in a spirit of playfulness and enabled Inuit children to recognize and cope with their normal antisocial feelings and emotional anxieties. The games ceased once a child learned to respond in a culturally appropriate, restrained manner.

Not all verbal games presented such emotional minefields for children. One traditional game that Ulukhaktok elder Mabel Nigiyok taught to high school students as part of a cultural lesson provided a humorous reminder of the social connections that are built up

Ulukhaktok students learning to play *maq*, 2001. (Photo by author)

through sharing and doing things for others. The students were asked to sit on the floor, close together in a semicircle with their legs out straight as if lining the walls of a snowhouse. In the first round Mabel went along the line and lightly kicked each student on the sole of the shoe and told the students to respond "maq," which was, according to Mabel, also the name of the game. In the next round, she asked each student a question about who made or how they obtained an item of clothing. The third round consisted of the students holding out their hands while Mabel made silly comments about the color of their skin. In round four, the questioner (but in this case a student stand-in for Mabel) walked on the tops of the students' flexed feet as if on a balance beam. More questions, such as "Who made your hair?" or "Where did you get your nose?" followed. The desired responses were clever and absurd, and the game generated gales of laughter, but the content of questions also forced the students to reflect on the nature of their social relationships.[9]

SOLITARY PLAY

Inuit also encourage solitary play. Anthropologist Jean Briggs noted that Inuit children develop the ability to amuse themselves at young ages. She described the play of a five-year-old girl:

I never ceased to be amazed at her capacity for absorbing herself in scarcely perceptible pursuits for hours on end, sitting or lying quietly on the ikliq [living/sleeping platform] and demanding no attention from anyone. She might scrape a discarded bit of hide with her mother's scraping tool, wave a sock vaguely in the air, twist and untwist an empty plastic bag, or run cardboard dogs, which her mother had made for her, up and down the tent pole that edged the ikliq. One of her favorite activities was drawing.[10]

Traditional solitary games included string figures and cup-and-pin games, though string figures were sometimes associated with storytelling. There was a seasonality associated with some games. Inuit in many regions played string games (*ajaraaq*) in the late fall in order to catch the sun in the string and draw out the time before the sun disappeared for the winter. They also played cup-and-pin (*ajagaq*) in the late winter to symbolically pull the sun up above the horizon.

I have heard that when the sun was just returning they used to play a lot of *ajagaq*. When this game is played one has to throw a bone up and try to poke the stick through one of the holes in the bone. So the idea was that by throwing the ajagaq bone up in the air they would appear to be trying to get the sun higher in the same manner that the bone was going higher. They did this when the sun had just started to come out, and at the same time string games, *ajaraaq*, were discouraged; otherwise the sun might get tangled up in the strings and keep falling down, making its progress much slower.[11]

CONTEMPORARY SPORTING EVENTS

Today, playing and watching sports are a significant form of recreation in many Inuit communities, occupying youth especially. In fact, teens in Ulukhaktok told anthropologist Richard Condon that involvement with sports, even more than chronological age, was a way to distinguish teenagers from adults.[12] There is some national variation in the sports that are popular in contemporary Inuit communities. Canadian Inuit, like other Canadians, play ice hockey, while basketball, an American game, is the rage in many Inupiaq communities. One Canadian Inuk, Jordin Tootoo, from Rankin Inlet, Nunavut, plays professional hockey with the National Hockey League team the Nashville Predators.

Basketball, both high school and intercity league, dominates public life in Noorvik, in Alaska's Northwest Arctic Borough, from October through April.[13] It is played with passion by all segments of the population of this Inupiaq village of approximately 600 people, and often draws an enthusiastic crowd of spectators to the small gymnasium. Despite the competitiveness of play, basketball games are a place where the *Inupiat Ilitquisiat* (see Chapter 2) values of cooperation and humility are on display.

Star players know they are admired, yet when they speak at rallies, they tend to stress the helpfulness of the coaches or otherwise deflect attention from themselves. . . . Shouting, and a lot of it, occurs at the emotionally charged basketball games in Noorvik. Spectators yell out encouragements to their teams and may hoot loudly to distract a player of the opposite team when he/she shoots for a basket. However, booing is unusual.[14]

Although ice hockey was played occasionally in Ulukhaktok in the Inuvialuit Settlement Region in the 1960s and 1970s, it was only after the arrival of television in 1980 that the game that is so central to Canadian national identity became popular in the community. Richard Condon attributed increases in overt forms of competition in all kinds of sports play to television.[15] In contrast to the cooperative and humble character that Sprott observed among basketball players and spectators in Noorvik, Ulukhaktokmiut bring a particularly aggressive style of play to hockey competitions, but this, too, is Inuit in character. Many young Inuit in Ulukhaktok see their game as emulating the style (including the fighting) of the National Hockey League; however, there are distinct differences. Ice hockey and other organized team sports are played in an individualistic manner, and fights during hockey games often consist of "hitting people from behind and skating away (what [Ulukhaktok] players call 'bothering') instead of dropping the gloves and fighting it out on the ice."[16] The individualism of hockey play in Ulukhaktok mirrors the value that Inuit in the Central Canadian Arctic place on self-sufficiency and independence. But, like the song contests of the past, hockey provides a venue where an individual can legitimately act on hostile feelings toward another person. Although the ideal is not always achieved, the hostility displayed on the ice is not supposed to extend to other venues and arenas of activity.

Other forms of contemporary recreation include snowmobile and dog teams racing. Spring ice fishing provides an opportunity for families to spend time together on the land. And for some contemporary Inuit hunting has become an important leisure as well as a subsistence activity. There is a small Alpine skiing hill outside Nuuk, Greenland. Greenlanders also engage in cross-country running, Nordic

Youth skateboarding in Nuuk, Greenland, August 2008. (Photo by Peter V. Hall)

(cross-country) skiing, soccer, and kayaking as well as hunting and fishing. Greenlanders participate in Danish and other Nordic sports federations, and Greenland is a member of the Arctic Winter Games International Committee.

NOTES

1. Butler, Gwynneth, and Joe Karetak (1980) *Inuit Games,* Rankin Inlet: Keewatin Inuit Association.

2. Noah Piugaattuk quoted in MacDonald, John (1998) *The Arctic Sky: Inuit Astronomy, Star Lore, and Legend,* Toronto: Royal Ontario Museum, 120.

3. Larson, Mary A. (2003) "Festival and Tradition: The Whaling Festival at Point Hope," in *Indigenous Ways to the Present: Native Whaling in the Western Arctic,* Allen P. McCartney, ed., Edmonton: Canadian Circumpolar Institute Press, 348.

4. Ibid.

5. Paraschak, Vicky (2003) "Sport Festivals and Race Relations in the Northwest Territories of Canada," in *Sport, Racism and Ethnicity,* Grant Jarvie, ed., London: RoutledgeFalmer, 80.

6. Quoted in Paraschak, "Sport Festivals and Race Relations in Northwest Territories of Canada," 82.

7. Kleivan, Inge (1971) "Song Duels in West Greenland—Joking Relationship and Avoidance," *Folk* 13: 17.

8. Briggs, Jean L. (1998) *Inuit Morality Play: The Emotional Education of a Three-Year-Old,* New Haven, CT: Yale University Press, 5.

9. Stern, Pamela (2005) "Wage Labor, Housing Policy and the Nucleation of Inuit Households in Holman, NWT Canada," *Arctic Anthropology* 42(2): 70.

10. Briggs, Jean L. (1970) *Never in Anger: Portrait of an Eskimo Family,* Cambridge, MA: Harvard University Press, 119.

11. François Quassa quoted in MacDonald, *The Arctic Sky,* 117.

12. Condon, Richard G. (1987) *Inuit Youth: Growth and Change in the Canadian Arctic,* New Brunswick, NJ: Rutgers University Press, 65.

13. Sprott, Julie (1997) "Christmas, Basketball, and Sled Dog Races: Common and Uncommon Themes in the New Seasonal Round in an Iñupiaq Village," *Arctic Anthropology* 34(1): 68–85.

14. Ibid., 52.

15. Condon, *Inuit Youth.*

16. Collings, Peter, and Richard G. Condon (1996) "Blood on the Ice: Status, Self-Esteem, and Ritual Injury among Inuit Hockey Players," *Human Organization* 55(3): 257.

9

EXPRESSIVE AND POPULAR CULTURE

Prior to contact with Europeans, Inuit literature in the form of stories, verse, and song was transmitted orally. Stories and songs entertained and educated children in tents and snowhouses, but were also performed for larger gatherings in *qaggit* (sing. *qaggiq,* large ceremonial snowhouses of the Central Arctic) and *qargit* (sing. *qargi,* "men's houses," in Inupiaq North Alaska). Performances often included drum dancing; singing; throat singing; contests of strength, endurance, and physical skill; and shamanic performances in addition to storytelling. Christian missionaries and other colonial administrators disrupted this traditional form of expressive culture. For example, there are documented cases where missionaries and/ or police ordered Inuit in Alaska and Canada to cease drum dancing.[1] Introduced diseases such as influenza and measles, which devastated communities, also disrupted traditional social organization. Qargit in Alaska fell into disuse in the 1890s, and with the move to permanent, government-organized settlements in the 1950s and 1960s, Canadian Inuit stopped building qaggiq except for very special public events such as the establishment of Nunavut Territory in April 1999. Nonetheless, despite disruption, Inuit never abandoned their unique forms of expressive culture and these traditional elements have been adapted to and for new venues. As discussed in the previous chapter, Inuit continue to engage in traditional contests of strength and skill at festivals and at international events such as the Arctic Winter Games, but the physical contest as a representation of masculine competition is also present in a stylized form in the very contemporary Greenlandic short film, *Eskimo Weekend* (2002). Many stories and songs that were not recorded by early ethnographers or by the handful of Inuit historians have been lost. Yet, the Canadian Inuk poet, writer, and graphic artist Alootook Ipellie (1951–2007) noted that he "found inspiration from reading words of wisdom such as those spoken" to and recorded by the ethnographer Knud Rasmussen during the Fifth Thule Expedition 1921–24 across the North American Arctic.[2]

INUIT LITERATURE

Inuit stories of the past fell into two broad categories: *unipkaat,* historical tales in which the protagonists were identifiable persons, and *quliaqtuat,* stories that have more of a mythical character (see Chapter 2). Both contain elements that may appear surreal to the non-Inuit listener. Although traditional Inuit literature was oral, Inuit readily adopted writing and printing, and more recently, video technologies to record their stories and for many other purposes.

Memoirs and Oral Histories

As discussed in Chapter 2, Christian missionaries developed the first orthographies or writing systems used by Inuit, and with the introduction of orthographies for writing Inuktitut, Inuit in Canada, Greenland, and Alaska adopted and adapted Western forms of writing to communicate among themselves and to document their lives. While some of these like the first Greenlandic newspaper, *Atuagagdliutit* (Readings), were initiated by non-Inuit, many were not. One of the best-known Inuit chroniclers was Peter Pitseolak (1902–73) who, prior to the establishment of consistent government administration, kept records of births and deaths and chronicled events in the lives of the Inuit near present-day Cape Dorset, documenting a way of life that was changing rapidly. As Pitseolak biographer, Dorothy Harley Eber, put it, "it was always his intention to leave a record."[3] Eber spearheaded the effort to translate and publish a portion of Peter Pitseolak's writings as two volumes: *Peter Pitseolak's Escape from Death* and *People from Our Side.* Peter Pitseolak was also an avid amateur photographer, and with his second wife, Aggeok (1906–77), worked out a method to develop his film in a tent-lined snowhouse and to print his pictures in a cabin built of salvaged lumber. The photographs offer an intimate and sensitive portrait of Inuit camp life in the 1940s and 1950s just prior to the establishment of government-administered towns in the Canadian Arctic. Peter Pitseolak also shot 8-millimeter black-and-white movies and recorded stories on audiotape. After his death, more than 1,500 negatives and photographs were purchased and preserved by the government of Canada.

Taamusi Qumaq (1914–93) of Puvirnutuq, Nunavik (northern Quebec) was another chronicler of Inuit culture and history, creating both an Inuktitut dictionary and a museum. The latter he called *Saputik,* meaning "Weir." It was to trap the items that might otherwise be lost to the "river of time." Both Peter Pitseolak and Taamusi Qumaq were ordinary individuals who found new ways to tell Inuit stories. Both were motivated to record Inuit culture in order to preserve knowledge of a passing way of life.

In Greenland, Hinrich Rink, the Inspector for South Greenland (a position analogous to colonial governor), invited Greenlanders to send in traditional Inuit stories. The result was *Tales and Traditions of the Eskimo* (1875), which consists of blended, unattributed versions of various Inuit tales. Individual Inuit in other parts of the North worked with anthropologists and other researchers to record what was understood as a passing way of life. These included Simon Paneak (1900–75), an Inupiaq from Anatuvuk Pass, who worked with several anthropologists between the 1950s and his death. As a consequence, Paneak played an influential role in shaping the academic literature about the Nunamiut (inland Inupiat). Beginning in the late 1960s Paneak recorded memories of his life, Nunamiut history, and traditional stories in a nonstandard English accompanied by freehand maps and line drawings. These have been published as *In a Hungry Country: Essays by Simon Paneak* (2004). In the 1920s, William A. Oquilluk (1896–1972) began recording the history of the Inupiat from the Seward Peninsula based upon the stories he learned from his grandfather. Toward the end of his life, Oquilluk worked with Laurel Bland to produce *People of Kauwerak: Legends of the Northern Eskimo* (1973). The book tells how the Inupiat people came into being as a result of four disasters: an earthquake, a flood, a cooling climate that led to starvation, and finally the 1918 influenza pandemic. According to Oquilluk,

Each one [of the disasters] killed most of the people, leaving only a few to survive on the land. Those who survived, each time, made the population

Inuit children's author Michael Kusugak reading his book *A Promise Is a Promise* to children in Rankin Inlet, Nunavut, 1992. (Photo by Tessa Macintosh, PW&S/NWT Archives/G-1995-001: 7500)

grow up again in Northwestern Alaska. Each time those few left told their story of what happened in other centuries to the young ones while they were growing up. If someone writes these stories down, it should bring understanding and thoughtfulness to anyone who reads them.[4]

Recording the past continues today. In the last decade, students at Nunavut Arctic College in Iqaluit have worked with several anthropologists and Inuit elders to produce a series of books on topics from Inuit perspectives including childrearing, traditional law, health and medicine, shamanism and cosmology, and dreams.

A number of other Inuit have written memoirs. These include *I, Nuligak* (1966) by an Inuvialuit man also as known as Bob Cockney (1895–1966); *Life among the Qallunaat* (1978) by Canadian Inuk Minnie Aodla Freeman; and *Memoirs of Hans Hendrik, the Arctic Traveler, Serving under Kane, Hayes, Hall and Nares, 1853–1876* (1878) by Greenlander Hans Hendrik (1834–89), to name just three. Hendrik was a West Greenlander, but lived for a time among the people of North Greenland, married a woman from that community, and may have attempted to convert them to Christianity. He was also involved in one of the most bizarre episodes in the history of Arctic exploration.

Beginning in 1853 Hendrik participated in several polar-exploring expeditions. In 1871, he and his wife and four children signed onto the third Arctic expedition led by the American Charles Francis Hall. Several disasters befell the voyage. First Hall died under mysterious circumstances. The ship, the *Polaris,* became trapped in the ice and then broke free, stranding Hendrik and his family, another Inuit couple who were Hall's primary guides, and several members of the ship's crew on an ice floe. They drifted south for seven months and 1,500 miles and were eventually rescued off the coast of Newfoundland. The entire party survived the ordeal largely because of the hunting and other work done by the Inuit members.

Newspapers and Magazines

As noted above, the first Inuktitut-language newspaper, *Atuagagdliutit,* began publishing in Greenland in 1861. The paper was founded by Hinrich Rink as part of a larger project to enhance Greenlanders' self-respect and to provide a route to social enlightenment. The first two editors, Rasmus Berthelsen (1827–1901) and Lars Møller (1842–1926), both Inuit, received some of their education in Denmark. During its first decades the paper provided a venue where ordinary Greenlanders debated and discussed matters of social importance. In particular, they debated the nature of the Greenlandic identity—whether it derived from the traditional hunting life or instead resided in the use of the Greenlandic language and love of the country. *Atuagagdliutit* also published poems, travel narratives, and fiction, both translated and written by Greenlanders. *Atuagagdliutit* merged with the Danish-language paper, *Grønlandsposten,* in 1952 and is now published as a bilingual paper: *Atuagagdliutit/Grønlandsposten.* While there have been many other Inuktitut-language newspapers, none has even come close to achieving *Atuagagdliutit's* longevity.

Alaska's first statewide Native newspaper, the *Tundra Times,* was published from 1962 to 1991 and briefly again between 1993 and 1997. Inupiaq Howard Rock (1911–76) was the founding editor and continued in that post until his death. Rock was an artist, with no training in journalism or writing, but was assisted in the start-up by a non-Native journalist named Tom Snapp who had been working for the Fairbanks newspaper, the *News Miner.* Financing for the *Tundra Times* came from a Massachusetts philanthropist, Dr. Henry S. Forbes. While Inupiat were concerned about a number of civil and indigenous rights issues, the catalyst for the paper was Project

Chariot, a plan by the U.S. Atomic Energy Commission to use a nuclear weapon to excavate a harbor at Cape Thompson in northwest Alaska. At the first meeting of Inupiat Paitot (see Chapter 6), Rock proposed a newspaper as a way to share information among Alaska Natives about this and other pressing issues. At the time, the mainstream news organizations in the state rarely covered issues important to the Native population. Although never a financial success, the *Tundra Times* became an important forum for discussing Native issues. It was nominated for a Pulitzer Prize for its coverage of the Alaska Native Claims Settlement Act (ANCSA), and broke a story about slave-like conditions endured by the Aleut residents of the Pribilof Islands at the hands of the U.S. government.

Other Inuit newspapers, including *Atuaqnik,* which was published in Nunavik for 18 months in 1979 and 1980, and *Tusagakasat,* which was published in Baker Lake, Nunavut, by the Reverend Armand Tagoona (1926–92), were also forums where Inuit shared news and discussed issues of concern. Several contemporary Inuit political and cultural organizations publish magazines, but these tend to be highly positive celebrations of Inuit culture rather than vehicles for analytical or investigative journalism.

Novels and Short Stories

Fiction is perhaps the least known of the Inuit literary genres, in part, because very little of it is available in English. Greenlandic fiction often presents a romanticized vision of an idealized indigenous past, even when the setting is in the future. The first Greenlandic novel, *Sinnattugaq* (*The Dream*, 1914), by Mathias Storch (1883–1957), and the second, *Ukiut 300-nngornerat* (*The 300th Anniversary*, 1931), by Augo Lynge (1899–1959), use futuristic settings as a vehicle for social criticism. In the latter, the author imagines Greenland in the year 2021. The climate is warming; the nations of Europe are in political union; Greenland's capital, Nuuk, is an important fishing port with urban amenities; and air travel is commonplace. In the novel Greenlanders are able to take their rightful place alongside Danes because they are no longer incapable of managing their own affairs.

Where the early novels critiqued the presumed failings of Greenlanders, later fiction served as an indictment of Danish colonialism. Hans Anthon Lynge's *Umiarsuup tikinngilaattaani* (*Just before the Ship Came In*, 1982) is set in a village where Greenlanders wait for Home Rule while observing the incompetence of a supposedly more technologically and intellectually advanced Dane. A recent short story by

Kelly Berthelsen, "NASA-p isertaasa isertugaanersaa" ("NASA's Most Secret Secret," 2001), presents Greenlanders enjoying the benefits of globalization while at the same time Greenlandic shamans travel to the moon without the aid of technology and drink coffee with Apollo astronauts.

Poetry

Traditional Inuit drum songs are often regarded as poetry and translations of their texts are frequently included in collections of Native North American poetry. Modern Inuit poets include Inupiaq Fred Bigjim, Greenlander Aqqaluk Lynge, and Canadian Inuk Alootook Ipellie. Both Ipellie and Bigjim write in English. Lynge writes in Greenlandic, but many of his poems have been translated into English. A recent bilingual collection is *The Veins of the Heart to the Pinnacle of the Mind* (*Taqqat Uummammut Aqqutaannut Takorluukkat Apuuffiannut*, 2009).

MUSIC AND DANCE

As discussed in previous chapters, music was incorporated into contests that allowed disputes to be aired, diffusing tensions. But also Inuit made, and continue to make, music purely for amusement and entertainment. Traditional Inuit music included drum songs (*pisiit*) and throat singing.

Drum songs are usually accompanied by dance. The drums are narrow-rimmed hoops of wood or bone, with an attached handle, and a membrane of gut or tanned hide. Modern drums sometimes use a membrane made of rubber. The style of both drumming and dancing varies from region to region. In the Central Canadian Arctic, for example, the drumming and dancing is performed by a single individual who rotates the drum from side to side, striking the underside of the drum on alternate sides of the frame with a short, fat stick while moving about the dance floor. The singing is done by a separate chorus. In contrast, in Inupiat and Inuvialuit communities, there may be as many as 15 seated drummers/singers who provide the musical accompaniment for multiple dancers. The dancers' arms and hands freed from drumming frequently pantomime the lyrics of the song. Prior to conversion to Christianity, Inupiat danced wearing masks.

Drum songs are sometimes called *ai-jai-jai* songs, after a refrain that is repeated throughout the song for the sake of melody. The songs can be spontaneous compositions, but many are learned and repeated on social occasions. The lyrics frequently describe past events. Ethnomusicologist Beverley Cavanagh regards these songs as a form of record-keeping or reporting, a way that people, particularly before the development of writing, preserved a record of memorable events.[5] In addition to describing actual events, drum songs can also express the desire of the singer for hunting success, health, or love. Frequently, the lyrics express strong thoughts or emotions, but in keeping with Inuit norms of expression, do so in an indirect manner.

The Netsilingmiut shaman, Orpingalik, told ethnographer Knud Rasmussen that "songs are thoughts, sung out with the breath when people are moved by great forces and ordinary speech no long suffices."[6] Rasmussen collected drum song lyrics from Orpingalik as well as from the Iglulingmiut shaman Aua such as this one describing a caribou hunt:

I came creeping along over the marsh
With bow and arrows in my mouth.
The marsh was broad and the water icy cold,
And there was not cover to be seen.
Slowly I wriggled along,
Soaking wet, but crawling unseen
Up within range.
The caribou were feeding, carelessly nibbling the juicy moss,
Until my arrow stood quivering, deep
In the chest of the bull.
The terror seized the heedless dwellers of the plain.
The herd scattered apace,
And trotting their fastest, were lost to sight
Behind sheltering hills.[7]

Drum singing was infrequent in the 1940s, 1950s, and 1960s, perhaps due to pressure from Christian missionaries or other non-Natives who regarded it as pagan or primitive, but has been revived across the North as an expression of Inuit culture and identity. Inuit drumming and dancing is frequently presented at festivals and cultural events, and sometimes great effort is made to perform traditional dances in traditional ways. For example, in 1982, Inupiaq elders presented a four-part "carefully researched and rehearsed re-enactment of the Eagle-Wolf Dance of the Messenger Feast, using the recollections of aged dance-leaders, early historical eye-witness accounts, and close examination of nineteenth century photographs"

Ulukhaktok residents Jimmy Memogana (left) and Buddy Alikamek drum sing while Roberta Memogama dances, 2001. (Photo by author)

for an Elders' Conference at Nome.[8] But drum songs are not a static, historical art performed only at special events. There is considerable innovation in drum singing, and in addition to public performances, drum singing continues to be done by small groups in intimate settings simply for pleasure.

Drum songs are performed by men and women, but throat singing is a women's activity in which pairs of singers alternate rapidly producing meaningless words or syllables and using each other's mouth as resonators in a kind of vocal game. The singers stand very close together, sometimes grasping each other's arms. Together, they alternate producing a series of short, rapid, rhythmic voiced and unvoiced sounds, which in combination are meant to imitate the sounds of animals, the wind, or other everyday sounds. The game ends when one of the pair runs out of breath, is unable to maintain the rapid pace, or dissolves in laughter. Like drum dancing, throat singing is now part of displays of Inuit culture performed at festivals and public spectacles. But it has also moved into some hybrid and world music venues. Canadian Inuk, Tanya Tagaq, for example, has collaborated with artists as diverse as the string ensemble, the Kronos Quartet, and Icelandic pop singer, Bjork, making vocal music based on the sounds of Inuit throat singing. Tagaq grew up in Cambridge Bay, Nunavut, but taught herself to throat sing only after leaving the North. In contrast with traditional throat singing, Tagaq produces the vocal sounds without a partner.

Early encounters with non-Natives made a significant contribution to the Inuit musical repertoire. Inuit borrowed and adapted the musical instruments and styles brought by the newcomers. Moravian missionaries in Labrador encouraged the establishment of brass bands and string ensembles, and a tradition of playing on rooftops developed there. Music was also a part of missionary work in Greenland, and Inuit catechists learned to compose psalms and hymns in a European style, but Inuit were also "able to transpose their own musical preferences onto the repertoire that the [missionaries] brought them."[9] Christian religious themes underlie the music of Greenlanders Rasmus Berthelsen, the editor of *Atuagagdliutit* who wrote the Christmas hymn "Guuterput quisinnermiu" ("Our Lord in Heaven"); Jonathan Petersen (1881–1961); and Henrik Lund (1875–1948), as well as the contemporary Canadian gospel singer-songwriter, Susan Aglukark. From Scottish and American whalers Inuit adopted the fiddle and the accordion and learned reels, square dances, and polkas. These religious and the secular forms are part of contemporary Inuit indigenous music, to which new styles continue to be added.

Vaigat music developed in Greenland in the 1940s and 1950s. It is built upon the big band swing and country-and-western dance music that was popular with American military personnel stationed in Greenland during World War II. Vaigat has lyrics in Greenlandic, some of which are loose translations of American song lyrics. The lyrics are consciously nonpolitical, and often concern nature, home, and everyday life.

Country-and-western music is also popular in the Canadian Arctic where it is widely played on radio. One of the most popular Inuit performers of this genre is Charlie Panigoniak who lives in Rankin Inlet, Nunavut. Panigoniak writes and sings songs in Inuktitut based on his personal experiences of life in the North. Though his music is clearly patterned on country-and-western music in the style of Johnny Cash, he adds vocal effects borrowed from both throat singing and drum songs.

Inuit musicians today contribute to every genre of music. Greenlander Rasmus Lyberth is a successful folk musician, while Canadian M.O. (Mosha Folger) and Greenlanders Nuuk Posse, Maasi Pedersen, Prussic, and others compose and perform hip-hop. There are numerous individual artists and bands that make rock music. The Greenlandic band SUME, which became popular in the 1970s, was among the first. Their lyrics dealt explicitly with the widespread aspirations of Greenlanders for independence from Denmark.

More contemporary Inuit rock and hip-hop musicians (and others, including Susan Aglukark) attack social problems as well as politics with their song lyrics. The despair that comes from being trapped in the hostile city is a subject tackled by North Greenlander Ole Kristiansen's "Zoo inuillu" ("Zoo and the People"). Canadian Lucie Idlout's song "Lovely Irene" deals with domestic violence, while her "E5-770, My Mother's Name" is a commentary on the disk numbers that the Canadian government assigned to Inuit to be used in place of names in the 1940s and 1950s (see Chapter 1).

Nuuk, Greenland, has an especially vibrant music scene. "The local music life is varied and vivid, it ranges from groups from different music schools; the city orchestra playing big band and jazz music; rock bands; rapper groups; country-and-western-like local music groups, etc."[10] Contemporary youth music, both hip-hop and rock, is striking for its attention to urban social problems. As Pedersen notes, where the musicians of the 1970s were part of the Home Rule/anti-Danish colonialism movement, the current young generation has only known Home Rule and "has no passionate feelings about the post-colonial traumatic Greenland-Denmark issue."[11] They do, however, have passionate feelings and traumatic experiences of abandonment by parents who abused alcohol while blaming their problems on colonialism. Where Greenland's early social critics expressed nostalgia for a traditional hunting way of life in their literature, this is not the solution sought by contemporary critics. Malik Kleist, lead singer of the very popular rock band Chilly Friday, explained,

We don't write nationalistically. You know, now the sun is shining, nature is beautiful and look a nice seal. . . . Our texts are more personal and much stronger. Deeper, isn't that what you call it? They are about suicide, drunkenness and children being left on the streets, or children playing out in the middle of the night because they don't dare going [sic] home. So far a lot of people have hidden behind the excuse that the Danes destroyed our hunting culture. That became an excuse for drinking and wallowing in self-pity, but in modern Greenland, we have to move on.[12]

Kleist's statement contrasts markedly with the suggestion that music and other genres of performance provide a very tangible way to bridge "older nomadic hunting cultures and Inuit modernity."[13]

The varied ways that Inuit incorporate music into their daily lives reflect the great versatility of music as a form of expressive culture as well as the diversity of Inuit culture. While quite a number of Inuit are working to revive older musical forms, others are incorporating traditional styles into new forms or building entirely new Inuit musical genres. Language also matters. Among the contemporary musicians Charlie Panigoniak writes and performs in Inuktitut, and many of the Greenlandic artists use Kalaallisut, but also include Danish and English at times. Susan Aglukark sings mostly in English while incorporating some Inuktitut in her lyrics, such as a translation of "Amazing Grace." Lucie Idlout, however, sings in English.

Both Tanya Tagaq and Lucie Idlout present themselves as musicians who happen to be Inuit, rather than as Inuit musicians. According to Tagaq, "I am Inuit, I am a woman, but I'm just expressing me. I would be expressing myself no matter where I was from or what culture was in me. . . . I think girls that are doing traditional throat-singing are representing the culture more accurately."[14] Idlout takes an almost identical position, but very much in keeping with the traditional Inuit value of speaking only for oneself and of one's own experience.

I don't like to be promoted [as an Inuk singer-songwriter]. Because all I'm doing is I'm writing about life, and life as I experience it and life as I understand and feel. . . . I don't understand why we should have to be pigeon-holed. It's beautiful for people who are doing traditional music. I love that. I love traditional music. I love listening to it. I don't personally appropriate any elements of that into my music and I don't see why I should have to, for that matter.[15]

RADIO AND TELEVISION IN THE NORTH

The development of satellite broadcasting technology in the 1960s made it possible for television to reach most of the world, including the Arctic. Prior to that, however, Inuit had little exposure to television as a medium of expression or as a medium of advertising. The arrival of television coincided with many changes in Inuit communities, and television contributed to those changes. It would be a mistake, however, to assume that Inuit have been passive recipients of externally created television programming.

The Canadian government launched its first Arctic telecommunications satellite, which it called *Anik,* meaning "Brother" in Inuktitut, in 1969. It began television broadcasting in Inuit communities through the Northern Service of the CBC (Canadian Broadcasting

Corporation) in 1973, but television programming reached most Canadian Inuit communities only in the late 1970s. The service, at first, consisted only of a single channel, CBC North; it included no Inuktitut-language programming or even any programs produced in the North.

While most Inuit communities eagerly accepted television, the residents of Igloolik, Nunavut, voted twice to refuse television service, and several Inuit organizations protested, arguing that English-language non-Native television constituted a form of cultural genocide. To its credit, the Canadian government responded with financial support for studios and training in television production for Inuit in several Nunavut and Nunavik communities. After two years of training and 18 months of trial broadcasting, the government agreed to fund the establishment of an Inuit television production company. The Inuit Broadcasting Corporation (IBC) was established in 1981 by Inuit Tapirisat of Canada (now Inuit Tapiriit Kanatami) and went on the air in 1982 with four hours a week of programming.

IBC produced a number of innovative children's and public affairs programs that were popular with Inuit viewers, but because it was forced to share the CBC North broadcast channel it had very little airtime. The government increased funding to IBC in 1983, enabling it to expand its activities, but then almost immediately withdrew the extra funding. IBC suffered additional funding cuts in 1985, 1990, 1993, and 1996. It responded with a one-hour film, *Starting Fire with Gunpowder* (1991), to document the social and cultural value of television by Inuit for Inuit.

IBC produces nearly all of its programs in Inuktitut and actively resists making shows in English. Still, some Inuit have felt that IBC is too closely allied with non-Native advisors and too restricted by its reliance on government funding. IBC joined a consortium of northern aboriginal broadcasters, Television Northern Canada (TVNC) in 1990. TVNC received its own satellite uplink in 1992. It became part of Aboriginal Peoples Television Network (APTN) in 1999 and is currently included as part of most basic cable television packages throughout Canada. This has largely solved the timeslot problem that existed when IBC was forced to share a channel with CBC North, but it has diluted the impact of Inuktitut-language programming as just one more aboriginal broadcaster. Since 2001 APTN has been allowed by the Canadian Radio and Television Commission to have 30 percent of its programming come from international sources. Aboriginal broadcasting is just one of many cable television channels available to Inuit viewers. Sports programs, physical comedies, and action films are especially popular with Inuit viewers, perhaps because these types of programs can be understood without specific cultural knowledge.

Native broadcasters in Alaska have been much less successful in producing and broadcasting indigenous television programming, although PBS affiliates in Kotzebue and Barrow are able to broadcast some locally produced programs. Again money is a problem, and cuts to funding in the mid-1990s forced Alaska Native broadcasters throughout the state to share programming. While this means that every station has the ability to broadcast more indigenous programming, the need to share requires that programs be produced in English rather than in indigenous languages.

Radio Greenland (*Kalaalllit Nunaata Radioa* or KNR) is Greenland's primary television and radio broadcaster. In 1980 KNR became one of the first institutions to come under the jurisdiction of the Home Rule government. KNR produces some television programming, primarily news and public affairs, in Kalaallisut, but also broadcasts Danish and other international programs.

Radio, much more than television, has been a critical medium for the Inuit communities, and an important source of locally produced, Inuktitut-language broadcasting. In Greenland, radio broadcasts support the local music industry. In Canada there are local volunteer-run radio stations in most Inuit communities, and the CBC affiliate stations in the larger towns also broadcast regional news and public affairs in Inuktitut. A number of Inuit political leaders in Canada, such as Nellie Cornoyea (former Premier of the Northwest Territories), began their public lives as reporters and news readers on CBC radio.

INUIT IN FILM

In 1922, Robert Flaherty introduced Inuit to mass audiences with the film *Nanook of the North*. Though promoted as a true picture of life among primitive hunters, *Nanook* is neither an accurate representation of precolonial Inuit life nor of the lives of the Inuit actors in Flaherty's fictionalized account. In Flaherty's rendering Nanook and his companions are "untouched, untroubled, and disease free"[16] and cheerfully naïve as they engage in a constant struggle with the elements. The *Wedding of Palo* (1937), made by Danish ethnographer Knud Rasmussen, presented a more realistic picture of Inuit culture, but it too relied on common stereotypes to tell a fictionalized story about rivalry of two men for the affections of a marriageable woman.

The commercial success of *Nanook* contributed to decisions of Hollywood studios to make a number of films on location in Alaska. Alaska Natives were cast in supporting roles, and Inupiaq actor Ray Wise played the romantic lead in several pictures. Wise, who changed his surname to Mala after the character he played in MGM's *Eskimo* (1934), became involved in the film industry as a result of meeting Arctic explorer and filmmaker Frank Kleinschmidt in 1922 when he was just 14 years old. Wise eventually made his way to Hollywood where he worked as a cameraman before becoming a successful actor. Wise tried his hand at scriptwriting, producing a script that depicted the actual lives of Inupiat of the time. The film, which Wise titled *Modern Eskimos,* was never made. The productions that Wise starred in, in contrast, perpetuated stereotypes of Inuit as happy-go-lucky primitives who existed in an almost lawless state, rubbing noses, trading spouses and abandoning children and the elderly to the elements without remorse.

The representation of Inuit in Hollywood movies says more about the audiences' concerns and preoccupations than it does about Inuit realities past or present. Inuit (and the Arctic landscape) in these films often serve as foils for the perceived ills of modern, technological civilization.

INUIT AS FILMMAKERS

The development of inexpensive digital video technologies has made it possible for peoples all over the world to become filmmakers. Inuit are no exception and have turned to filmmaking in order to produce both documentaries and fictionalized stories. *Qallunaat! Why White People Are Funny* (2006) is a farcical comedy presenting a world in which Inuit study white people or Qallunaat rather than the other way around. The film, which is the result of collaboration between non-Native filmmaker Mark Sandiford and Inuit writer Zebedee Nungak, builds on Nungak's satirical writings about an imaginary field of study he dubs "Qallunology" or the study of white people. Qallunology is a satirical critique of the objectification of Inuit culture by anthropologists and other social scientists. Much of the film is set in an imaginary Inuit research center known as QSI, or the Qallunaat Studies Institute, and follows the work of Inuit social scientists as they collect data from research subjects (played by actual Arctic social scientists) and report with great seriousness about rather trivial linguistic habits of white people.

Igloolik Isuma Productions, founded in 1990 by Zacharias Kunuk, Paul Apak Angilirq (1954–98), Pauloosie Quilitalik (1939–2007), and

Norman Cohn, has been highly successful in producing Inuktitut-language films. The production company, based in Igloolik, Nunavut, is best known for its feature-length films *Atanarjuat: The Fast Runner* (1999), *The Journals of Knud Rasmussen* (2005), and with the Inuit women's film group, Arnait Video Collective, *Before Tomorrow* (2008). Igloolik Isuma has also produced a number of shorter films documenting Inuit life as well as a 13-episode dramatic television series, *Nunavut (Our Land)*, set in the 1940s, just prior to settlement in government-created towns. In 2007, Igloolik Isuma launched isuma.tv as an Internet portal to showcase the work of indigenous filmmakers from around the world.

Each of the Igloolik Isuma feature-length films is distinct. *Atanarjuat*, set long in the past, presents a traditional Inuit legend. It is a story of jealousy and rivalry between two families. Jealousy leads to betrayal, murder, a naked run across the ice, and ultimately, banishment of the murderers. The film is visually stunning and the narrative and style of presentation are less linear than most commercial productions. In *The Journals of Knud Rasmussen*, the filmmakers imagine what transpired in the early 20th century when their ancestors abandoned shamanism for Christianity (see Chapter 7). *Before Tomorrow*, based on the novel *For morgendagen* by Danish writer Jørn Riel, presents the trials of a grandmother and grandson left alone in the world when disease wipes out their entire community.

The Igloolik Isuma and Arnait filmmakers may seem to be doing nothing more than documenting their culture, but in fact, they work from a consciously political perspective to produce Inuit stories for Inuit audiences and to work in a purposely Inuit way. One of the techniques they employ, particularly for their historical films such as the *Nunavut* dramatic series, is for an actor to play his or her namesake or *atiq* (see Chapter 1). In other words, the actors are improvising their lives and their relationships from an earlier time period. These "living fictionalizations," as the filmmakers describe their production techniques, support the continuation of specifically Inuit styles of social interaction and comportment as the "actors are actually hunting, sewing, traveling, and answering to their Inuktitut names while living in camps with the camera running."[17]

Notable films by Greenlanders include *Eskimo Weekend* (2002), by visual and performance artist Inuk Silis Høegh, and a documentary, *Inuk Woman City Blues* (2002), by singer and actress Laila Hansen. Contemporary Greenlandic music features prominently in both filmic portraits of urban Inuit life. Like the earlier novel by Greenlander Maaliaaraq Vebaek, *A Meeting in the Bus* (1981), *Inuk Woman*

City Blues reveals the despair and misery of Greenlandic women living in Copenhagen. *Eskimo Weekend,* although it ends on a hopeful note, also reveals a kind of despair—that of youth living in the capital, Nuuk, with little to do but play music, drink alcohol, and pursue sexual liaisons. *Heart of Light* (1998), co-written by Jacob Grønlykke and Hans Anthon Lynge, also deals with despair wrought by colonialism and redemption that comes from a return to tradition. Though not as obviously based in Inuit storytelling traditions as the work of Arnait and Igloolik Isuma, these films are indeed Inuit cultural productions. What makes them uniquely Inuit, aside from the Greenlandic identity of the performers and filmmakers, are the subtle uses of specifically Inuit symbolic references and characters as well as the fact that even in the fictional *Eskimo Weekend,* the actors play parts strikingly close to their own lives. The latter, similar to the *atiq*-technique of acting employed by Igloolik Isuma for its historical productions, fits with the Inuit practice of speaking only from personal knowledge and experience.

As consumers of music, film, and television, Inuit are well connected to the global marketplace and have access to and interest in the latest productions. The almost-universal availability of the Internet and digital media sites such as YouTube, MySpace, and Facebook enables ordinary Inuit to more easily participate as contributors to global media culture as well as to be consumers.

NOTES

1. Kulchyski, Peter, and Frank James Tester (2007) *Kiumajut (Talking Back): Game Management and Inuit Rights 1900–70,* Vancouver: University of British Columbia Press, 167–69.

2. Ipellie, Alootook (2008) "Walking Both Sides of an Invisible Border," in *The Journals of Knud Rasmussen: A Sense of Memory and High-Definition Inuit Storytelling,* Gillian Robinson, ed., Montreal: Isuma Distribution, 60.

3. Eber, Dorothy Harley (1998) "Peter Pitseolak and the Photographic Template," in *Imaging the Arctic,* J.C.H. King and Henrietta Lidchi, eds., London: British Museum Press, 57.

4. Oquilluk, William A., with Laurel L. Bland (1973) *People of Kauwerak: Legends of the Northern Eskimo,* Anchorage: Alaska Methodist University Press, xvii.

5. Cavanagh, Beverley (1987) "Problems in Investigating the History of an Oral Tradition: Reconciling Different Types of Data about Inuit Drum Dance Traditions," *Anuario Musical* 42: 29.

6. Rasmussen, Knud (1931) *The Netsilik Eskimos, Report of the Fifth Thule Expedition (1921–24),* Vol. 8, Copenhagen: Gyldendalske Boghandel, 321.

7. Aua quoted in Rasmussen, Knud (1929) *Intellectual Culture of the Iglulik Eskimos, Report of the Fifth Thule Expedition (1921–24)*, Vol. 7, No. 1, Copenhagen: Gyldendalske Boghandel, 239–40.

8. Johnston, Thomas F. (1991) "Contemporary Emphases in Northern Eskimo Dance," *International Review of the Aesthetics and Sociology of Music* 22(1): 53.

9. Gordon, Tom (2007) "Found in Translation: The Inuit Voice in Moravian Music," *Newfoundland and Labrador Studies* 22(1): 307.

10. Pedersen, Birgit Kleist (2008) "Young Greenlanders in the Urban Space of Nuuk," *Etudes/Inuit/Studies* 32(1): 93.

11. Ibid., 94.

12. Quoted in Pedersen, "Young Greenlanders in the Urban Space of Nuuk," 95.

13. Diamond, Beverley (2008) *Native American Music in Eastern North America*, New York: Oxford University Press, 35.

14. Quoted in Cronshaw, Andrew (2008) "Getting Inuit," *Sing Out!* 52(1): 22.

15. Quoted in Diamond, Beverley (2002) "Native American Contemporary Music: The Women," *The World of Music* 44(1): 25.

16. Fienup-Riordan, Ann (1995) *Freeze Frame: Alaska Eskimos in the Movies*, Seattle: University of Washington Press, xiv.

17. Wachowich, Nancy (2006) "Cultural Survival and the Trade in Iglulingmiut Traditions," in *Critical Inuit Studies*, Pamela Stern and Lisa Stevenson, eds., Lincoln: University of Nebraska Press, 134.

10

VISUAL ARTS

Inuit arts, like many other aspects of Inuit culture, are nationally and regionally specific. This is the case both for art Inuit make for themselves as well as for those made for sale to non-Inuit collectors. Some archeologists suggest that artistic motifs were one important way that ancient Inuit communities, or polities as they have been called by some, asserted their distinctive identities. Still today, Inuit recognize regional differences on the basis of design elements on clothing and other material culture.

Inuit, like other Arctic peoples have not, until recently, separated function from aesthetics in the making of clothing, tools, and other items of material culture and had no perception of art as a distinct conceptual category. Nonetheless, the archeological record contains considerable evidence of well-formed aesthetic sensibilities. Masks, small wood and ivory sculptures in human and animal forms, were produced in Greenland and Canada during the late Dorset period. From the same time period in Alaska, archeologists have recovered masks and other items carved in ivory from graves near Point Hope, and highly decorated harpoon gear have been found in sites on the Bering Sea islands. By contrast, there is less evidence of artistic activity in the archeological sites of the Thule ancestors of modern Inuit. Although Inuit have replaced many items of traditional material culture with imported manufactured goods, Inuit aesthetics continue to permeate items made for local use such as parkas and boots, *umiaqs* (skin boats), *inukshuks* (stone monuments), and *ulus* (semilunar knives).

CREATION OF MARKETS FOR INUIT ART

European explorers and other early non-Native visitors in the Arctic collected souvenirs of their travels to Inuit communities, but the commercial market for Inuit art likely began with the large collecting expeditions mounted by, and on behalf of, museums in the United States, Canada, and Europe. These occurred mostly in the latter half of the 19th century. Inuit were encouraged to sell the sacred and everyday objects, which they supposedly no longer needed and which ethnologists and museum curators assumed would disappear. In Alaska, the Nome gold rush (1899–1909) produced a steady market for Inuit arts in North Alaska, but both on their own and with the encouragement of Christian missionaries and government administrators, Inuit in many different regions produced replicas and miniatures of traditional items to sell to the growing number of non-Native visitors. Contemporary Inuit commercial arts developed out of these early ad hoc marketing activities.

The art forms most often associated with Inuit—*tupilak* figurines, baleen baskets, Anaktuvuk caribou-skin masks, soapstone and whalebone sculptures, and graphic prints—are all recent forms produced for sale rather than for domestic use. For the most part they originated as tourist arts. It is a mistake, however, to discount their authenticity on that basis. Nor is it correct to assume that the quality is poor. Artists of all cultures and ethnic groups make their art for the market, and Inuit artists are no exception. Today, art is just one component of the mixed economies of Inuit communities (see Chapter 3). Through the materials employed and the motifs and symbols presented, Inuit art is very much representative of contemporary Inuit culture.

Tupilak figurines are small, grotesquely shaped sculptures carved of ivory by Greenlanders. Meant to represent an agent of sorcery or supernatural power, tupilaks were first produced as commercial art in the 1930s. According to Greenlandic anthropologist Robert Petersen, the sculptures that are sold as tupilaks did not exist prior to that time.[1] Rather they existed in the imagination and were brought into being through stories. Physical models of tupilaks were carved for the benefit of Danes and other Europeans who could not otherwise understand what these malevolent beings looked like. European purchasers proved to be most interested in the most grotesque and bizarre images and thus, tupilak figures became more monstrous and alarming in response to the market.

Baskets of baleen, the plastic-like substance with which bowhead whales strain plankton from sea water, are an Inupiaq art form dating from around 1915. The first baleen baskets were produced in Barrow, Alaska, at the instigation of Yankee whaler-turned-trader Charles Brower. These small, lidded baskets are woven of coiled baleen and topped with a carved ivory finial, usually in the shape of an animal such as a seal. Disks of ivory are used as starter pieces for attaching the first coils of the base and lid. Brower is reported to have asked Kinguktuk to make baskets similar to willow-root baskets from baleen that Brower might give as gifts. This art form did not attract other weavers until the 1930s when the fur market, which had replaced commercial whaling as an income generator for Inupiat, collapsed. Basket making then provided an alternate source of income.

The caribou-skin masks from the village of Anaktuvuk Pass, Alaska, originated in an entirely different way. Under the influence of Christian missionaries, Inupiat stopped making masks for religious purposes prior to 1900 (see Chapter 7), but it is also the case that the Nunamiut (inland Inupiat) residents of Anaktuvuk Pass did not use masks historically. Caribou-skin masks are a modern creation unrelated to any traditional Inuit religious practices, but they were initially created by a pair of Inupiaq hunters for local use. Bob Ahgook and Zacharias Hugo made the first caribou-skin masks in 1951 as part of costumes they wore to the community Christmas celebration. As part of the holiday festivities, performers disguised themselves and clowned to amuse fellow residents (see Chapter 7). The two men are said to have gotten the idea to wear masks from Halloween masks Hugo had seen in Fairbanks a few months earlier. University of Alaska researchers later purchased Ahgook's and Hugo's creations for the University Museum, but the price paid was low. It was several years before, through the efforts of a non-Native teacher, that a market for caribou-skin masks developed sufficiently for other residents of Anaktuvuk Pass to experiment with mask-making techniques. Ahgook and Hugo, who made the original masks, did not produce any for the market, although Hugo's wife, Doris, has.[2]

The mask-making technique used by Anaktuvuk mask makers today was developed by Justus Mekiana. It involves stretching a piece of wet caribou skin over a wooden form carved in the shape of a face. Openings for eyes and mouth are cut and, once the blank is

Caribou-skin mask from Anaktuvuk Pass,
Alaska. (Author's collection)

dry, strips of caribou, fox, or other fur are sewn or glued to the face
to create facial hair (eyebrows, mustache or beard if male) and a
parka ruff. The Anaktuvuk masks remain a tourist art, and are used
only rarely by Inupiat for local performances.

Canadian Inuit artists are widely known as printmakers, an art
form introduced by James Houston in Cape Dorset in the late 1950s.
Houston, an artist, was employed by the Canadian government to
help develop an art industry in Canadian Inuit communities. Cape
Dorset remains the most successful and best known of the Inuit
printmaking communities, but artists in Puvirnituq, Ulukhaktok (formerly Holman), Baker Lake, and Pangnirtung have also had success with printmaking.

Houston's involvement with Inuit artists dates to the previous decade. In 1948, he traveled to Inukjuaq on the east coast of Hudson
Bay on a sketching and painting trip. While there he purchased a
number of small carvings and other souvenirs from Inuit. Upon re-

turning south, he brought the items to the Handicrafts Guild in Montreal, which was easily persuaded that the items had commercial potential. The Guild raised money to send Houston on a more purposeful collecting expedition the following summer. He returned with more than 1,000 items, which when exhibited that fall, sold out completely in less than three days. Eventually, but with considerable reluctance, the Canadian government funded Houston's and the Handicrafts Guild's efforts to encourage an Inuit handicraft industry. While government financial backing was necessary, Houston's connections to the art world were also critical to turning small-scale production of handicrafts into a successful art industry.

CO-OPS AND THE CANADIAN ESKIMO ARTS COUNCIL

The Canadian government was slow to get involved in the day-to-day affairs of Inuit, but once it did become involved it insinuated itself into nearly every facet of Inuit life. Through the efforts of Houston and others, the northern administrators came to see art as an economic activity that could supplement or replace fur trading as a source of income for Inuit who were settling in the newly created towns and villages. All Inuit were regarded as potential artists, and the government came to believe that art could provide a steady income, and thus, reduce the need for welfare payments. Beginning in the 1960s the Canadian government encouraged the formation of producers' cooperatives both to manage the production and sale of Inuit arts and crafts and as a way for Inuit to gain experience with modern economic institutions. While not all of the co-ops have been financially successful, they are important institutions in the Canadian North, and have been especially important in fostering commercial Inuit arts.

In addition to the cooperatives, the government established the Canadian Eskimo Arts Council (CEAC) to serve as a combination advisory body, marketing arm, and quality control agent. Made up initially of non-Inuit "art experts," the CEAC met annually to select the drawings to be produced as prints, often rejecting images it deemed "not Inuit enough." It encouraged prints that could be characterized as primitivist, displaying bold colors and often depicting images of an Inuit life that no longer existed. Despite this colonialist approach, CEAC also developed exhibitions of Inuit art at top galleries and museums and promoted Inuit prints and sculpture as fine art. In this way the CEAC directly shaped the art Canadian Inuit made as well as the art-buying public's understanding of Inuit art. Once the market for Inuit art was established through a network of specialty galleries, Inuit artists grew increasing frustrated by CEAC's gatekeeping function, and during the mid-1980s a number of co-ops opted out of the CEAC approval process. The CEAC disbanded in 1989.

INNOVATION

Despite efforts of organizations like the Canadian Eskimo Arts Council to define Inuit art narrowly, when afforded the opportunity, Inuit artists have experimented with both imagery and media. One experimental artist was Peter Pitseolak (1902–73) who used photography to document camp life around present-day Cape Dorset during the 1940s, 1950s, and 1960s. Peter Pitseolak's photographs provide an intimate portrait of Canadian Inuit life just before and after the creation of permanent towns and villages. Peter Pitseolak is thought to have first learned about photography in the 1910s from *Nanook of the North* filmmaker Robert Flaherty, but obtained a camera only several decades later. His photographs are especially remarkable when one considers that he, in collaboration with his wife, Aggeok, developed the film and printed the photographs in snowhouses and northern cabins.

Other Inuit artists also borrowed and adapted artistic techniques learned from non-Natives. For example, Angokwazhuk, an Inupiaq carver better known as Happy Jack (c. 1870–1918), observed Yankee whalers making scrimshaw and adopted some of their techniques to produce intricate naturalistic and fantastical scenes on walrus tusks, which he sold to gold rushers in Nome. Happy Jack was probably the first Alaska Inuit artist who was able to earn a living solely from selling art.

FROM TOURIST ART TO FINE ART

Inuit commercial art has matured over the short period of its existence. Some of its early practitioners produced art for sale only reluctantly and in the absence of other income-producing activities. Many Inuit as well as many non-Native northern administrators seem to have regarded art-making as an occupation suitable for invalids who might otherwise be indigent. Anthropologist Nelson Graburn, for example, noted that many of the soapstone carvers in Salluit, Nunavik, whom he observed in the 1960s disliked carving and found it boring to make the carvings that Canadian art advisors deemed saleable. Many of them carved only in the absence of other money-making options.[3] In fact, many of the first commercially successful Inuit artists suffered from illnesses or disabilities that made other work, such as hunting, impossible. These included Happy Jack as well as the Greenlander Aron from Kangeq and several of the best-known Inupiaq graphic artists.

Aron from Kangeq (1822–69) was one of Greenland's earliest pictorial artists. He made woodcut prints and watercolor paintings illustrating traditional stories and historic events. Aron provided the illustrations and also contributed stories for *Tales and Traditions of the Eskimo* published in 1875 by Hinrich Rink. Aron's woodcut prints also appeared in *Atuagagdliutit,* Greenland's first newspaper (see Chapter 9). Aron's artistic and literary output constitutes an important record of Greenlandic social history.

Most of Aron's body of work, which included more than 300 drawings and paintings as well as 40 woodcut prints and 56 stories, was deposited at the Danish National Museum in Copenhagen and at the University Museum of Ethnography in Oslo by Rink's widow, Signe. In 1982, a number of pieces were returned to Greenland and are now in the collections of the National Museum of Greenland in Nuuk. There was a major exhibit of Aron's watercolors in the same year.

Graphic artists James Kivetoruk Moses (c. 1903–82) and his brother-in-law George Ahgupuk (1911–2001) were part of the second generation of Inupiaq artists from the Seward Peninsula in Alaska. Both took up art as a profession after sustaining injuries that limited their mobility. Faced with a shortage of paper, Ahgupuk became noted for his drawings on tanned and bleached caribou, seal, moose, and occasionally, fish skins. Ahgupuk produced scenes of contemporary daily village life as well as of traditional Inupiaq activities. He often finished his skin canvases with a woven border of red-dyed reindeer skin. Famed American artist Rockwell Kent became acquainted with Ahgupuk's work in the 1930s. Kent published several articles about him in *Time* magazine and the *New York Times* and facilitated his induction into the American Artists Group. This attention probably provided a boost to Ahgupuk's career; he was commissioned to illustrate a number of publications and produced artwork that decorated ceramics and other mass market souvenirs.

James Kivetoruk Moses is best known for brightly colored, realistic portraits and drawings of events from his earlier life as a hunter. His highly detailed works were often accompanied by narrative explanations of the events depicted that he dictated to his wife,

Ink on skin drawing by Inupiaq artist George Ahgupuk, depicting scenes of daily life. (Courtesy University of Alaska Museum of the North, UA 1967-98-177)

Bessie. The stories contributed to the sense of authenticity in Kivetoruk's drawings and enabled him to command a higher price from his non-Native customers.

REPRESENTATIONS OF DAILY LIFE

While there has been a tendency for Inuit artists to present images of traditional Inuit life, a significant portion of Inuit commercial art, past and present, depicts images drawn directly from the life experiences of the artists. Thus, the works of several of the artists discussed above, including Peter Pitseolak, George Ahgupuk, and James Kivetoruk Moses, provide windows onto ordinary life in the North, at least as that life is remembered. Other artists, notably Aron from Kangeq and Puvirnituq sculptor Davidialuk Amittuk (1910–76), used their art to depict the historical events recorded in stories. "Davidialuk wanted to portray dramatic events in the lives of real people in the remembered past: shamans who fought the missionaries, men who murdered each other over women, and people who starved because of broken taboos."[4]

Among contemporary artists, Canadian Inuk Annie Pootoogook depicts the mundane domestic scenes that constitute life in the North today: watching the news on television, dressing for work, bringing in the groceries, a couple embracing on the sofa. Many of her drawings display a sense of warmth and contentment through the very ordinariness of the scenes. In other drawings, however, she portrays another side of contemporary northern life that is all too commonplace. These include scenes of spousal assault and alcohol abuse. In their narrative quality, Annie Pootoogook's artwork echoes that of her mother, Napachie Pootoogook (1938–2002), and grandmother, Pitseolak Ashoona (c. 1904–83). Each of these Cape Dorset graphic artists drew upon their individual experiences as Inuit women to create scenes of daily life. Napachie, in particular, produced powerful images of women resisting forced marriage, of starvation and of infanticide.

ART AND NATIONAL IDENTITY

During the first decades of the 20th century Greenlandic pictorial art underwent a shift in which the Greenlandic landscape, rather than the Greenlandic people, became the visual focus of interest. The principal artists of this period, including Niels Lynge (1888–1965), Henrik Lund (1875–1948), Hans Lynge (1906–88), Pavia Petersen (1904–43), and Peter Rosing (1892–1965), were mainly catechists and pastors for whom depicting the beauty in the landscape was a form of religious reverence.

The romantic nationalism of these artists was evident in their work in which the beauty of the land also served as a metaphor for piety and the unspoiled nature of the Greenlandic people. In addition to painting, this group of artists also wrote poetry and plays proclaiming the beauty of the land. Henrik Lund, who was also known as "Endaleraq," wrote Greenland's national anthem, *Nunarput* ("Our Country").

Inuit art contributes to national consciousness in a very different way in Canada. There, the government officials who were responsible for the administration of Inuit communities promoted Inuit art as an authentic Canadian art form. Since the 1950s, the Canadian government has presented Inuit art as gifts to both foreign dignitaries and, on several occasions, to Queen Elizabeth. In the National Gallery of Canada in Ottawa, art made by Inuit is displayed alongside the work of non-Native Canadian artists. This official recognition of Inuit art as a genuine Canadian art has had the effect of reinforcing its social and psychological value among Inuit.

GENDER AND INUIT ART

Men predominate among the earliest-named Inuit artists, but this probably is more a consequence of the gender stereotypes that non-Natives brought to their interactions with Inuit than anything having to do with Inuit gender roles. For example, trader Charles Brower asked a man, Kinguktuk, to make the first baleen baskets, and many of the early baleen basket weavers were men. While it is possible that Brower chose Kinguktuk because container making was traditionally a male activity among Inupiat, it is more likely that Brower simply had more interactions with men than with women. Still today, baleen basket making is largely associated with men, but there are a number of Inupiaq women as well as married couples who weave baleen baskets. Non-Natives across the North viewed Inuit men as the appropriate breadwinners within a household and encouraged them to take up sculpture and other new art forms as a way to supplement or replace income from trapping or whaling. Canadian Inuit women were, however, encouraged to draw, and there is a mistaken perception that women are primarily graphic artists, while carvers are primarily men.

There is one area in which Inuit women do dominate; that is in skin sewing and textile arts. In Pangnirtung, Nunavut, for example, female weavers translate the drawings of both male and female

Ulukhaktok artist Agnes Nanogak Goose examining a drawing to be made into a print. (Richard G. Condon photo collection)

artists into limited edition tapestries. Elsewhere in the North, Inuit women apply traditionally feminine sewing skills to produce appliquéd wall-hangings as well as clothing and *kamiks* (boots).

FORMAL ART TRAINING

As noted above, in the past Inuit were often regarded as natural artists, but ones producing ethnic rather than fine art. Greenlanders Mathias Dalager (1770–1842) and Hans Zakaeus (d. 1819) were likely the first Inuit to be formally educated as artists. Zakaeus, also known as John Sacheuse, stowed away on a whaling ship headed to Scotland in 1816. There he met the painter Alexander Nasmyth and Arctic explorer Sir John Ross. Sacheuse joined Ross's 1818 expedition in search of the Northwest Passage as an interpreter. On this voyage, Ross became the first European to encounter Inughuit, Inuit from northwest Greenland whom Ross called "Arctic Highlanders." In addition to interpreting, Sacheuse made drawings of the expedition. His rendering of the first meeting of Inughuit and Europeans was reproduced in Ross's *Voyage of Discovery in His Majesty's Ships Isabella and Alexander* (1819). The image is a fascinating study of contrasts: sea water and sea ice, mountains and icebergs, massive European ships and small Inuit dog sleds, metal and ivory, light and dark, short fur-clad Inuit and tall uniformed Europeans. The image is the earliest known depiction of a "first meeting" between Europeans and an indigenous people produced by an indigenous artist.

While it was extremely rare for the first generations of Inuit artists to receive any formal art training, this is no longer the case. Quite a number of recent and contemporary Inuit artists have attended an art institute or have earned a degree in art. These include Inupiat artists Howard Rock (1911–76), Ronald W. Senungetuk, and Ken Lisbourne. Senungetuk, himself, became an art instructor, establishing the Native Arts Center in Fairbanks, Alaska, in 1965.

CONTEMPORARY INUIT FINE ARTS

Contemporary Inuit fine art is extremely diverse in both media and form. It is a hybrid art that uses traditional materials in new ways, new media to produce traditional forms, as well as ideas and themes from global and local sources to make personal and political statements. While only a small proportion of the Inuit are successful artists, their work often expresses the experiences and perspectives of the

wider community. A number of artists, including Canadians Alootook Ipellie (1951–2007), Annie Pootoogook, Manasie Akpaliapik,
Ovilu Tunnille, and Inupiaq Susie Bevins, have produced work ad-
dressing personal and Inuit experiences with alcohol abuse. Other
than the shared subject, the works are not at all similar, yet all can be
easily recognized as Inuit by the choice of materials and motifs.

Inuit art often comprises, wholly or in part, materials such as bone,
ivory, and animal skins previously used for domestic arts. Thus, production of these arts is tied to the continuation of subsistence hunting and collecting. The production of baleen baskets, caribou-skin
masks, and ivory carvings requires continued access to items such as
baleen, caribou skin, and walrus ivory. Artists either must be hunters
themselves or must have relationships with individuals who are.
Thus, these arts are embedded in uniquely Inuit social relations.

In the last few decades artist has become a recognized profession
in Inuit communities and Inuit commercial art has transformed from
something to be done to earn a little money into an acknowledged
form of aesthetic expression. Just as Canada's adoption of Inuit art as
a symbol of Canadian identity has been essential in creating a market for Inuit fine art, Alaska Native fine artists have benefitted from
a state law enacted in 1975 designating 1 percent of capital expen-
ditures on public buildings and facilities to be spent on art to be displayed at those sites. One Percent for Art, as the program is known,
supported acquisition and exhibition of Native art at the Anchorage International Airport, the Maniilaq Health Center in Kotzebue,
3MG Hospital at Elmendorf Air Force Base in Anchorage, and at the
Yukon-Kuskokwim Health Corporation in Bethel, and many other
sites. This has enabled Inupiat and other Alaska Natives to see images of their communities and cultures displayed as fine art in
public buildings around the state. However, contemporary Alaska
Native artists remain marginalized from mainstream art markets
and rarely have "access to audiences outside Alaska [or to] the kind
of critical, complex analysis devoted to other contemporary Native
and non-Native artists."[5] In contrast, contemporary Greenlandic artists participate in global art circles. Julie Edel Hardenberg and Inuk
Silis Høegh both produce work that questions the perceived role of
indigenous artists to guard and interpret traditional culture in the
modern world. One of Hardenberg's installations, entitled "Made In"
(1995), consisted of a series of passport photo self-portraits enacting
different ethnicities in order to challenge assumptions about visual
representation and identity. Høegh, better known for filmmaking
(see Chapter 9), collaborated with Danish artist Asmund Havsteen-

Mikkelsen to create a series of performance artworks called "Melting Baricades," which imagined the invasion of Europe by a Greenlandic army.

Some observers have suggested that printmaking and other contemporary Inuit arts have antecedents in traditional Inuit art forms such as engraved ivory and inlayed and appliquéd decoration on clothing. Such claims, however, seem rooted in a misplaced desire to show that contemporary Inuit commercial arts are authentic traditional Inuit arts. The error is in thinking that authenticity derives from a romanticized and timeless past. For the most part the objects that are recognized today as Inuit art were not part of traditional Inuit material culture, but rather are made explicitly for the market. Significantly, many collectors expect Inuit art to contain materials or symbols that are readily identified with their images of Inuit culture. Many collectors also like to imagine Inuit culture as separate and unchanging. Thus, Inuit arts, like other ethnic arts made for the market, are sometimes disparaged for their commercial qualities.

Inuit and other Native peoples' art made for the tourist market is frequently labeled as mere craft by art experts and not worthy of serious attention. Further, since the forms are often recent innovations rather than items of traditional material culture, others dismiss them as inauthentic. Nonetheless, tourist art is real art as well as an artifact of a living Inuit culture, and thus, reflects genuine Inuit aesthetics and thematic motifs.

NOTES

1. Petersen, Robert (1964) "The Greenland Tupilak," *Folk* 6(2): 73–88.
2. Blackman, Margaret B. (1997) "In Their Own Image: The Anaktuvuk Pass Skin Mask," *American Indian Art Magazine,* Autumn: 58–67.
3. Graburn, Nelson H. H. (1969) *Eskimos without Igloos: Social and Economic Development in Sugluk,* Boston: Little, Brown.
4. Graburn, Nelson (1998) "Weirs in the River of Time: The Development of Historical Consciousness among Canadian Inuit," *Museum Anthropology* 22(1): 24.
5. Biddison, Dawn (2004) "Representing Indigenous Cultures: Alaska Native Contemporary Art Exhibits in Anchorage," *Etudes/Inuit/Studies* 28(1): 39.

11

HEALTH AND MEDICINE

One of the most devastating consequences of the European colonization of North America was the introduction of infectious diseases to indigenous peoples who had no previously acquired immunity. While there is debate about the speed and magnitude of the demographic collapse suffered by Native North Americans, there is no doubt that infectious diseases such as measles, smallpox, diphtheria, tuberculosis, and influenza brought by non-Natives severely reduced and even wiped out entire communities.

With some exceptions, Inuit encounters with non-Natives did not occur until the 18th and 19th centuries and, in some regions, not until the early 20th century. While this did not fully protect Inuit from introduced diseases—diseases often traveled ahead of direct contact with non-Natives—it does mean that the impact of epidemics on Inuit communities is better documented than for Native American communities affected in the 1600s. For example, a missionary-teacher in Point Hope, Alaska, described the devastating effects of an epidemic of bronchopneumonia in the summer of 1894, which sickened three-quarters of the local Inupiat population over a two-month period. "So many people were sick and dying that bodies were left in the streets as a prey to the dogs."[1] The poor state of Inuit health in the postcontact period supported the view, common among American, Canadian, and Danish authorities, that Inuit culture was dying. It also helped establish the incorrect assumption, still widespread, that prior to contacts with whalers, traders, and other non-Natives Inuit were disease-free.

Relatively little is known about the state of Inuit health prior to the arrival of non-Natives. Accounts of the earliest explorers generally describe Inuit as robust and healthy. The cold climate of the Arctic certainly helped reduce the number of disease vectors, and Inuit probably suffered few, if any, infectious diseases. Injuries from accidents were probably the primary causes of premature death. Available data suggest that Inuit had good dental health, and the traditional diet, based on meat, would have protected them from tooth decay.

Diet, and particularly the practice of eating meat raw or fermented, did, however, expose Inuit to several zoonotic infections including trichinosis and botulism. Trichinosis is caused by ingesting roundworms in raw meat. Since the trichinosis-carrying worms can be found in walrus and other sea mammals, the infection was probably quite common prehistorically. Trichinosis can affect eyesight, cause

Man wearing snow goggles, c.1947. (Osborne/NWTArchives/ N-1990-006: 0389)

muscle weakness, and can occasionally lead to death, but these are rare, and most infections cause only mild gastric symptoms. Still, a serious outbreak in Disko Bay in West Greenland in the 1940s, likely caused by eating infected walrus, sickened some 300 people, 33 of whom died.[2] Botulism is much more likely to be fatal, but may have been rare in the past. All of the documented cases come from the late 19th and early 20th centuries, and most involve eating meat from whales or seals that had washed up on shore.

Medical historian Robert Fortuine believes that ancient Inuit may have suffered from a number of chronic conditions including cataracts, arthritis, and earaches. Inuit also experienced snowblindness, a painful, usually temporary, condition caused by overexposure to ultraviolet light. Snow goggles, which Inuit used in springtime when they were most susceptible to the reflection of ultraviolet light on snow, helped to prevent the problem.

TRADITIONAL MEDICINE

Little is also known of the specific ways that Inuit treated illnesses and injuries. In most cases illness, and even accidents and misfortunes, were understood to have a spiritual cause and required a spiritual treatment (see Chapter 7). In those cases *angakkuit* (sing. *angakkuq*) or shamans held séances in order to determine the source of illness and to restore health. "A classic healing ritual consisted of a public shamanic séance with the sick person in the circle, drummers playing and some of the people attending, a number of whom went into trance themselves."[3] The main goal of a healing séance was to require the patient to publicly confess the violations of taboos that had caused the illness (see Chapter 7). Few non-Natives were allowed to witness a shamanic healing séance and those who did were generally more interested in debunking its efficacy than in understanding and describing the practice.

Not all illnesses required the services of a shaman, but could be cured by the application of plant or animal extracts to the affected body part. Information about the healing properties of plant and animal substances was shared among women. Elders interviewed about traditional medicine by students from Nunavut Arctic College indicated that many remedies were worked out by trial and error. "We found out what worked through experimentation. Everybody relies on doctors now. Back then we experimented with different things to find out what was effective."[4] Like traditional herbalists in Western culture, Inuit healers sometimes selected substances for their physical resemblance to the body part to be healed. Inuit also used charms and amulets for protection against illness and injury, as well as to produce desirable qualities in a child.

Inupiat in Alaska treated arthritis, rashes, headaches, and other ailments by lancing the affected area or a nearby joint to remove pus or other substances from the body. Archeological remains indicate that the practice dates to the Thule period (c. 1000 c.e.). This treatment, referred to today as "poking," is still practiced in northwest Alaska, but sometimes only after biomedical treatments fail to cure the problem.

MIDWIFERY

Until quite recently, women were usually assisted in childbirth by other women; however, there are many descriptions of women giving birth while traveling, and assisted only by their husbands. Some women did develop extra knowledge about pregnancy and childbirth and became known for their midwifery skills. Traditional midwives paid particular attention to the positioning of the laboring woman's body. Many different birthing positions were used, but midwives stressed the need to have the body aligned properly in order to speed delivery.

The woman would be positioned so that she was uncomfortable so the baby would come sooner. It was not very often that labour would carry on to the next day. Some would deliver their babies quite quickly. . . . She was not allowed to be comfortable, but the midwife would keep a close eye on the woman in labour. She would make sure her legs were positioned properly. She would make sure her legs were not spread too wide. The midwife would keep the position of the spine in mind, as well as the tail bone.[5]

Fast, easy deliveries were a general concern that permeates both childrearing and the prenatal advice still given to women. Pregnant women were, and still are, told to stay active, to walk constantly, and to resist any urge to be sedentary. Young girls were routinely exhorted to "rise quickly from bed and go outside, never to linger in doorways, and to respond quickly and obediently to the requests of elders" in order to ensure quick and easy labors.[6] It should be noted that Inuit associated long labors with the birth of girls, and many Inuit have a cultural preference for boys.

EPIDEMICS

Diseases brought by explorers, traders, commercial whalers, and even medical personnel created a severe crisis in Inuit communities, and the epidemics that ensued may have been the single most important cause of the changes in Inuit culture and communities that followed contact with non-Natives. A smallpox epidemic in Greenland in 1734 reportedly killed 2,000 people. Influenza killed nearly half the Inupiat population near Barrow in the 1860s and 1870s. Inuit around the Mackenzie River Delta in the western Canadian Arctic suffered an epidemic of scarlet fever (1865) as well as a combined influenza and measles epidemic (1900–2). The influenza pandemic of 1918 was especially severe in Inuit communities. There were outbreaks of polio in the Canadian Arctic and Greenland in the 1940s and 1950s. These are just a few examples. Large numbers of Inuit, in every region of the North, died as a direct consequence of infection by introduced diseases. Population became redistributed and reorganized and concentrated in a smaller number of communities. But epidemics also contributed to demographic collapse indirectly. Survivors, weakened by disease, were often unable to secure sufficient winter food supplies, leading to a second round of deaths by starvation.

Inuit methods of treating illness, especially shamanism, were ineffective against the new diseases. A substantial number of early Christian missionaries were medical doctors, and by providing health care, they insinuated themselves into Inuit communities at a time when Inuit were most vulnerable. The missionaries used the health crisis brought on by the epidemics to wage war on shamanism. Some missionary physicians refused to treat Inuit patients who also sought cures from *angakkuit*. "The missionaries viewed the struggle [against shamanism] as a spiritual, not a medical one, but an important effect was that Christianity and shamanistic healing could not comfortably coexist."[7]

Many of the epidemic diseases that afflicted Inuit were rapid, acute infectious ones and caused severe mortality, but the population of most Inuit communities was too small and dispersed to provide a reservoir for continuous infection. Tuberculosis, syphilis, and gonorrhea, on the other hand, while also highly infectious, develop slowly, and thus became major causes of chronic poor health for Inuit. Tuberculosis was probably the most significant cause of illness and premature death for Inuit in the 20th century. In the 1950s Greenlanders and Inupiat had mortality rates from the disease up to 30 times higher than the national averages in Denmark and the United States, respectively. In Canada the disparity in tuberculosis death rates between Inuit and the rest of the population may have been even higher.

Prior to World War II there were very few medical facilities serving Inuit in the North. The exception was Greenland, where health services were established in every district by 1925. In the Canadian Arctic the government generally ignored questions about Inuit health. There were mission hospitals in Pangnirtung, Chesterfield Inlet, Aklavik, and in Labrador, but for the most part Inuit in Canada were left without access to biomedical health care.

Antibiotics effective in the treatment of tuberculosis were developed in the late 1940s, and in the 1950s northern administrators initiated programs to eradicate the disease among Inuit. In all three countries, the eradication program involved X-ray screenings followed by evacuation of those with active infections to hospitals outside the North. Greenlanders were evacuated to Denmark until 1959. The TB screening program in the Canadian North was especially problematic for its lack of sensitivity to basic human rights. Between 1950 and 1969, the Coast Guard ship *C.D. Howe* sailed to Inuit communities in the central and eastern Canadian Arctic, stopping usually for no more than a day. Inuit were given chest X-rays aboard ship, and no one found to be infected was permitted to disembark even to gather clothing or bid their loved ones goodbye. According to Robert Williamson, a northern administrator turned anthropologist,

The ship was deep in misery. It was terrible because it was the ship which carried the Inuit away from their homes to the sanatoria in the south. And they were herded together in the foc'sle, in the hold of the ship in three-tiered bunks, mass-fed, mass-accommodated. In the stormy seas they were sick, they were terrified, they were demoralized. They were frightened of what was happening to them, of what was likely to happen to them.[8]

Patients could be gone for many years, with little or no contact from their families and little understanding of the medical procedures being performed. Children were evacuated without a parent and sometimes returned home unable to speak Inuktitut. Others' records were lost, and they did not go home at all. Inuit who died in hospital were buried there, and oftentimes no notice was given to their kin. In 1956 one out of every seven Canadian Inuit was in a TB sanatorium in southern Canada.[9] But the program was effective. New infections were contained and the tuberculosis hospitals closed by the early

1970s. Still, however, some Inuit avoid seeking medical treatment as a result of the trauma they experienced from TB treatment.

HEALTH TRANSITIONS

Vaccination and development of effective treatments have brought many infectious diseases under control in Inuit communities across the North. Decreases in overall and infant mortality rates have contributed to an increase in life expectancy. But like other minority communities, contemporary Inuit face a number of health challenges related to poverty, poor access to care, and cultural difference. Differences in data collection and reporting make comparisons between regions difficult, but Inuit continue to lag behind the majority populations in Denmark, Canada, and the United States in widely used indicators of health status.

With the decrease in mortality Inuit have experienced health transitions similar to other peoples. What this means is that infectious diseases are no longer the primary causes of death. These have been replaced by diseases, such as heart disease and Type 2 diabetes, that are linked to smoking, obesity, and a sedentary lifestyle and by diseases, like cancer, that are most common in aging populations. Accidents and suicides also account for a disproportionate number of deaths, especially among young Inuit throughout the North.

Substance abuse, especially of alcohol, is another serious health problem in Inuit communities, and contributes to high rates of accidents, suicide, and domestic violence. For many years, Inuit did not have the power to control the sales and distribution of alcohol in the North. Government policies in the Canadian North, for example, publically discouraged making alcohol available to Inuit, while in practice the policies often encouraged unhealthy and binge drinking. In several places in the Canadian North, Inuit community leaders' petitions to limit deliveries of alcohol were ignored. At present municipalities in Alaska and the Canadian Arctic can enact local alcohol availability policies. Many have chosen to ban alcohol completely. This has worked to reduce alcohol-related injuries in a number of places, but in others it has resulted in bootlegging and other forms of illegal substance abuse.

FOOD SECURITY

Diet and nutrition are essential components of good physical and good mental health. Thus, any discussion of health must take food security, or the ability to procure safe and healthy food, into consideration. Food security is more than preventing hunger or malnutrition, but entails the ability to obtain "adequate amounts of safe, nutritious, culturally acceptable food . . . in a dignified and affordable manner."[10] Inuit diets changed considerably as a result of contact with non-Natives and transition to a cash economy (see Chapter 3), and today contain both traditional Inuit or country foods and commercial or market foods.

The Arctic ecosystem contains relatively few plant foods and these are available for only a few weeks in summer. Thus, while there was regional variation, the traditional Inuit diet consisted almost entirely of animal flesh. Sea mammals, especially seal, walrus, and whale, were especially important to Inuit in many parts of the North. Contrary to what might be expected, the traditional Inuit diet of meat was a healthy diet that provided all of the vitamins and micronutrients required. It was low in sugars and saturated fats and high in protein. Because country foods were eaten raw, frozen, or very lightly cooked, they retained their vitamins and micronutrients. In fact, traditional Inuit communities had no history of the vitamin deficiency diseases such as scurvy or rickets that affected peoples with grain-based diets. These diseases were well documented among Arctic explorers and commercial whalers, and were only avoided when these groups added Inuit foods to their diets.

While non-Natives in the Arctic learned to survive by eating Inuit foods, Inuit developed a taste for the commercial foods brought by the visitors. At first these consisted of a relatively limited number of market foods, notably sugar, jam, flour, and tea. But as Inuit throughout the North became more enmeshed in a cash economy and had access to more market foods, these were added to the diet. Market foods are appealing to Inuit for the same reasons that they appeal to non-Native peoples: taste and convenience.

Many, if not most, Inuit continue to consume traditional foods in traditional ways, but they also use country foods in new ways as components of stews and other prepared dishes. Consequently, country foods comprise a much smaller proportion of the diet than at any time in the past. Also, with the addition of market foods, many Inuit are able to limit their consumption of country foods to those they like best. Consequently, Inuit today consume fewer species of animals than was necessary in the past.

Inuit regard food as directly tied to health, and country foods are "still highly valued for their taste, freshness, substance, and economy. While people depend heavily upon store-bought food, many

Country food market, Nuuk, Greenland, 2008. (Photo by Peter V. Hall)

report that it is not as satisfactory since it 'has no blood' and therefore 'makes you hungry right away.'"[11] For example, Inupiat in Kotzebue note that foods available in the store are "riddled with additives and preservatives" and believe that eating them weakens the blood and makes people susceptible to illness.[12] And young and old residents of Clyde River, Nunavut, told anthropologist Kristen Borré that sharing and consuming Inuit foods, especially seal meat, "creates a healthy human body and soul" and thus, protects Inuit from physical and mental illness.[13] The emotional and existential value of eating seal is reflected in statements made to Borré by many residents of Clyde River. For example,

Seal blood is in all Inuit who [were raised] eating animals. Seal blood gives us our blood. Seal is life-giving.[14]

Hunting is time-consuming and modern hunting equipment is expensive, so that Northerners with wage labor jobs may find it difficult to make time for hunting, while those without jobs may lack

Imported fruit in a Nuuk supermarket, 2008. (Photo by Peter V. Hall)

the necessary tools (see Chapter 3). Arctic residents without the means or ability to obtain food from hunting may find it extremely difficult to purchase a nutritious diet. Stores in the largest communities, such as Barrow, Alaska, Iqaluit, Nunavut, and Nuuk, Greenland, stock a variety of fresh and frozen meats and produce. Transportation costs and monopoly pricing, however, make food shopping expensive. In small and remote communities the selection of locally available market foods is often extremely limited. Dietary surveys indicate that low-quality market foods like soft drinks, frozen pizza, and potato chips comprise a large proportion of the calories eaten, especially by young Inuit, increasing the incidence of obesity, Type-2 diabetes, tooth decay, and other diet-related illnesses. To counteract this, the Canadian government created a Food Mail Program to subsidize the delivery of nutritious, high-quality perishable and staple foods from southern suppliers to northern communities. Though the program improves access to more nutritious market foods, there are some suggestions that the subsidies may encourage Inuit and other Northerners to incorporate more market foods in their daily consumption if those are less expensive than hunting.

Greenlanders have long been able to purchase country foods at supermarkets or from a *kalaalimineerniarfik* (outdoor market stall), but these kinds of markets for country foods do not exist in Alaska or the Canadian Arctic. Sharing, especially within extended families, continues to be the primary way that country foods are distributed in Canadian and Alaskan Inuit communities, and helps to ensure access to nutritious foods (see Chapter 3).

In recent years there have been questions regarding the safety of northern country foods, many of which are contaminated by methylmercury, cadmium, lead, and other heavy metals as well as industrial chemicals and pesticide residues known as persistent organic pollutants (POPs). In almost all cases these contaminants originate outside the Arctic, are transported there on air currents, and the Arctic becomes a sink for pollutants.

POPs in the Arctic environment, including polychlorinated biphenyls (PCBs) and DDT, and heavy metals are a particular threat to human health because they are stored in the fat tissues of animals and are thus passed up the food chain. They are also transmitted to human fetuses in utero and to breast-fed infants. Fish and marine mammals, which still compose a substantial part of the Inuit diet, are especially prone to contamination from POPs.

High levels of POPs in the breast milk of Inuit women were first identified in the 1980s. Researchers from Laval University in Quebec City working with the Kativik Regional Board of Health found that the breast milk of Inuit mothers in Nunavik had levels of PCBs more than five times higher than two comparison groups of non-Native mothers in regions of southern Quebec.[15] Following these and other studies, Canadian Inuit took the lead in the development and adoption of an international treaty banning the use of some POPs (see Chapter 12).

Contaminants in food are a problem for human health because they can affect children's motor and mental development, can lower immunity to infections, and may affect the endocrine system in ways that cause problems for growth and sexual development. In adults heavy metals are thought to contribute to heart disease and several cancers. It is difficult to know, however, exactly what levels of exposure to these food contaminants are dangerous.

The presence of contaminants in northern country foods creates a public health dilemma. Should Inuit limit their intake of nutrient-rich country foods in order to avoid ingesting POPs and heavy metals? Or should they limit their intake of market foods, especially given that the imported foods available in most Arctic communities are generally higher in fat, sugars, carbohydrates, and calories and low in proteins, essential micronutrients, and other important components for human nutrition? The relationship between diet and health is complex. The traditional reliance on fish and marine mammals, which are high in n-3 fatty acids, was thought to protect Inuit from heart disease and other circulatory disorders. Recent research, however, has questioned this assumption as data on the past incidence of heart disease are poor. Other factors such as cigarette smoking, obesity, and reduced physical activity appear to contribute to cardiovascular disease incidences among Inuit similar to the national rates in the United States, Canada, and Denmark.

While there seems to be some evidence that the micronutrients in country foods "interact with heavy metals and modulate toxicity,"[16] worry about ingesting contaminants may cause some Inuit to choose to eat more market foods or to feed those to their children. As noted above, the market foods available in most Inuit communities tend to be less nutritious and higher in saturated fats and sugars than country foods. This is true even of the so-called better foods subsidized by the Canadian Food Mail Program. As well, eating—and the hunting, sharing, and preparation that precede it—is a social and cultural activity. Diets based on market foods do not provide many Inuit with the same emotional well-being as diets containing country food.

ACCESS TO CARE

Access to health care is much better today than in previous periods, but the remoteness of most Inuit communities as well as language and/or cultural differences between patients and the overwhelming majority of doctors and nurses in the North remain obstacles to good health care. Shortages of medical professionals and high turnover among non-Native medical personnel means that patients rarely have an opportunity to develop relationships of trust and confidence with their providers.

Greenland is divided into health districts, each with a clinic or small hospital and a dental clinic, staffed by medical officers. Doctors make regular, brief visits to villages in the districts, but many villages have a health aide as the only resident medical staff. Advanced diagnostic and specialist care are available in Nuuk or Denmark, though specialists do make scheduled visits to regional hospitals. Nonetheless, distance to clinics is a problem for both patients and their families from villages, especially cases where patients have serious illnesses as villagers "are usually unable to travel easily and cheaply to visit loved ones in hospital. They also feel constrained by their inability [because of language differences] to deal directly with the doctor."[17]

Alaska Natives receive health care from the Indian Health Service (IHS), which is part of the U.S. Public Health Service. The IHS contracts with tribal organizations and regional nonprofit Native corporations to provide services in each region of the state. This nominally local control, however, does not translate into cultural sensitivity on the part of non-Native doctors and nurses.[18] There are small hospitals in regional centers like Barrow and Kotzebue, but patients who need specialized care travel to Anchorage, Fairbanks, or even Seattle. The Alaska Native Medical Center in Anchorage treats indigenous patients. Villages are served by health aides, and in some places traditional healers are employed as "tribal doctors." In the Northwest Arctic Borough, the village clinics are connected via video to the hospital in Kotzebue, eliminating the need for some medivacs.

Health care in Canada is the responsibility of provincial and territorial governments. Each community in the Canadian Arctic has a health center staffed by nurse-practitioners who are the primary care providers. As in Greenland, physicians make regular scheduled visits to communities, but most patients who require diagnostic, specialist, or even hospital services must fly to a regional center or to a

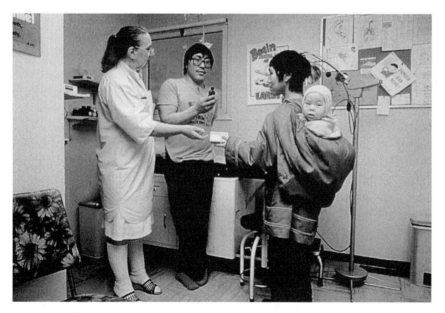

Nurse and patients at Pelly Bay, Nunavut Health Centre, 1981. (Photo by Bob Wilson, PW&S/NWT Archives/G-1995-001: 1297)

city in southern Canada. Also as in Greenland, patients and their families find the travel and the language and cultural differences to be an added source of stress.

Beginning in the mid-1970s, pregnant Canadian Inuit women were required to deliver their babies in southern hospitals. In general, this meant that women were evacuated approximately two weeks prior to their expected due dates, and had to leave their partners, their families, and often young children behind for an indefinite period of time. The experience was often one of loneliness, boredom, and worry. In a number of places in the Canadian North, Inuit have fought to bring childbirth back to their communities and to involve Inuit midwives in labor and delivery. In 1986, Inuit in Nunavik established a midwifery training program and birthing center in Puvirnituq, which combines Inuit and southern midwifery practices. The success of the program enabled additional birthing centers to open in Inukjuak in 1998 and in Salluit in 2004. There are plans to open a fourth maternity center in Kuujuaq. The three currently operating Inuulitsivik Maternities serve the seven Inuit communities on the coasts of Hudson Bay and Hudson Strait. Eighty percent of births to women from Hudson coast communities between 1986 and 2005 occurred in one of these birthing centers, allowing Inuit there to reclaim control of an important social institution.

There is also a birthing center in Rankin Inlet, Nunavut, but the protocols used there for determining risk result in far more evacuations than occur in the Nunavik maternity centers.[19] Advocating for Inuit-led childbirth is political as well as medical, and Pauktuutit/ Inuit Women's Association in Canada has been active in this aspect of self-determination. To support its goals, in the 1990s, it conducted interviews with dozens of Inuit women to document birthing experiences and traditional midwifery.

Health care is essential to an individual's and a community's sense of power over their own lives, and is an area that Inuit are working to exert more control. The observations of Peter Bjerregaard and Thomas Stensgaard regarding the health care system in Greenland could be extended to the entire Inuit region substituting only the names of the countries and the languages.

It is a system created by Danes and staffed by Danes who are trained in a Danish framework. While both the Danish and Greenlandic languages are used in the health care system, all record keeping is done in Danish. It is a recurrent topic of discussion, when speaking of how Greenland is run and administered, that there is a wish for a more Greenlandic and less Danish way of doing things.[20]

NOTES

1. Quoted in Fortuine, Robert (1989) *Chills and Fever: Health and Disease in the Early History of Alaska,* Fairbanks: University of Alaska Press, 211.

2. Fortuine, Robert (1961) "Current Status of Animal-Borne Diseases among the Eskimos," *Canadian Journal of Comparative Medicine and Veterinary Sciences* 25: 185–89.

3. Turner, Edith (1989) "From Shamans to Healers: The Survival of an Inupiaq Eskimo Skill," *Anthropologica* 31: 5.

4. Jayko Pitseolak quoted in Joamie, Alacie, Akisu Joamie, Jayko Pitseolak, Malaya Papatsie, Elisapee Ootoova, and Tirisi Attagutsiak (2001) *Interviewing Inuit Elders: Perspectives on Traditional Health,* Frederic Laugrand and Michelle Therrien, eds., Iqaluit: Nunavut Arctic College, 209.

5. Elisapee Ootoova quoted in Joamie et al., *Interviewing Inuit Elders,* 28.

6. Stern, Pamela R., and Richard G. Condon (1995) "Puberty, Pregnancy, and Menopause: Lifecycle Acculturation in a Copper Inuit Community," *Arctic Medical Research* 54: 25.

7. Fortuine, *Chills and Fever,* 192.

8. Robert Williamson quoted in Grygier, Pat Sandiford (1994) *A Long Way from Home: The Tuberculosis Epidemic among the Inuit,* Montreal: McGill-Queens University Press, 87.

9. Ibid., xxi.

10. Myers, Heather, Stephanie Powell, and Gerard Duhaime (2004) "Setting the Table for Food Security: Policy Impacts in Nunavut," *Canadian Journal of Native Studies* 24(2): 426.

11. Condon, Richard G., Peter Collings, and George Wenzel (1995) "The Best Part of Life: Subsistence Hunting, Ethnicity, and Economic Adaptation among Young Adult Inuit Males," *Arctic* 48(1): 42.

12. Cassady, Joslyn (2008) "'Eating for Outsiders': Cancer Causation Discourse among the Iñupiat of Arctic Alaska," *International Journal of Circumpolar Health* 67(4): 380.

13. Borré, Kristen (1991) "Seal Blood, Inuit Blood, and Diet: A Biocultural Model of Physiology and Cultural Identity," *Medical Anthropology Quarterly* 5(1): 53.

14. Elderly hunter quoted in Borré, "Seal Blood, Inuit Blood, and Diet," 54.

15. Dewailly, Eric, Albert Nantel, Jean-P. Weber, and François Meyer (1989) "High Levels of PCBs in Breast Milk of Inuit Women from Arctic Quebec," *Bulletin of Environmental Contaminations and Toxicology* 43: 641–46; Dewailly, E., A. Nantel, S. Bruneau, C. Laliberté, L. Ferron, and S. Gingras

(1992) "Breast Milk Contamination in PCDDs, PCDFs and PCBs in Arctic Quebec: A Preliminary Assessment," *Chemosphere* 25(7–10): 1245–49.

16. Kuhnlein, H. V., and H. M. Chan (2000) "Environment and Contaminants in Traditional Food Systems of Northern Indigenous Peoples," *Annual Review of Nutrition* 20: 604.

17. Nuttall, Mark (1992) *Arctic Homeland: Kinship, Community and Development in Northwest Greenland,* London: Belhaven Press, 105.

18. Cassady, "Eating for Outsiders."

19. Douglas, Vasiliki K. (2006) "Childbirth among the Canadian Inuit: A Review of the Clinical and Cultural Literature," *International Journal of Circumpolar Health* 65(2): 128.

20. Bjerregaard, Peter, and Thomas Stensgaard (2008) "Greenland," in *Health Transitions in Arctic Populations,* T. Kue Young and Peter Bjerregaard, eds., Toronto: University of Toronto Press, 36.

12

INUIT IN INTERNATIONAL POLITICAL ARENAS

Prior to World War II, Inuit traveled freely across international borders and maintained relationships with Inuit and other indigenous peoples in distant communities. Pre-20th-century trade fairs are one notable example of this (see Chapter 6). Inuit are renowned travelers, and there are many examples of individuals and small groups who covered long distances to trade or to explore. World War II, and the subsequent Cold War, subjected Inuit to the borders erected by national governments, but in recent years Inuit individuals and organizations have pursued multiple means to break down barriers imposed by national governments and to engage in a new internationalism.

INUIT-LED GOVERNMENTS AS INTERNATIONAL ACTORS

As discussed in Chapter 6, Inuit in every region of the North American Arctic have achieved some level of local self-government, but as far as international law is concerned Inuit-led governments do not have the status of sovereign nations. Thus, they cannot conclude treaties with foreign governments or in engage in unilateral diplomatic activities. Under international law, their jurisdiction over international affairs is limited to the authority granted them by treaties or other international documents signed by the United States, Canada, or Denmark. Nonetheless, Inuit and other northern residents often have interests in or concerns about international matters that differ from the interests of their national governments. For example, Greenlanders strongly objected to joining the European Economic Community (EC) as part of Denmark. Denmark's 1972 referendum on membership in the EC passed overwhelmingly despite the fact that more than 70 percent of Greenlanders voted against the measure.[1]

Greenlanders did benefit from EC membership in that the European countries invested between $10 and $25 million a year in Greenland for infrastructure and education. Nonetheless, Greenlanders felt disadvantaged by the EC's control over fishing quotas. According to former Prime Minister Lars Emil Johansen, Greenlanders found it "unfair and humiliating that Greenlandic politicians had to go to Brussels to bargain with the EC about the right of local fishermen to catch cod and shrimp off their own coastline."[2] In addition, Greenlanders accused Germany of fishing illegally in Greenlandic waters. Once Greenland achieved Home Rule (see Chapter 6), it was able to withdraw from the EC, which it did in 1985. Since that time, the European Union (EU), as the EC is now known, has paid an annual fee to the Home Rule government for fishing rights along Greenland's coast. In 1992, Greenland opened a diplomatic office in Brussels, where the EU is headquartered, and in the last few years some in Greenland have suggested that they rejoin the EU.

In the 1970s and 1980s, Greenlanders felt culturally distant from Europe, and that likely also played a part in their desire to withdraw from the EC. Nonetheless, their agreements with the EU have never referenced Greenlanders' status as an indigenous people. That contrasts with the relationship both Greenlanders and Inupiat have with another international body, the International Whaling Commission (IWC).

In the late 19th and very early 20th centuries, overhunting by commercial whalers severely threatened whale stocks. In 1948, the International Whaling Commission was created to regulate commercial whaling, but prior to 1977 it did not concern itself with indigenous whaling. In 1977, the IWC became concerned that the population of bowhead whales was dangerously low and that Inupiat whalers were striking, but not landing, too many whales. As a result it moved to ban indigenous subsistence hunts of bowhead whales.

Inupiat and Yupik whalers disputed the IWC's scientific data. Furthermore, they argued that the IWC had not considered the economic, social, and cultural benefits that whaling conveys to Inupiat and

Yupik communities. With financial support from the North Slope Borough, they formed the Alaska Eskimo Whaling Commission (AEWC) and undertook their own scientific studies of bowhead whale populations. As a result, the IWC and the AEWC developed a new protocol for managing subsistence whale hunting that does take into account that Inupiat are an indigenous people engaging in a traditional activity (see Chapter 3). The hunt remains closely managed, and AEWC receives an annual quota for strikes and kills, but it, rather than any other agency, makes the decisions about how the quota is allocated among whaling communities. The AEWC also participates in IWC meetings as part of the U.S. delegation. Greenlanders' whaling activities are also regulated by the IWC, which in 1985 decided to cut Greenland's quota for minke whales in half and forbid the hunting of humpback whales. However, in both places, the IWC does sanction whaling only because it accepts that it is of tremendous social and cultural value to Inuit. The nonindigenous communities in Iceland, Norway, and Japan that also engage in small-scale subsistence whaling do so in defiance of the IWC.

INUIT CIRCUMPOLAR COUNCIL

The year 1977 is an important date in the history of Inuit international affairs. Inuit from Greenland, Canada, and Alaska met in Barrow, Alaska, to establish the Inuit Circumpolar Conference (ICC). It was the first international gathering of Inuit from across the North, and built on some of the ideas generated by the Arctic Peoples Conference held in Copenhagen in 1973. Although the Arctic Peoples Conference attendees resolved to create an organization of circumpolar peoples, that did not happen. The establishment of the Inuit Circumpolar Conference as the international political body for Inuit was the vision of Eben Hopson, who was then mayor of Alaska's North Slope Borough. Delegates from Alaska, Canada, and Greenland attended a pre-Conference agenda-setting meeting in Barrow in March 1976, and the first assembly of the Inuit Circumpolar Conference occurred in June of the following year. Hopson hoped that delegates from the Soviet Union would also participate in the meeting, but invitations extended through the Soviet embassies in Copenhagen and Washington, D.C., were not acknowledged. The Lilly Foundation provided the funding for both meetings.

While the aims behind establishment of the Inuit Circumpolar Conference were wide-ranging and concerned issues of self-determination and indigenous rights generally, as well as language and culture, communications, education, and energy resource development, it was this last subject that provided the specific impetus for the meeting. The discovery of oil at Prudhoe Bay had led to construction of the Trans-Alaska Pipeline and had spurred further exploration for oil and gas on and offshore, including in the Beaufort Sea adjacent to the North Slope Borough. At the time the relationship between Inupiat in the North Slope Borough and oil companies could only be characterized as one of tension and distrust. In particular, Hopson and other Inupiat were anxious to prevent offshore drilling for oil, which they believed posed a serious threat to bowhead whaling. Hopson signaled this in his welcoming speech to the delegates:

Our language contains the memory of four thousand years of human survival through conservation and good managing of Arctic wealth. Ours is the language of the very environment that challenges the environmental safety of existing offshore technology. Our language contains the intricate knowledge of the ice that we have seen no others demonstrate. Without our central involvement, there can be no safe and responsible resource development.[3]

Hopson laid the groundwork for the ICC's subsequent engagement in all spheres of international environmental policy, so that today Inuit are recognized as "legitimate political stewards of the Arctic ecosystem."[4]

The first General Assembly passed 17 resolutions concerning specific and general matters of self-determination, citizenship, land claims, subsistence hunting, and resource management. Of these, the first resolution established the Inuit Circumpolar Conference as the "international organization of Inuit to study, discuss, represent, lobby and protect our interests on the international level."[5] It set forth guiding principles and established the procedures for its creation as an enduring institution. Finally, it elected a committee of men only, to take the organization forward.

Hans-Pavia Rosing, from Greenland, was elected as the first president of the ICC at the second General Assembly held in Nuuk, Greenland, in 1980. He was reelected to a second three-year term at the third assembly in Iqaluit, Nunavut, in 1983, resigning in 1986 to become the Greenland Home Rule minister of economic affairs. Rosing was replaced by Canadian Inuk Mary Simon. She was formally elected at the General Assembly held later that year in Kotzebue and reelected at the next meeting in 1989 in Sisimiut, Greenland. Meeting in Inuvik, Northwest Territories, Canada, in 1992, the General Assembly selected Eileen P. MacLean (1949–93) of Barrow as its president, but she

1992 General Assembly, Inuit Circumpolar Conference, Inuvik, NWT. (Photo by Tessa Macintosh, PW&S/NWT Archives/G-1995-001: 7757)

was forced to resign due to illness. MacLean was succeeded by Caleb Pungowiyi, a Yupik Eskimo from St. Lawrence Island, Alaska. The next General Assembly was held in Nome, Alaska, in 1995 and Canadian Inuk Rosemarie Kuptana was selected to be the ICC president. She served until 1996, and was replaced in 1997 by Greenlandic poet and politician Aqqaluk Lynge. The General Assembly met in Nuuk in 1998 and elected Lynge to a full, now four-year term. At the 2002 General Assembly in Kuujjuaq, the ICC reorganized so that Inuit from each participating country were to choose a national president. Sheila Watt-Cloutier from Canada was selected to be the chair of the ICC Executive Council, which also includes the four national presidents who serve as vice-chairs and an additional member from each country. Patricia Cochrane from Nome, Alaska, was selected the ICC chair in 2006. In June 2009 the Executive Council named James (Jimmy) Stotts, an Inupiaq from Barrow, to replace Cochrane who had resigned.

From its beginning, the ICC has served as a vehicle for Inuit in one country to engage in political debate in another nation, using their status as the nongovernmental organization representing Inuit internationally as a basis for their intervention. For example, in 1982 the Inuit Circumpolar Conference coordinated testimony of Greenlanders before Canada's National Energy Board opposing the shipping of liquefied natural gas in Arctic waters. In another example, Inupiat from Alaska took a position in support of Nunavik Inuit and opposed Quebec's possible succession from Canada.

The ICC along with the World Council of Indigenous Peoples commissioned Canadian Justice Thomas R. Berger to conduct a review of the Alaska Native Claims Settlement Act (ANCSA) (see Chapter 6). In 1984 and 1985 Berger conducted a series of community hearings and roundtable discussions, known as the Alaska Native Review Commission. The ICC selected Berger because of his previous experience conducting hearings for the Canadian government on the proposed Mackenzie Valley Pipeline. Berger's findings and recommendations were published as *Village Journey*. Berger was highly critical of the ANCSA particularly for its failure to protect Alaska Native peoples' rights to subsistence hunting, fishing, and collecting and for the absence of any provision in the ANCSA that would prevent loss of traditional lands. According to Berger,

For Alaska Natives, the loss of their lands would be catastrophic. The severance of ties with traditional life and the foreclosure of any possibility that the villages might achieve a greater measure of self-sufficiency would have serious implications for non-Native Alaskans, as well. Without its Native villages, without the subsistence way of life, Alaska would not be Alaska.[6]

To prevent the potential loss of Alaska Natives' land through sale or bankruptcy, Berger recommended reestablishing and strengthening tribal governments and the transfer of land title from the Native corporations to the tribes.

The ICC describes its principal goals as:

- strengthen unity among Inuit of the circumpolar region;
- promote Inuit rights and interests on an international level;
- develop and encourage long-term policies that safeguard the Arctic environment; and
- seek full and active partnership in the political, economic, and social development of circumpolar regions (http://www.inuitcircum polar.com).

It has pursued these goals in an incremental, but substantial, way. In support of Inuit subsistence rights the ICC began sending a representative to the meetings of International Whaling Commission in 1980. Its primary authority to speak and act on behalf of Inuit throughout the North comes from its recognition, since 1983, as an official nongovernmental organization (NGO) within the United Nations (UN). This designation gives the ICC consultative status within the United Nations Economic and Social Council (ECOSOC). The ICC became especially active in the UN Working Group of the Rights of Indigenous Peoples, a division of the ECOSOC, and participated in drafting the United Nations Declaration on the Rights of Indigenous Peoples.

United Nations Declaration on the Rights of Indigenous Peoples

On September 13, 2007, after 25 years of diplomatic work, the UN General Assembly adopted the Declaration on the Rights of Indigenous Peoples. Only four member nations, Canada, the United States, Australia, and New Zealand, voted against the resolution. Despite the objections of these four nations, the Declaration is, in fact, the international community's statement affirming that all indigenous peoples have fundamental rights to their cultures and languages, health and security. The ICC "sees itself as being at the vanguard of indigenous rights generally, especially with regard to self-determination."[7] Early drafts of the Declaration did not contain references to the rights of indigenous peoples to self-determination, or their right to agree on their relationship with national governments, or the right to agree to the development of resources on their lands. The Inuit organization was particularly active in assuring that the final declaration contained language affirming indigenous peoples' right to self-determination, or the right to "freely determine their political status and freely pursue their economic, social and cultural development"[8] and to develop governments that reflect their particular distinct cultural values.

Siberian Peoples

Prior to the 1983 ICC General Assembly in Iqaluit, Canadian Inuit John Amagoalik and Peter Ittinuar, who was also a Member of Parliament, made overtures to the Soviet Ambassador to Canada hoping to gain permission for some Siberians to attend the meeting. They were told that their "attempts were repugnant to Soviet policy,"[9] and it was several more years before any Siberians were allowed to participate. The ICC responded by creating an empty seat for the Russians and continuing to press for them to attend. Delegates from Russia were permitted to attend as observers in 1989, in part as a result of ongoing lobbying efforts to the Soviets by Aqqaluk Lynge. With the end of the Cold War and the dissolution of the Soviet Union, Russian Yupik became full members of the ICC in 1993.

The dissolution of the Soviet Union, however, created a difficult economic situation in Siberian indigenous communities. The situation was particularly desperate in Chukotka, where the governor, Alexander Nazarov, was especially hostile to indigenous peoples. There were profound shortages of food, heating oil, and other basic supplies. In their reports to the 1998 General Assembly, representatives of the ICC for Russia reported that between 1992–97 mortalities of Yupik in Chukotka may have been as high as 20 percent of the population as a direct result of the economic, social, and environmental collapse.[10]

The various national offices of the ICC and other Inuit organizations responded to the humanitarian crisis in Chukotka. ICC-Canada worked directly with other NGOs and officials of the Canadian government to deliver emergency food aid and blankets to people living in three Yupik communities in December 1998. Governor Nazarov was replaced by Roman Abramovich in December 2000. As a result, in the summer of 2001, the ICC was able to negotiate a Memorandum of Cooperation for the ICC to engage in development work and capacity-building in Chukotka.

Arctic Council

The ICC has been active on a number of other diplomatic fronts. In 1991, it organized a summit of Arctic indigenous leaders, which by leading the way for international collaboration in the Arctic, served as a precursor to the 1996 establishment of the Arctic Council. The Arctic Council is a nonbinding, multilateral forum where the eight Arctic nations (Canada, Iceland, Denmark, Norway, Sweden, Finland, Russia, and the United States) meet to discuss matters of shared concern. The Arctic Council, through its working groups, has supported substantial research on environmental and sustainability issues. The ICC and five other indigenous NGOs are permanent participants in the Arctic Council, and former ICC President, Mary Simon, served as Canada's first ambassador to the Arctic Council.

Environmental Initiatives

The ICC has long insisted that Inuit, as subsistence users, are the best stewards of the Arctic ecosystem. In 1986 it developed the Inuit Regional Conservation Strategy (IRCS), which explicitly joined the issues of environmental protection with sustainable development. The IRCS was the first truly regional conservation strategy, and was unique at the time by promoting the recognition of indigenous knowledge in the creation of environmental policy and conduct of environmental management. A driving motivation was the protection of Inuit culture and subsistence activities through continued ability to engage in hunting and fishing. The IRCS was awarded a Global 500 award from the United Nations Environmental Programme in 1998.

The ICC actively participated in the Earth Summit held in Rio de Janeiro in June 1992 as well as in the 2002 World Summit on Sustainable Development (sometimes referred to as "Rio plus 10") in Johannesburg, South Africa.

In her role as president of ICC-Canada, Sheila Watt-Cloutier was part of the Canadian delegation that negotiated an international treaty to reduce and eliminate persistent organic pollutants (POPs) such as DDT, PCBs, and dioxins from the environment. These chemicals and their residues are transported by air currents and concentrate in the Arctic, where they become part of the human food chain and contaminate breast milk (see Chapter 11). One of the dilemmas faced by negotiators concerned DDT, a pesticide long banned in North America, but still used to combat malaria-carrying mosquitoes in parts of Africa. Watt-Cloutier specifically addressed this in her speeches to the delegates.

I stated in my speech "I cannot believe that a mother in the Arctic should have to worry about contaminants in the life-giving milk she feeds her infant. Nor can I believe that a mother in the South has to use these very chemicals to protect her babies from disease. Surely we must commit ourselves to finding and using alternatives. While adopting elimination, not perpetual management, as an ultimate goal, the POPs convention must simultaneously ensure that cost-effective alternatives, particularly for DDT, are made available in the developing world." I also reminded delegates of what I said in Montreal on the first session: that a "poisoned Inuk child, a poisoned Arctic, and a poisoned planet are all one in the same," and that we were all in this together.[11]

The legally binding agreement, known as the Stockholm Convention on Persistent Organic Pollutants, was adopted in 2001 and was signed by more than 120 nations, including Canada and the United States. It was the first global agreement that specifically referenced the Circumpolar Arctic and Arctic indigenous peoples. The ICC's involvement played a critical role in this. As one of the technical advisors noted, the success in influencing the debate on POPs led to Inuit being regarded as credible participants in more recent climate change debates. "There is every reason to believe that Arctic voices and Arctic perspectives can help persuade global decision-makers to strengthen their commitments to reduce emissions of greenhouse gases that most scientists believe is at least a contributing cause of current climate change."[12]

The Right to Be Cold

The warming of the Earth is accelerating. This is most apparent in the Arctic where, in the past 100 years, average temperatures have increased at almost twice the average global rate. In parts of the Inuit North average temperatures have risen as much as 3.5°C just since 1970.[13] For Inuit and other Arctic residents, global warming has had wide-ranging social, cultural, and economic consequences. As just a few examples, winter storms are causing severe coastal erosion in areas of coastal northwest Alaska and will require that a number of Inupiat communities be relocated. In winters past, the coastline was protected from erosion by landfast sea ice. Thinning of sea ice and longer annual periods without ice have also made ocean travel by hunters dangerous and unpredictable. At the same time reductions of ice are endangering the survival of many animal species that Inuit rely on, and making it more feasible for governments and corporations to consider mining and oil exploration on Inuit lands and near Inuit communities.

On land, permafrost is melting in many parts of the Arctic, changing the configuration of streams and lakes and causing erosion and slumping. Just as traditional Inuit architecture (see Chapter 5) was engineered to use the climatically induced features of the Arctic environment, contemporary Arctic infrastructure such as houses, roads, and airport runways have all been engineered to take advantage of the stability of permanently frozen ground. As this disappears, costly infrastructure is becoming damaged and lost. While Inuit are concerned that global warming will threaten subsistence uses of their lands, they are equally concerned that the totality of effects will erode their rights to self-determination.

The ICC has been especially effective in communicating the serious threats that global warming poses. For example, in 2004, Canadian Sheila Watt-Cloutier, who was then the international chair of the ICC, testified to the effects of global climate change on Inuit communities before the U.S. Senate Committee on Commerce, Science and Transportation. Watt-Cloutier's and the ICC's argument is that human-induced climate change is not only an environmental issue or an environmental and an economic issue. According to Watt-Cloutier, global climate change is at its core a human rights issue and that Inuit have "the right to be cold." Frustrated with the actions of the U.S. government under President George W. Bush with regard to global warming, in December 2005, Watt-Cloutier led a group of 62 Canadian and American Inuit hunters and elders in filing a petition to Inter-American Commission on Human Rights, a department of the Organization of American States (OAS), alleging that the United States violated Inuit cultural and environmental human rights by contributing to global warming through its unwillingness to reduce its own greenhouse gas emissions. In the 175-page petition, the ICC and the petitioners alleged that the United States through its actions and omissions had violated "the Inuit's fundamental human rights protected by the American Declaration of the Rights and Duties of Man and other international instruments. These include their rights to the benefits of culture, to property, to the preservation of health, life, physical integrity, security, and a means of subsistence, and to residence, movement, and inviolability of the home."[14]

The OAS rejected the petition, but invited Watt-Cloutier to testify at a March 2007 hearing on climate change and human rights. For these efforts to combat the human causes of global warming, Watt-Cloutier was nominated along with former U.S. Vice President Al Gore and the Intergovernmental Panel on Climate Change (IPCC) for the Nobel Peace Prize in 2007 for her work to stop climate change. The Nobel committee, however, did not include her when it made the award to Gore and the IPCC.

Aqqaluk Lynge has also been active in the politics of climate change. In May 2007, as president of ICC-Greenland, he testified at public hearings in Great Britain against the expansion of Stansted airport, arguing that the mainly holiday travel that originates from that facility would contribute to global warming for unimportant reasons. In contrast, he claimed, Inuit hunt for important reasons.

The serious consequences affecting my people today will affect your people tomorrow. Most flights from Stansted are not for an important purpose. They are mostly for holidays and leisure. Is it too much to ask for some moderation for the sake of my people today and your people tomorrow? . . . For generations, Inuit have observed the environment and have accurately predicted weather, enabling us to travel safely on the sea-ice to hunt seals, whales, and polar bears. We don't hunt for sport or recreation. Hunters put food on the table. You go to the supermarket, we go on the sea-ice. When we can no longer hunt on the sea-ice, we will no longer exist as a people.[15]

Inuit Nunaat and Arctic Sovereignty

In 1975 a group of hunters from the tiny village of Niaqornat in northwest Greenland stopped an icebreaker traveling through nearby Uummannaq Fjord. The ship was on its way to a zinc and lead mine, and in the process was destroying the ice that served as the primary transportation route of local Inuit hunters. Using their dog teams, the hunters blocked the icebreaker's passage, and local politicians negotiated an agreement that kept ships from calling at the mine between December and June. A few years later, Inuit in the Nunavut community of Baker Lake brought a lawsuit against the Canadian Minister of Indian Affairs and Northern Development and six mining companies to force the closure of a uranium mine that Inuit feared would disrupt their subsistence hunting for caribou. And in 1971, Inupiat from the North Slope Borough filed suit against the U.S. Secretary of the Interior for failing to stop mineral and oil companies from trespassing on Inupiat lands. The timing of these events is not a coincidence. The 1970s was a time when many in the global community viewed the Arctic as a natural resource frontier that was available for exploitation and development. They did not, however, consider the interests, needs, or opinions of the peoples who lived in the Arctic.

In the first decade of the 21st century, oil companies and mining firms are again looking at the Arctic as a site ripe for development. But this time, Inuit are in a much better position to exercise control over development. As part of the ICC efforts to assert Inuit authority over activities on Inuit lands, in April 2009, the organization issued a Declaration on Arctic Sovereignty over *Inuit Nunaat* ("the lands of the Inuit"). The Declaration is not about stopping resource development, but about asserting Inuit rights to self-determination with regard to development.

The organization changed its name from Inuit Circumpolar Conference to Inuit Circumpolar Council in 2006. The ICC remains the sole international nongovernmental organization representing approximately 160,000 Inuit and Yupik peoples of Greenland, Alaska, Canada, and Russia. The focus on the protection of the Arctic environment that drove the very first meeting in Barrow continues as the primary focus of the organization. In the years since its founding, the ICC has become a significant participant in Arctic policy making. It "has grown into a powerful political actor in Arctic governance [and has] acquired the legitimacy to help determine the very definition of the region as a whole."[16]

NOTES

1. Rasmussen, Lars Toft (1987) "Greenlandic and Danish Attitudes to Canadian Arctic Shipping," in *Politics of the Northwest Passage,* F. Griffiths, ed., Montreal: McGill-Queens University Press, 138.

2. Johansen, Lars Emil (1992) "Greenland and the European Community," *Etudes/Inuit/Studies* 16(1–2): 35.

3. Hopson, Eben (1977) Welcoming Address Inuit Circumpolar Conference, June 13, 1977, retrieved July 14, 2009 from http://www.ebenhopson.com/icc/ICCKeynote.html.

4. Shadian, Jessica (2006) "Remaking Arctic Governance: The Construction of an Arctic Inuit Policy," *Polar Record* 42(3): 252.

5. Inuit Circumpolar Conference (1977) "Resolution ICC 77-01," *1977 Inuit Circumpolar Conference Booklet,* retrieved July 14, 2009 from http://www.ebenhopson.com/icc/ICCBooklet.html.

6. Berger, Thomas R. (1985) *Village Journey: The Report of the Alaska Native Review Commission,* New York: Hill and Wang, 116.

7. Nuttall, Mark (2005) *Protecting the Arctic: Indigenous Peoples and Cultural Survival,* 2nd ed., London: Routledge, 29.

8. United Nations (2007) United Nations Declaration on the Rights of Indigenous Peoples, retrieved July 15, 2009 from http://www.iwgia.org/sw248.asp.

9. Ipellie, Alootook (1984) "Editorial," *Inuit Today, Special Edition: Inuit Circumpolar Conference, Iqaluit '83,* 4.

10. Inuit Circumpolar Conference (1998) *Proceedings of the 8th General Assembly of the Inuit Circumpolar Conference, July 24–31, 1998,* retrieved July 15, 2009 from http://www.inuitcircumpolar.com.

11. Watt-Cloutier, Sheila (2003) "The Inuit Journey towards a POPs-free World," in *Northern Lights against POPs: Combating Toxic Threats in the Arctic,* David Leonard Downie and Terry Fenge, eds., Montreal: McGill-Queens University Press, 260.

12. Fenge, Terry (2001) "Climate Change and Canadian Inuit," *IPS Update* 1(2): 5.

13. Intergovernmental Panel on Climate Change (2007) *Climate Change 2007: Synthesis Report,* Geneva, Switzerland: Intergovernmental Panel on Climate Change, retrieved July 16, 2009 from http://www.ipcc.ch.

14. Watt-Cloutier, Sheila (2005) *Petition to the Inter American Commission on Human Rights Seeking Relief from Violations Resulting from Global Warming Caused by Acts and Omission of the United States,* 5, retrieved July 16, 2009 from http://www.ciel.org.

15. Lynge, Aqqaluk (2007) "Aqqaluk Lynge: Global Warming Is Not Just a Theory to Us," *The Independent,* May 30, retrieved July 30, 2009 from http://www.independent.co.uk.

16. Shadian, "Remaking Arctic Governance," 250.

GLOSSARY

aboriginal title—Collective ownership of land on the basis of prior and continuous occupation. Aboriginal title is extinguished by modern land claims agreements signed in Canada and the United States (Alaska).

acculturation—The process of adopting introduced cultural traits from socially or politically dominant peoples.

alienation—With respect to land or other property, refers to the involuntary loss of ownership and/or use rights.

Anglican Church—The Church of England, known as the Episcopal Church in the United States.

atiq—Name soul or namesake, *atiit* (pl.).

Circumpolar North—The geographic region surrounding the North Pole.

cosmology—Spiritual beliefs.

country food—Traditional foods procured through subsistence hunting and collecting; also known as land foods.

dialect—A regional variation of a language.

egalitarian—Having no status differences.

ethnonym—Name by which a people or culture is known.

extended family—Family organized to include three or more generations.

extinguishment—Legal ending of the right to make a claim of aboriginal title to land.

fictive kin—People regarded as relatives despite an absence of genetic or marital ties.

First Nations—Term used in Canada to refer to the peoples called Indians or Native Americans in the United States.

food security—Usually defined as access to adequate amounts of safe, nutritious, culturally acceptable food.

Francophone—A person who speaks French.

Greenlandization—Replacement of Danish language and Danish values in the governance and everyday life of Greenlanders.

High Arctic—Northernmost region of Greenland and the Canadian Arctic, notable for its sparse vegetation.

indigenous peoples—The original inhabitants of a region that has been incorporated into a nation-state dominated by other peoples.

indigenous rights—Recognized rights to land or self-determination based on one's status as an indigenous person.

Inuit Nunaat—Political term meaning the lands of the Inuit peoples.

inuk—Singular form of Inuit, an Inuit person.

inukshuk—Literally, "resembles a person," a marker of piled stones.

Inuktitut—Literally, "in the manner of an [Inuit] person," the Inuit language.

Inupiaq—Language of the Inupiat; also the adjectival form of Inupiat.

Inupiat—The Inuit people of north and northwest Alaska; "the real people" in the Inupiaq language.

Inuvialuit—The Inuit people of the western Canadian Arctic.

Inuvialuk—An Inuvialuit person.

Kalaalliit Nunaat—Greenland, literally "the land of the Greenlanders."

Kalaallisut—Name of the Greenlandic dialect of Inuktitut.

Kalaallit—Greenlander, Kalaalliit (pl.).

kamiks—Skin boots.

land claims—Modern negotiations to determine aboriginal title to traditional lands.

maktak—Skin and outer layer of fat of a whale.

material culture—Artifacts and physical possessions and manufactures of a people.

monolingual—Speaking one language only.

neoeskimos—Literally, "new Eskimos," archeologically known Thule period ancestors of modern Inuit.

nuclear family—A family organized as a married couple and their offspring.

orthography—A standardized system for writing a language.

paleoeskimos—Literally "old Eskimos," archeologically known peoples who inhabited the North American Arctic prior to the arrival of the ancestors of modern Inuit.

photoperiod—Amount of time that is daylight.

pisiit—Drum songs, *pisiq* (sing.).

polyandry—Marriage of one woman to two or more men.

polygyny—Marriage of one man to two or more women.

public government—Term used in Canada to refer to a nonethnic, democratically elected government that is chosen by all citizens.

qaggiq—A dance house, usually a temporary structure built of snow, used for late-winter celebrations by Inuit in the Canadian Arctic; also the gathering for celebration.

qargi—Inupiaq "men's house," usually a permanent semisubterranean structure that was the site of political and social activity. Large villages usually had several *qargit* (pl.).

qarmaq—A semisubterranean stone-and-sod house with a skin or canvas roof. A traditional form of housing built by Inuit in the central and eastern Canadian Arctic.

quliaqtuaq—(Inupiaq dialect) stories that concern people and/or events that can be identified, *quliaqtuaq* (pl.).

qulliq—Soapstone oil lamp used for heating and light.

skraellings—Indigenous peoples of North America referred to in Norse sagas.

social housing—Government-subsidized housing, usually provided as part of poverty relief programs.

social organization—Ongoing, institutionalized relationships between people in a community.

TEK—Traditional ecological knowledge; refers to a holistic approach to understanding the world; often contrasted with scientific management systems.

tuniit—A mythic people who may represent the Dorset Eskimos who occupied Greenland and the Canadian Arctic at the time of the Thule expansion.

ulu—Semilunar-shaped knife used by women.

umialik—Inupiaq whaling captain; the title refers to the fact that these traditional political leaders were boat owners.

umiaq—Small, usually skin-covered, boat, *umiat* (pl.).

unipkaaq—(Inupiaq dialect) story concerning people and events of the distant, mythic past, *unipkaat* (pl.).

vernacular—Everyday language or esthetics.

zoonotic infections—Infections passed to humans from animal vectors.

APPENDIX: PLACES MENTIONED IN THE TEXT

Aklavik—Town near the mouth of the Mackenzie River in the Inuvialuit Settlement Region of Canada.

Akulivik—Village on the east coast of Hudson Bay in Nunavik.

Anaktuvuk Pass—Inland Inupiaq village located in the Brooks Mountain Range, part of Alaska's North Slope Borough.

Arctic Archipelago—Canadian Arctic island group bounded by Baffin Island in the east and Banks Island in the west.

Arviat—Nunavut town on the west coast of Hudson Bay, formerly called Eskimo Point.

Baffin Island—Largest and easternmost island in the Canadian Arctic Archipelago.

Baker Lake—Nunavut town, inland from the west coast of Hudson Bay.

Barrow—Administrative center for the North Slope Borough, located at the northernmost point of Alaska.

Bathurst Inlet—Tiny village on the mainland Arctic coast in the western region of Nunavut.

Beaufort Sea—Region of the Arctic Ocean bordering Alaska and Canada.

Belcher Islands—Small group of island in southeastern Hudson Bay, included within the Nunavut Territory.

Bering Sea—Area of the Pacific Ocean between Alaska and Russia.

Bering Strait—Body of water separating Alaska from Russia.

Cambridge Bay—Town on the southeast coast of Victoria Island in Nunavut.

Cape Denbigh—Site of archeological remains on Alaska's Bering Sea coast.

Cape Dorset—Town on southwest Baffin Island famous for its art industry.

Cape Thompson—Traditional settlement and hunting area near Point Hope, Alaska, once proposed as a site for nuclear testing.

Chantrey Inlet—Mouth of the Back River, Nunavut.

Chesterfield Inlet—Town on west coast of Hudson Bay, in Nunavut.

Chukchi Sea—Area of the Arctic Ocean between Alaska and Russia.

Chukotka—Easternmost district of the Russian Arctic.

Cumberland Sound—Body of water off the east coast of Baffin Island, at present-day Pangnirtung, Nunavut.

Davis Strait—Waterway separating Greenland from Baffin Island.

Grise Fjord—Northernmost town in Canada, located on Ellesmere Island in Nunavut.

Herschel Island—Site of former commercial whaling station in the Beaufort Sea.

Hudson Bay—Body of water bordering Nunavut, Nunavik, and the Canadian provinces of Ontario, Quebec, and Manitoba.

Igloolik—Town of about 1,200 people, just west of the northern part of Baffin Island in Nunavut.

Inukjuak—Town in Nunavik located on the east coast of Hudson Bay.

Inuvialuit Settlement Region—Administrative area encompassing the traditional lands of Inuit from Inuvik, Aklavik, Paulatuk, Tuktoyuktuk, Sachs Harbour, and Ulukhaktok in the western Canadian Arctic.

Inuvik—Multi-ethnic administrative town near the mouth of the Mackenzie River in Canada's Northwest Territories.

Iqaluit—Largest community and capital of the Nunavut Territory, located on southern Baffin Island.

Ittoqqortoormiit—Village in East Greenland.

Ivujivik—Nunavik town at the entrance to Hudson Bay.

Kaktovik—Easternmost Inupiaq village located adjacent to the Prudhoe Bay oil fields.

Killiniq—Abandoned village at the entrance to Hudson Strait.

Kotzebue—Largest community and administrative seat of the Northwest Arctic Borough, Alaska, located at the end of a narrow peninsula.

Kugluktuk—Westernmost town in Nunavut, located on the Arctic coast near the mouth of the Coppermine River, formerly called Coppermine.

Kuujjuaq—Nunavik town just inland from the Ungava Bay coast.

Labrador—Mainland portion of the Canadian province of Newfoundland and Labrador, easternmost Inuit region in Canada.

Mackenzie Delta—Traditional Inuvialuit lands where the Mackenzie River empties into the Beaufort Sea.

Maniitsoq—West Greenland town.

Niaqornat—Village in northwest Greenland.

Nome—Multi-ethnic town on Alaska's Seward Peninsula.

Noorvik—Inupiaq village located approximately 45 miles east of Kotzebue in Alaska's Northwest Arctic Borough.

North Slope Borough—County-like administrative district covering the lands north of the Brooks Range in Alaska.

Northwest Arctic Borough—County-like administrative district in northwest Alaska.

Northwest Territories—Administrative district of the Canadian Arctic and Subarctic.

Norton Sound—Body of water just south of the Seward Peninsula in Alaska.

Nunatsiavut—Inuit lands of northern Labrador.

Nunavik—Arctic Quebec, Canada.

Nunavut—Traditional Inuit lands in the eastern and Central Canadian Arctic, contiguous with the area designated as the Nunavut Territory.

Nunavut Territory—Administrative district of the central and eastern Canadian Arctic, created through the division of the Northwest Territories in 1999.

Nuuk—City of approx. 15,000 people in west central Greenland, capital of Greenland.

Pangnirtung—Town on the east coast of Baffin Island.

Pelly Bay—Village in central Nunavut.

Point Barrow—Northerly most point in Alaska, site of the present-day town of Barrow.

Point Hope—Westernmost village in Alaska's North Slope Borough.

Prudhoe Bay—Site of oil fields on the Beaufort Sea coast of Alaska.

Puvirnituq—Town on the east coast of Hudson Bay in Nunavik.

Qaanaaq—Village in northwest Greenland.

Rankin Inlet—Second-largest town in Nunavut, located on the west coast of Hudson Bay.

Resolute—Town in north central Nunavut.

St. Lawrence Island—Large island between the Alaska mainland and Siberia, part of Alaska.

Salluit—Town in Nunavik on the coast of Hudson Strait.

Seward Peninsula—Area of western Alaska protruding into the Bering Strait.

Siberia—The Russian Arctic.

Sisimiut—Large town in West Greenland.

Taimyr Peninsula—Area on north central Siberia projecting into the Arctic Ocean.

Taloyoak—Town in the Nunavut Territory previously known as Spence Bay.

Ulukhaktok—Village on the west coast of Victoria Island in the Inuvialuit Settlement Region of Canada's Northwest Territories, formerly called Holman.

Uummannaq—Village in northwest Greenland.

FURTHER READING

PRINT RESOURCES

Alia, Valerie. *Names, Numbers, and Northern Policy: Inuit, Project Surname and the Politics of Identity*, Halifax, NS: Fernwood Publishing, 1994.

Alia, Valerie. *Names and Nunavut: Culture and Identity in Arctic Canada*, New York: Berghahn Books, 2007.

Aupilaarjuk, Mariano, Tulimaaq Aupilaarjuk, Lucassie Nutaraakuk, Rose Iqallijuq, Johanasi Ujarak, Isidore Ijituuq, and Michel Kupaaq. *Interviewing Inuit Elders: Cosmology and Shamanism*, edited by Bernard Saladin d'Anglure, Iqaluit: Nunavut Arctic College, 2001.

Bennett, John, and Susan Rowley, eds. *Uqalurait: An Oral History of Nunavut*, Montreal: McGill-Queens University Press, 2004.

Bigjim, Frederick Seaguyak, and James Ito-Adler. *Letters to Howard: An Interpretation of Alaska Native Land Claims*, Anchorage: Alaska Methodist University Press, 1974 (also available at http://www.ankn.uaf.edu/Curriculum/ANCSA/letters.html).

Billson, Janet Mancini, and Kyra Mancini. *Inuit Women: Their Powerful Spirit in a Century of Change*, Lanham, MD: Rowman and Littlefield, 2007.

Blackman, Margaret B. *Sadie Brower Neakok: An Iñupiaq Woman*, Seattle: University of Washington Press, 1989.

Briggs, Jean L. *Inuit Morality Play: The Emotional Education of a Three-Year-Old*, New Haven, CT: Yale University Press, 1998.

Briggs, Jean L. *Never in Anger: Portrait of an Eskimo Family*, Cambridge, MA: Harvard University Press, 1970.

Campbell, John Martin, ed. *In a Hungry Country: Essays by Simon Paneak,* Fairbanks: University of Alaska Press, 2004.

Chance, Norman A. *The Iñupiat and Arctic Alaska: An Ethnography of Development,* Chicago: Holt, Rinehart and Winston, 1990.

Condon, Richard G. *Inuit Youth: Growth and Change in the Canadian Arctic,* New Brunswick, NJ: Rutgers University Press, 1987.

Dahl, Jens. *Saqqaq: An Inuit Hunting Community in the Modern World,* Toronto: University of Toronto Press, 2000.

Dahl, Jens, Jack Hicks, and Peter Jull, eds. *Nunavut: Inuit Regain Control of Their Lands and Their Lives,* Copenhagen: International Work Group for Indigenous Affairs, 2000.

Damas, David, ed. *Handbook of North American Indians: Arctic,* Washington, D.C.: Smithsonian Institution Press, 1984.

Downie, David Leonard, and Terry Fenge, eds. *Northern Lights against POPs: Combating Toxic Threats in the Arctic,* Montreal: McGill-Queens University Press, 2003.

Duffy, R. Quinn. *The Road to Nunavut: The Progress of the Eastern Arctic Inuit since the Second World War,* Montreal: McGill-Queens University Press, 1988.

Duhaime, Gérard, ed. *Sustainable Food Security in the Arctic: State of Knowledge,* Edmonton: Canadian Circumpolar Institute Press, 2002.

Ekho, Naqi, and Uqsuralik Ottokie. *Interviewing Inuit Elders: Childrearing Practices,* edited by Jean Briggs, Iqaluit: Nunavut Arctic College, 2000.

Fair, Susan W. *Alaska Native Art: Tradition, Innovation, Continuity,* edited by Jean Blodgett, Fairbanks: University of Alaska Press, 2006.

Fienup-Riordan, Ann. *Freeze Frame: Alaska Eskimos in the Movies,* Seattle: University of Washington Press, 1995.

Gedalof, Robin, ed. *Paper Stays Put: A Collection of Inuit Writing,* Edmonton: Hurtig, 1979.

Grant, Shelagh. *Polar Imperative: A History of Polar Sovereignty in North America,* Vancouver: Douglas & McIntyre, 2010.

Grygier, Pat Sandiford. *A Long Way from Home: The Tuberculosis Epidemic among the Inuit,* Montreal: McGill-Queens University Press, 1994.

Henderson, Ailsa. *Nunavut: Rethinking Political Culture,* Vancouver: University of British Columbia Press, 2007.

Ipellie, Alootook. *Arctic Dreams and Nightmares,* Penticton, BC: Theytus Books, 1993.

Joamie, Alacie, Akisu Joamie, Jayko Pitseolak, Malaya Papatsie, Elisapee Ootoova, and Tirisi Attagutsiak. *Interviewing Inuit Elders: Perspectives on Traditional Health,* edited by Frederic Laugrand and Michelle Therrien, Iqaluit: Nunavut Arctic College, 2001.

Jorgensen, Joseph G. *Oil Age Eskimos,* Berkeley: University of California Press, 1990.

Kaalund, Bodil. *The Art of Greenland, Sculpture, Crafts, Painting,* translated by Kenneth Tindall, Berkeley: University of California Press, 1983.

King, J.C.H., Birgit Pauksztat, and Robert Storrie, eds. *Arctic Clothing of North America—Alaska, Canada, Greenland*, Montreal: McGill-Queens University Press, 2005.

Kulchyski, Peter, and Frank James Tester. *Kiumajut (Talking Back): Game Management and Inuit Rights 1900–70*, Vancouver: University of British Columbia Press, 2007.

Lee, Molly, and Gregory A. Reinhardt. *Eskimo Architecture: Dwelling and Structure in the Early Historic Period*, Fairbanks: University of Alaska Press, 2003.

Leroux, Odette, Marion E. Jackson, and Minnie Aodla Freeman. *Inuit Women Artists: Voices from Cape Dorset*, Vancouver: Douglas & McIntyre, 1994.

Lowenstein, Tom. *Ancient Land, Sacred Whale: The Inuit Hunt and Its Rituals*, London: Bloomsbury, 1993.

Lynge, Aqqaluk. *The Veins of the Heart to the Pinnacle of the Mind (Taqqat Uummammut Aqqutaannut Takorluukkat Apuuffiannut)*, translated by Marianne Stenbaek, Hanover, NH: International Polar Institute Press, 2009.

MacDonald, John. *The Arctic Sky: Inuit Astronomy, Star Lore, and Legend*, Toronto: Royal Ontario Museum, 1998.

Marcus, Alan Rudolph. *Relocating Eden: The Image and Politics of Inuit Exile in the Canadian Arctic*, Hanover, NH: University Press of New England, 1995.

Mashner, Herbert, Owen Mason, and Robert McGhee, eds. *The Northern World, A.D. 900–1400*, Salt Lake City: University of Utah Press, 2009.

McCartney, Allen P., ed. *Hunting the Largest Animals: Native Whaling in the Western Arctic and Subarctic*, Edmonton: Canadian Circumpolar Institute Press, 1996.

McCartney, Allen P., ed. *Indigenous Ways to the Present: Native Whaling in the Western Arctic*, Edmonton: Canadian Circumpolar Institute Press, 2003.

McGhee, Robert. *Ancient People of the Arctic*, Vancouver: University of British Columbia Press, 1996.

Mitchell, Donald Craig. *Take My Land, Take My Life: The Story of Congress's Historic Settlement of Alaska Native Land Claims, 1960–1971*, Fairbanks: University of Alaska Press, 2001.

Mitchell, Marybelle. *From Talking Chiefs to a Native Corporate Elite*, Montreal: McGill-Queens University Press, 1996.

Morgan, Lael. *Art and Eskimo Power: The Life and Times of Alaskan Howard Rock*, Fairbanks: Epicenter Press, 1988.

Nuttall, Mark. *Arctic Homeland: Kinship, Community and Development in Northwest Greenland*, London: Belhaven Press, 1992.

Nuttall, Mark. *Protecting the Arctic: Indigenous Peoples and Cultural Survival*, 2nd ed., London: Routledge, 2005.

Odess, Daniel, Stephen Loring, and William W. Fitzhugh. "Skraeling: First Peoples of Helluland, Markland, and Vinland." In *Vikings: The North Atlantic Saga*, edited by William W. Fitzhugh and Elisabeth I. Ward, 193–205, Washington, D.C.: Smithsonian Institution Press, 2000.

Oquilluk, William A., with Laurel L. Bland. *People of Kauwerak: Legends of the Northern Eskimo*, Anchorage: Alaska Methodist University Press, 1973.

Oswalt, Wendell H. *Eskimos and Explorers*, 2nd ed. Lincoln: University of Nebraska Press, 1999.

Pitseolak, Peter, and Dorothy Harley Eber. *People from Our Side*, Montreal: McGill-Queens University Press, 1993.

Stern, Pamela R. *Historical Dictionary of the Inuit*, Lanham, MD: Scarecrow Press, 2004.

Stevenson, Marc G. *Inuit, Whalers, and Cultural Persistence: Structure in Cumberland Sound and Central Inuit Social Organization*, Oxford: Oxford University Press, 1997.

Tester, Frank James, and Peter Kulchyski. *Tammarniit (Mistakes) Inuit Relocation in the Eastern Arctic 1939–63*, Vancouver: University of British Columbia Press, 1994.

Thomas, Lesley. *The Flight of the Goose: A Story of the Far North*, Seattle: Far Eastern Press, 2005.

Wachowich, Nancy, with Apphia Agalakti Awa, Rhoda Kaukjak Katsak, and Sandra Pikujak Katsak. *Saqiyuq: Stories from the Lives of Three Inuit Women*, Kingston and Montreal: McGill-Queens University Press, 1999.

Wenzel, George W. *Animal Rights, Human Rights: Ecology, Economy and Ideology in the Canadian Arctic*, Toronto: University of Toronto Press, 1991.

Wenzel, George W. *Sometimes Hunting Can Seem Like a Business*, Edmonton: Canadian Circumpolar Institute Press, 2008.

NONPRINT RESOURCES ON INUIT CULTURE, HISTORY, AND COMMUNITY

Web Sites:

Alaska Native Knowledge Network, a Web site hosted by the University of Alaska, Fairbanks with detailed information about histories, cultures, and indigenous knowledge of Alaska Native peoples, http://www.ankn.uaf.edu.

Alaskool, curriculum materials for teachers concerning the histories, languages, and cultures of Alaska Native peoples, http://www.alaskool.org.

Avataq Cultural Institute, Web pages and digital archives of the cultural organization of the Nunavik Inuit, http://www.tradition-orale.ca.

Eben Hopson Memorial Archives, digital collection of speeches, photographs, and other materials related to life of the Inupiaq leader, as well as documents related to the founding of the Inuit Circumpolar Conference, http://www.ebenhopson.com.

Greenland.com, information about the culture and history of Greenland provided by the Greenland Tourism and Business Council, http://www.greenland.com.

Interviewing Inuit Elders, the series of books produced by Nunavut Arctic College are available as free downloads from http://nac.nu.ca/OnlineBookSite/index.html.

Inuit Circumpolar Council, Web pages and digitally archived documents of the Inuit Circumpolar Council, http://www.inuitcircumpolar.com.

Inuit Circumpolar Music, a blog about contemporary Inuit music and musicians containing reviews and links to musicians' personal Web sites, http://pisiit.blogspot.com.

Inuit Tapiriit Kanatami, Web pages and digital archives of the national Inuit organization in Canada, includes access to back issues of Inuktitut magazine, http://www.itk.ca.

IsumaTV, webportal to film work by indigenous people created and maintained by the Igloolik Isuma Productions, includes material from the video libraries of the Inuit Broadcasting Corporation and Nunavut Independent Television Network, http://www.isuma.tv.

Kitikmeot Heritage Society, digital museum exhibits, curricula materials, and publications on the history, culture, and archeology of the Central Canadian Arctic, http://www.kitikmeotheritage.ca.

Listening to Our Past, short video clips and texts of interviews with Nunavut Inuit Elders on topics related to traditional knowledge and recent history of the people and communities in the Nunavut Territory, http://www.tradition-orale.ca.

NunatsiaqOnline, online version and searchable archives of Nunatsiaq News, a weekly newspaper published in Iqaluit, http://www.nunatsiaqonline.ca.

SIKU News, web-based news consolidator covering Inuit and other Circumpolar communities, http://www.sikunews.com.

Films, Videos, and DVDs:

Atanarjuat, The Fast Runner. 2001. Igloolik, NU: Igloolik Isuma Productions.
Before Tomorrow. 2008. Igloolik, NU: Igloolik Isuma Productions.
Ce Qu'il Faut Pour Vivre (The Necessities of Life). 2009. Montreal: Seville Pictures.
Eskimo Weekend. 2002. Nuuk: Techno Suaasat.
Heart of Light. 1998. Buena Park, CA: Vangard Cinema.
Inuuvunga—I am Inuk, I am Alive. 2004. Ottawa: National Film Board of Canada.

The Journals of Knud Rasmussen. 2009. Igloolik, NU: Igloolik Isuma Productions.

On Thin Ice—Le Voyage d'Inuk. 2009. n.p.: C'est la Vie Films.

Qallunaat! Why White People are Funny. 2006. Ottawa: National Film Board of Canada.

Starting Fire with Gunpowder. 1991. Ottawa: National Film Board of Canada.

The White Dawn. 1974. Hollywood, CA: Paramount Pictures.

INDEX

Aariak, Eva, 97
Aboriginal rights, 29, 49, 86, 90–92, 129, 175, 179
Aesthetics, 76, 143–44
Aggeok, 126, 148
Aging, 19
Aglukark, Susan, 134, 135, 136
Ahgupuk, George, 149, 150
Akpaliapik, Manasie, 154
Alaska Eskimo Whaling Commission (AEWC), 48, 175. *See also* International Whaling Commission
Alaska National Interest Lands Conservation Act (ANILCA), 49–50
Alaska Native Claims Settlement Act (ANCSA), xxvii, 49, 92–94, 130, 178; amendments to, 94; extinguishment, 92; Native corporations, 92, 93–94, 100–101
Alaska statehood, xxvii, 91

Alcohol, xvii, 141; abuse of, 33, 58, 99, 110, 111, 135, 141, 154, 153; regulation of, 163
Alutiiq people, xxiii
Amagoalik, John, 179
Amittuk, Davidialuk, 150
Animal rights movements, 46–48, 78–79
Animals, relationships to, 9–10, 26, 40, 79, 104, 165
Angilirq, Paul Apak, 139
Archaeology, xi–xv, xxiii, 41, 83, 85, 143, 160. *See also* Arctic Small Tool tradition; Dorset culture; Thule culture
Architecture, 10, 59–60, 71–76, 148, 182; modern housing, 59, 72–74, 78; traditional housing, 71–72, 82
Arctic Council, xxix, 180
Arctic Peoples Conference, xxvii, 175
Arctic Slope Native Association, 91

Arctic Small Tool tradition, xii, xxv
Arctic Winter Games, 118, 124, 126
Arnait Video Collective, xxx, 140,
    141
Aron from Kangeq, 149, 150
Art, 8, 16, 26, 50, 78, 126, 129, 140,
    143–55; Canadian Eskimo Arts
    Council, 147–48; fine art, xxvii,
    147–50, 153–55; One Percent for
    Art program, xxviii, 154; tourist
    art, 119, 144–46, 155
Ashoona, Pitseolak, 151
Atuagagdliutit, xxvi, 23, 126, 129,
    134, 149
Aua, 111, 132

Baleen, 37, 82, 144, 145, 152, 154
Baleen whales. *See* Bowhead
    whales
Bathurst Mandate, 97
Belkachi culture, xii
Berger, Justice Thomas R., 29–30,
    178
Berthelsen, Kelly, 131
Berthelsen, Rasmus, 129, 134
Bevins, Susie, 154
Bigjim, Fred, 131
Birnik culture, xii
Bowhead whales, xiv, xv, 41, 82,
    145; Inuit hunting of, xi, 10,
    41–44, 48–49, 174–75, 176
Broadcasting, xxi, xxviii, 136–38;
    Inuit Broadcasting Corpora-
    tion, xxviii, 137; radio, 26, 134,
    136, 138; television, 57, 78, 122,
    136–38, 140–41, 150
Brower, Charles, 145, 152
Bureau of Indian Affairs, 27,
    30–31, 101

Calendars, 63–64
Canadian Eskimo Arts Council,
    147–48
Children, 6, 12, 14, 22, 24, 57, 60,
    76, 111–12, 116, 119–22, 125, 135,
    160, 167, 168; adoption, 5; child-
    hood, 17–18, 27–28; relationships
    with parents, 3, 18. *See also*
    Naming
Chilly Friday, 135
Christianity, xxvi, 6–7, 14, 16,
    72, 75, 78, 112, 113, 126, 134,
    161; conversion to, 103, 106–9,
    110–11, 131, 140; Inuit ministers
    and missionaries, 24, 108–9, 128
Christmas, 65, 76, 78, 112, 113, 117,
    134, 145; feasts, 44, 112
Climate change, xii, xiii, xiv–xvi,
    xxv, xxix, xxx, 79–80, 101, 130
Cochrane, Patricia, 177
Cockney, Bob. *See* Nuligak
Cohn, Norman, 140
Cold War, xiii, xviii, xxvii, 61, 174,
    179. *See also* Military activity
Colonial administration of Inuit
    communities, xxii, 8, 10, 34, 57,
    58–59, 60, 73, 82, 85, 86, 88, 97,
    106, 111, 117, 125, 130, 135, 141
Colonization of Inuit lands, xvi,
    xviii, xix, 62, 81, 86–87, 90, 106–7,
    157; by Norse, xiii, xv–xvi, xix,
    xxv, 69, 106
Co-management, 49, 90, 101, 181,
    182–83

Dalager, Mathias, 153
Declaration on Arctic Sovereignty,
    xxx, 184
Declaration on the Rights of
    Indigenous Peoples, xxx, 179
Denbigh Flint complex, xii–xiii
Diet, 38, 158; country foods, 38,
    39–41, 164; food security,
    163–68; market foods, 164,
    167–68. *See also* Hunting; Shar-
    ing; Subsistence; Whaling
Disk numbers. *See* Names and
    naming
Distance Early Warning (DEW)
    line. *See* Military activity

Dogs, xii, xiv, xxvi, 46, 72, 117, 121, 123, 153, 157, 184
Dorset culture, xii–xiii, xv, xxv
Drug abuse, 33, 99, 110. *See also* Alcohol
Drum dancing. *See* Music

Eagle-Wolf Dance. *See* Messenger Feast
Education, xviii, xxvii, 27–32, 33, 58, 59, 61, 74, 87, 99, 100, 107, 174; Inuit control of, xxi, 29–31, 88, 95, 96, 101, 175–76; post-secondary, 30, 31–32, 65, 76, 84, 90, 105, 110, 128, 159; residential schools, xxx, 28, 29, 30, 31, 90; traditional, 27, 125. *See also* Children; Inuktitut; Kalaallisut
Egede, Hans, xvi, xxv, 86, 106
Employment, xviii, 10, 18, 28, 38, 42, 51, 57–58, 59, 66, 93–94, 99–100
Energy development, xxvii, 94–95, 176. *See also* Oil and gas
Environmental initiatives, 180–83
Epidemics, 107, 157, 161–63
European Economic Community. *See* European Union
European exploration, xvi, xvii, 128–29, 144, 153, 158, 161, 164
European Union, 174

Festivals. *See* Messenger Feast; Nalukataq
Fifth Thule Expedition (1921–24), 24, 104–5, 111, 126
Films and filmmaking, 5, 26, 87, 138; about Inuit, xxvi, 138–39, 148; by Inuit, xviii, xxx, 103, 126, 137, 139–41, 154
Flaherty, Robert, 138, 148
Folger, Mosha, 134
Forced relocations. *See* Migration
Freeman, Minnie Aodla, 129
Frobisher, Martin, xvi, xxv

Fur trade, 44–47, 78–79, 117, 145, 147; traders, xxii, 24, 45, 73, 78, 86, 117, 145, 152, 161

Games, 27, 64, 112, 115–124; traditional, 75, 116, 117, 118, 120–22
Gender, xxix, 3, 6, 9–12, 74, 76, 151–53
Gender parity proposal, xxix, 97
Global warming. *See* Climate change
Greenlandization, 22

Hansen, Laila, 140
Happy Jack, 148, 149
Hardenberg, Julie Edel, 154
Hendrik, Hans, 108, 128–29
Hensley, Willie, 90, 93
High Arctic Exiles, 63
Høegh, Inuk Silis, 140, 154
Homelessness, 66
Home Rule in Greenland, xxi, xxviii, xxx, 88, 89, 130, 135, 174; implementation of, xxi, 138; opposition to, 89
Hopson, Eben, 30–31, 101, 175–76
Houston, James, 146–47
Human rights, xxix, 162, 182–83. *See also* Aboriginal rights
Hunter Support Programs, 38–39, 95
Hunting, xiv, xix, xxviii, 2–3, 9, 10, 31, 39, 41, 42, 44, 46, 57, 60, 62, 64, 69, 78, 79, 82, 86, 87, 124, 129, 132, 135, 140, 149, 165–66, 168, 181. *See also* Subsistence

Idlout, Lucie, 135, 136
Igloolik Isuma Productions, 139–41
Independence culture, xii
Indian Reorganization Act (IRA), xxvi; IRA tribal governments, 100–101
Indigenous rights. *See* Aboriginal rights

International Whaling Commission (IWC), 47–49, 79, 174–75
Internet, 78, 140, 141
Inuit Circumpolar Conference. *See* Inuit Circumpolar Council
Inuit Circumpolar Council, xviii, xxviii, xxix, 25, 89, 175–84
Inuit Qaujimajatuqangit (IQ), 33–34, 97
Inuit Tapiriit Kanatami (ITK), xxvii, 63, 66, 137
Inuit Tapirisat of Canada. *See* Inuit Tapiriit Kanatami
Inuktitut, xi, xxi, xxvi, 21–25, 27–30, 67, 99, 108, 126, 127, 129, 134, 136, 137, 138, 140, 162. *See also* Kalaallisut
Inupiaq Ilitquisiat, 33–34, 109, 122
Inupiat Paitot, 91, 130
Inuvialuit Final Agreement, xxviii, 94
Ipellie, Alootook, 126, 131, 154
Ipiutak culture, xiii
IQ. *See* Inuit Qaujimajatuqangit
Ittinuar, Peter, 179

James Bay and Northern Quebec Agreement (JBNQA), xxviii, 61, 95, 96; Inuit opposition to, 95
Johansen, Lars Emil, 88, 174
Journalism, 129–30. *See also Atuagagdliutit*; *Tundra Times*

Kalaallisut, xxi, 21–23, 86, 88, 136, 138
Kinship, 39, 41, 55–56, 58, 59, 82, 86
Kleinschmidt, Samuel, 23, 107
Kleist, Malik, 135
Kristiansen, Ole, 135
Kunuk, Zacharias, 26, 139
Kuptana, Rosemary, 177

Land claims, xxi, xxii, xxvii, xxix, 29, 33, 48, 50, 66, 86, 90–96, 101, 176. *See also* Alaska Native Claims Settlement Act; Inuvialuit Final Agreement; James Bay and Northern Quebec Agreement; Nunavut Land Claims Settlement
Leadership, 10, 29, 33, 43, 55–56, 82–83, 93, 138, 163
Lisbourne, Ken, 153
Literacy, 24, 25, 29, 30, 32, 86
Literature, 22–23, 24, 26, 125–31, 135, 149; fiction, 130–31, 140–41; poetry, 131, 151
Little Ice Age, xv–xvi, xxv
Lund, Henrik, 109, 134, 151
Lynge, Aqqaluk, 131, 177, 179, 183
Lynge, Augo, 130
Lynge, Hans, 151
Lynge, Hans Anthon, 130, 141
Lynge, Niels, 151

MacLean, Edna P., 176–77
Marine Mammals Protection Act, 46
Marriage, xiv, 1–3, 10, 12–15, 16, 55, 64, 66, 85, 117, 151; spouse exchange, 16–17, 112, 139
Masks, xiii, 112, 143; dancing with, 111, 119, 131; from Anaktuvuk Pass, 119, 144, 145–46
Medieval Warm Period. *See* Climate change
Messenger Feast, xxvi, xxix, 75, 111, 116, 132
Midwifery, 4–5, 160, 170
Migration: forced relocations, 61–63; from Asia, xii; into permanent towns and villages, xxvi, xxviii, 10, 57–58, 59, 60, 140; seasonal, 56, 64, 71, 82; Thule, xiv, xxv; urban, xviii, 15, 59, 65, 66–67, 140–41. *See also* High Arctic Exiles
Military activity, xxi, 61, 87, 90–91, 134; Distant Early Warning (DEW) line, 61. *See also* Cold War

Mining and mineral exploration, xxi, 49, 50–51, 88, 89, 90, 96, 102, 182, 184
Missionaries. *See* Christianity
Møller, Lars, 129
Moses, James Kivetoruk, 149–50
Motzfeldt, Jonathan, 88
Music, xxix, 66, 131–36; drum songs, 75, 106, 112, 116, 125, 131–33, 134, 159; hip hop, 134; rock, 135; throat singing, xxix, 125, 131, 133–34, 136; Vaigat music, 134

Names and naming, 4–9, 12; *atiq*, 4, 7, 140, 141; disk numbers, xvii, 7–8, 135; Project Surname, xxvii, 8–9
Nanook of the North, xxvi, 138–39, 148
Newspapers. *See* Journalism
Norse. *See* Colonization
North Slope Borough, xxii, xxvii, 30, 32, 43, 48, 51, 100–101, 111, 117, 175, 176, 184
Northwest Passage, xvi, xvii, 153
Norton culture, xiii
Nuligak, 128
Nunavut Implementation Commission (NIC), 97
Nunavut Land Claim, xxii, xxix, 29, 50, 94, 96
Nunavut Legislative Assembly, xxix, 76, 97–99
Nunavut Territory, xxii, 29, 74, 96, 99–100; creation of, 96, 125; government of, 22, 29–30, 33
Nungak, Zebedee, 139
Nuuk Posse, 135

Oil and gas, 50–51, 90, 91–92, 176, 182, 184; Prudhoe Bay, xxvii, 30, 48, 51, 91, 101, 176
Old Bering Sea culture, xiii
Olsen, Moses, 88

Oquilluk, William A., 70, 79, 127–28
Oral traditions, 22, 25–26, 85, 109
Orpingalik, 132

Paleoeskimos, xii, xxvi, 41
Paneak, Simon, 127
Panigoniak, Charlie, 134, 136
Pauktuutit/Inuit Women's Association, 10, 97, 170
Peck, the Rev. Edmund James, 24, 108
Pederson, Maasi, 134
Persistent organic pollutants (POPs), 167, 181
Petersen, Jonathan, 134
Petersen, Pavia, 151
Petersen, Robert, 144
Pitseolak, Peter, 24, 126–27, 148, 150
Political parties, 88–89, 96, 97, 99
Pootoogook, Annie, 150–51, 154
Pootoogook, Napachie, 151
Pre-Dorset culture, xii
Project Chariot, 91, 129–30
Protests, 31, 88, 91–92, 118, 137
Prussic, 135
Punuk culture, xiii
Pungowiyi, Caleb, 177

Quilitalik, Pauloosie, 139
Qumaq, Taausi, 127

Radio. *See* Broadcasting
Radio Greenland, 138
Rasmussen, Knud, xxvi, 6, 64, 103, 111, 126, 132, 139, 140
Relocations. *See* Migration
Ringed seal, xv, 46
Ritual, 14, 42, 64, 85, 104, 109–10, 111, 112–13, 159
Rock, Howard, 129–30, 153
Rosing, Hans-Pavia, 176
Rosing, Peter, 151

Sacheuse, John. *See* Zakaeus, Hans
Schooling. *See* Education

Sedentization, 57–58. *See also* Migration

Self-determination, 38, 50, 89–102, 110, 170, 175, 176, 179, 182, 184

Self-governance, xviii, xxx, 33, 50, 81–85, 86, 90, 95, 96–97, 100–102, 173

Self Rule in Greenland, xix, xxx, 89

Senungetuk, Ronald W., 153

Sewing, 10, 17, 28, 43, 78, 104, 105, 141, 152–53

Sexuality, 3, 12, 14, 15, 16–17, 72, 106, 112, 141

Shamanism, 16, 75, 103–6, 107–11, 112, 125, 128, 132, 140, 150; healing, 104–5, 159, 161; shamanic flight, 26, 105–6, 131; taboos, 105, 109

Sharing, 10, 19, 33, 34, 38–41, 42, 44, 79, 82, 111, 120–21, 165, 167, 168

Simon, Mary, 176, 180

Song duel, 85, 99, 106, 118, 119

Snowhouse. *See* Architecture

Soul flight. *See* Shamanism

Sovereignty, xxx, 62, 184

Spirits, 103–6, 110, 111

Storch, Mathias, 130

Storytelling. *See* Oral traditions

Stotts, James (Jimmy), 177

Subsistence, xv, xxvi, 13, 16, 33, 37–41, 45–50, 51–52, 57, 58, 59, 60, 64, 93, 95, 101, 109, 116, 123, 154, 174, 175, 176, 178, 180–81, 182, 183, 184

SUME, 135

Syllabics. *See* Writing systems

Tagaq, Tanya, 133–34, 136

Tagoona, Armand, 130

Television. *See* Broadcasting

Third sex, 11–12

Thompson, Manitok, 97

Throat singing. *See* Music

Thule Inuit, xi, xiii, xiv–xv, xxv, 10, 41, 83, 143, 160

Time reckoning, xviii, 63

Trade, xiii, xvi, 51; fairs, 64–65, 81–82, 85, 111, 173; long distance, xiii, xiv, xvi, 69, 173. *See also* Fur trade

Trapping. *See* Fur trade

Tuberculosis, 157, 161–62

Tundra Times, xxvii, 91, 117, 129–30

Tunnille, Ovilu, 154

Vebaek, Maaliaaraq, 140

Violence, xiv, xvi, 16, 65, 66, 84, 99, 119, 135, 163

Warfare, 45, 57, 84, 86, 87, 134, 162, 173

Watt-Cloutier, Sheila, xxix, xxx, 177, 181–83

Whaling, xiv, xxi, 10, 31, 41–44, 47–49, 79, 83, 175, 183; commercial, xvii–xviii, 42, 45, 46, 47, 48, 79, 134, 161, 164. *See also* Alaska Eskimo Whaling Commission; International Whaling Commission

Wise, Ray, 139

Women, 66, 75, 77–78, 82, 83, 97, 104, 116, 117, 119, 133, 140, 141, 151–53, 159. *See also* Gender

Writing systems, 22–25, 86, 108, 109, 126

Yupik Eskimos, xiv, xviii, xxiii, 47, 48, 108, 174–75, 177, 179–80, 184

Zakaeus, Hans, 153

About the Author

PAMELA R. STERN is a sociocultural anthropologist and Adjunct Professor of Anthropology at Simon Fraser University in British Columbia, Canada. Her own research concerns how resource development affects citizenship, politics, and other aspects of everyday life in rural and remote regions of Canada. She is an author and editor of numerous scholarly works, including *Historical Dictionary of the Inuit* (2004) and *Critical Inuit Studies: An Anthology of Contemporary Arctic Ethnography* (2006), co-edited with Lisa Stevenson. She is currently working on a book about a former silver mining community in northern Ontario.